S0-CBG-441

GREAT NAVIGATORS
& DISCOVERERS

MAP OF THE WORLD, DESIGNED BY GIOVANNI MATTEO CONTARINI IN 1506

Probably the earliest printed representation of parts of America, the voyage round the Cape of Good Hope in 1498 of Vasco da Gama, and the Indian peninsula.

GREAT NAVIGATORS & DISCOVERERS

BY

J. A. BRENDON

B.A. F.R.Hist.S.

WITH ILLUSTRATIONS AND MAPS

Essay Index Reprint Series

BOOKS FOR LIBRARIES PRESS, INC.

FREEPORT, NEW YORK

First Published 1930
Reprinted 1967

LIBRARY OF CONGRESS CATALOG CARD NUMBER: 67-26720

PRINTED IN THE UNITED STATES OF AMERICA

FOREWORD

THIS collection of slight sketches overlooks many subjects it might well have included. But, while the names of great seamen are legion, the number of a book's pages is limited. The compiler, therefore, has been faced by a hard problem of selection; he could not hope to satisfy all possible critics. His aim has been to set out the stories of twenty-four representative sailors, and, at the same time, to show how the peoples of Europe made themselves the masters of the Seven Seas.

Most of his heroes won fame as navigators and explorers rather than as fighters. A few essentially fighting adventurers, however, also are dealt with. This, perhaps, can be logically justified. Paul Jones and Admiral Cochrane, for example, did not—in the manner of Columbus and Da Gama, Raleigh, Cartier, and Tasman—help to bring about the overseas expansion of Europe. Yet they played a big part in the establishing of that New World which Canning, "in order to redress the balance of the Old," strove to call into existence.

Why, it may be asked, do not any of the great seamen of modern times appear—Nansen and Peary, Amundsen, Shackleton, Scott? The question is easily answered. Sir John Franklin had the *Erebus* and the *Terror* (the ships in which he sailed in 1845) fitted with auxiliary engines. With this one exception, the men whose stories are told here were sailors all.

In a somewhat more compressed form the narratives have already been printed in the pages of *The Blue Peter*. To the Editor of that excellent "magazine of sea travel" thanks are due, and offered, for permission to assemble them in a book.

J. A. B.

CONTENTS

ILLUSTRATIONS

GREAT NAVIGATORS & DISCOVERERS

ILLUSTRATIONS

GREAT NAVIGATORS & DISCOVERERS

I. HANNO THE CARTHAGINIAN

c. 520 B.C.

A RECORD of the achievements of great navigators rightly, perhaps, should go back to the beginning, and so be made to include reasoned accounts of the voyage of the *Argo* and of the wanderings of the wise Odysseus. Yet who would essay to compile such a record? The traditional story of the Argonauts—the heroes who sailed with Jason from Thessaly in quest of the Golden Fleece—and the traditional history of Odysseus rest, no doubt, on foundations of fact. The foundations, however, overgrown by myth and legend, are hardly discernible.

Jason's fabled enterprise probably represents an attempt made by the Greeks of long ago to explore the Black Sea lands, and to enter into trading relations (symbolized by the Golden Fleece) with their inhabitants. The historian can say little more of it than that. Of the voyages undertaken by Odysseus after the fall of Troy he can say little more than that they represent a further step in the same direction.

Homer would have us believe that the ten years' siege of Troy—to which archæologists assign the date 1193–1184 B.C.—was brought about by the stealing of Greek women by Trojan men. This may have been the case. Pope's lines,

> What dire offence from am'rous causes springs,
> What mighty contests rise from trivial things,

are justified by history. Wars, none the less, whatever their occasions or ostensible origins, can generally be traced to quarrels explainable in terms of £ *s. d.*; one party aspires to a source of wealth enjoyed by the other, and the latter fears for its coveted possession. So the opinion may be ventured that the Greeks attacked Troy not merely because it was a city of women-stealing brigands, but because it commanded the Dardanelles—the gateway to the trade route which Jason had laboured to capture. The fall of Troy opened that gateway to them. *Ergo*, the subsequent adventures of Odysseus.

In unearthing the buried remains of old Ægean culture, Schliemann, Sir Arthur Evans, and their fellow-workers have shown that the *Iliad*—Homer's story of the siege of Troy—contains a deal of truth. Surely we may assume that the *Odyssey* contains as much. One day, perhaps, it too will be revealed, and with it the facts underlying the story of Jason. Pending that day we must concede to the Phœnicians, rather than to the early Greeks, the title "the fathers of navigation."

The people whom we, borrowing a sobriquet of Greek invention, style Phœnicians—'red men,' a name eminently suited to a race of sun-tanned sailors—hailed originally from Arabia. They settled in Syria about 1500 B.C., and, within a century and a half, made their cities, Tyre and Sidon, the chief commercial centres of the world. Subsequently they established colonies and trading depots all round the Mediterranean. Carthage, their great stronghold in Northern Africa—famous in song for the story of Queen Dido, and in history for the martial deeds of Hannibal—was founded in 850 B.C.

It has been suggested that the Phœnicians learned the elements of the navigating art while they were pastoral tribesmen, dwelling on the shores of the Persian Gulf. Be this as it may, ere the days of Hiram (*c.* 975 B.C.), that king of Tyre whose exploits Solomon sought to emulate, they had carried the art far forward, and were ranging over the Mediterranean in vessels of no mean size, well planned and well constructed.

In the Louvre at Paris may be seen a model of a Phœnician galley of that time. Ships of later date were mostly larger than this. The general design, however, remained unaltered, likewise the arrangement of the oars, and the single mast amidships, with its one square sail and its crow's-nest for the convenience of the pilot. The sail was used for running only; the oars, as in the long-ships of the Vikings, were worked usually by freemen. A speed of a 100 miles a day was commonly maintained.

In their ships, we have said, the Phœnicians ranged all over the Mediterranean. They ranged farther than that. Through the much-discussed Suez Canal projected (*c.* 1300 B.C.) by Pharaoh Seti I they made their way, in quest of gold and spices, to the

Queen of Sheba's capital (which stood, probably, near the spot where Aden stands to-day), and so on to India for cotton goods and ivory, even to Ceylon. Westward they sailed far beyond the Strait of Gibraltar or "Pillars of Hercules" (so named after a Phœnician deity, not the Greek hero), and, while they scoured the north-west coast of Africa and the west coast of Spain, they pushed

PHŒNICIAN MERCHANT GALLEY OF THE ROMAN IMPERIAL EPOCH

From a bas-relief in the Louvre

boldly northward to Cornwall to procure tin and copper to feed Tyrian factories.

There is ample proof that such voyages were made by them. Yet only one authentic, first-hand record of a specific expedition has come down to us. This, the record of a voyage undertaken by a Carthaginian navigator, a certain Hanno, deserves to be more widely known than it is.

In or about the year 520 B.C. the rulers of Carthage sent out Hanno with a fleet of sixty galleys to plant colonies on the Morocco coast. When he returned the navigator caused the story of his adventures to be engraved on a bronze tablet which he set up in the temple of Molech. The tablet has perished. But a Greek version of the writing on it has been preserved. Below is set out, almost in full, Thomas Falconer's translation:[1]

[1] *Vide* Falconer's *The Voyage of Hanno translated . . . and defended against the Objections of Mr Dodwell* (London, 1797).

When we had passed the Pillars on our voyage, and had sailed beyond them for two days, we founded the first city, which we named Thymaterium. Below it lay an extensive plain. Proceeding thence towards the west, we came to Soloeis,[1] a promontory of Libya, a place thickly covered with trees, where we erected a temple to Poseidon; and again proceeded for the space of half a day towards the east until we arrived at a lake lying far from the sea and filled with abundance of large reeds. There elephants and a great number of other wild beasts were feeding.

Having passed the lake about a day's sail, we founded cities near the sea, called Cariconticos and Gytte, Acra and Melita, and Arambys. Thence we came to the great river Lixus, which flows through Libya. On its banks the Lixitæ, a shepherd tribe, were feeding flocks, amongst whom we continued some time on friendly terms. . . .

Having procured interpreters from them, we coasted along a desolate country towards the south two days. Then we proceeded towards the east the course of a day. Here we found in a recess of a certain bay a small island, containing a circle of five stadia, where we settled a colony, and called it Cerne.[2] We judged from our voyage that this place lay in a direct line with Carthage, for the length of our voyage from Carthage to the Pillars was equal to that from the Pillars to Cerne.

We then came to a lake, which we reached by sailing up a large river called Chretes. This lake had three islands, larger than Cerne; from which, proceeding a day's sail, we came to the extremity of the lake, that was overhung by large mountains inhabited by savage men, clothed in skins of wild beasts, who drove us away by throwing stones, and hindered us from landing. . . .

Sailing thence, we came to another river[3] that was large and broad, and full of crocodiles and river-horses. . . .

Thence we sailed towards the south twelve days, coasting the shore, the whole of which is inhabited by Æthiopians, who would not wait our approval, but fled from us. Their language was not intelligible, even to the Lixitæ who were with us. Towards the last day we approached some large mountains covered with trees, the wood of which was sweet-scented and variegated. Having sailed by these mountains for two days, we came to an immense opening of the sea;[4] on each side of which, towards the continent, was a plain, from which we saw by night fire arising at intervals. . . . Having taken in water there, we sailed forwards five days near the land, until we came to a large bay.[5] . . . In this was a large island, and in the island a

[1] Cape Cantin. [2] Arguin Island. [3] The Senegal river.
[4] The mouth of the Gambia. [5] Gulf of Bissago.

PHŒNICIANS TRADING WITH ANCIENT BRITONS
From a drawing by Henry Evison

salt-water lake, and in this another island, where, when we landed, we could discover nothing in the daytime except trees, and in the night we saw many fires burning and heard the sound of pipes, cymbals, drums, and confused shouts. We were then afraid, and our diviners induced us to abandon the island.

Sailing quickly thence, we went past a country burning with fires and perfumes,[1] and streams of fire supplied by it fell into the sea. The country was impassable on account of the heat. We sailed quickly thence, being much terrified; and passing on for four days we discovered at night a country full of fire. In the middle was a lofty fire larger than the rest, which seemed to touch the stars. When day came, we discovered it to be a large hill called the Chariot of the Gods.[2]

On the third day after our departure thence, having sailed by those streams of fire, we arrived at a bay . . . at the bottom of which was an island [3] full of savage people, the greater part of whom were women, whose bodies were hairy and whom our interpreter called Gorillæ. Though we pursued the men, we could not seize any of them, but all fled from us, escaping over the precipices and defending themselves with stones. Three women were, however, taken, but they attacked their conductors with their teeth and hands, and could not be prevailed upon to accompany us. Having killed them, we flayed them and brought their skins to Carthage.

The modern names of some of the places mentioned are suggested in the footnotes. Others may be identified on a map. The so-called gorillæ were probably chimpanzees. Hanno's is the earliest description we have of such creatures; and his encounter with them seems to have decided the navigator to make for home. Thus his narrative abruptly ends: "We did not sail further on, our provisions failing us."

The Greek version of the narrative somehow came to be known as the *Periplus*, or *Circumnavigation*. On this account Pliny and certain other later writers erroneously credited Hanno with having sailed round Africa. Yet this feat was accomplished by a Phœnician navigator—and, it may be, by more than one. Herodotus has told us the story.

In or about 620 B.C., according to that historian, Pharaoh Necho

sent to sea a number of ships manned by Phœnicians, with orders to make for the Pillars of Hercules, and return to Egypt through them, and by way of the Mediterranean. The Phœnicians took their

[1] Bush fires. [2] Mount Sagres. [3] Sherbro Island.

departure from Egypt by way of the Erythræan Sea,[1] and so sailed into the southern ocean. When autumn came, they went ashore wherever they might happen to be, and having sown a tract of land with corn waited until the grain was fit to cut. Having reaped it, they again set sail; and thus it came to pass that two whole years went by, and it was not until the third year that they doubled the Pillars of Hercules, and made good their voyage home.

The truth of this story, long doubted, is now supported by archæological evidence, and the very circumstance which led Herodotus himself to treat it with suspicion tends further to confirm it. "On their return," wrote Herodotus, "they [the Phœnicians] declared—I for my part do not believe them, but perhaps others may—that in sailing round Libya they had the sun on their right hand."

Incidentally, it may be noted, the terms of Pharaoh Necho's instructions suggest that similar voyages had been made before that time. When were such voyages made again? Not, so far as we know, till the days of Vasco da Gama.

[1] Gulf of Suez.

II. LEIF ERICSSON

Born c. 970; *died c.* 1010

THE exploits of the old Norse navigators are known to us largely from Icelandic sagas. To most people the word 'saga' denotes a tale of fabulous adventure. By most people, therefore, the voyagings of the Vikings are regarded, like the voyagings of Odysseus, as mythical exploits. Yet many of the sagas, so far from being folklore, are sober chronicles of fact. Such, without question, is the *Saga of Eric the Red*, which tells us of Leif Ericsson and the first authentic discovery of North America.

The earliest extant version, *Hauk's-bok*, as it is known, is now preserved at the University of Copenhagen. But this vellum, in the beautiful handwriting of Hauk Erlendsson, a scholar who flourished at Iceland between 1400 and 1450, can hardly be the original manuscript. Hauk records events which happened at the beginning of the eleventh century. Had the story been handed down to him by word of mouth through nine generations it must have become fantastically distorted. In Hauk's narrative there is nothing even improbable; and the descriptions of men and beasts (peculiarly American) and of places and plants (likewise peculiarly American) will mostly bear the test of modern critical examination.

Save by the writer's heroes, those men and beasts, places, and plants were not seen by Europeans till the sixteenth century. Surely, therefore, old Hauk either copied an earlier manuscript, or edited the actual ship's logs. The latter may well have been in his possession, for he was descended from one who played a big part in the adventures chronicled. But enough! let us accept the evidence and retell the story.

About the year 870 a great king, Harold Fairhair, made himself lord of Norway in fact as well as in name. Many a proud jarl, or kinglet, then went forth to seek independence elsewhere. Some settled in Britain, some in France. Others sailed away over the Mediterranean to Sicily, Greece, and Syria. Others journeyed to Iceland. Before the close of the tenth century Iceland had a population of 50,000 souls, sprung from these jarls and their doughty vikings.

In 983 Eric the Red, a famous Icelandic chief, fell foul of his peers, and was outlawed. Nothing daunted, he gathered a few

ERIC THE RED ON THE GREENLAND VOYAGE
From a drawing by Stephen Reid

chosen followers, and, taking ship, struck out to the west. After many days' sailing he sighted land, and at length, having explored long stretches of uninviting coast, came upon a tolerably smooth and grassy plain. There, on the south-west coast of Greenland, not far from the modern Julianshaab, he settled. Greenland was the name which he himself gave to the land he had discovered. Said he: "Men will be more easily persuaded to come here if I give it a fair name."

In 986 the outlaw ventured back to Iceland to recruit settlers for his colony, and was so successful that he set out again for the west with twenty-five shiploads of emigrants—800 men, with their womenfolk and cattle.

On the voyage storms and icebergs wrought havoc in the fleet. Only fourteen of the vessels were safely brought to harbour. Nevertheless, within a few years, the west coast of Greenland had been colonized as far north as modern Godthaab, and it could soon boast 5000 Norse inhabitants. This is a fact as well established as any in mediæval history. The ruins of houses built by these early settlers, and other remains, are still to be seen. The colony continued in being for four hundred years. In 1407 hostile Eskimos extinguished it.

That the frequent passage of ships between Iceland and Greenland, and between Norway and Greenland, should have resulted in the discovery of land farther to the west cannot be deemed a matter for surprise. The Norse navigators had only the sun and stars to guide them. Sooner or later, cloud and a stiff north-easter must have brought one of them to America. The first to sight the American continent was a certain Bjarni Herjulfsson.

This Bjarni, after roaming at sea for several years, came home in 986 to Iceland, to drink the Yuletide ale with his father. But the old home was no more; Herjulf had migrated to Greenland with Eric the Red. His son resolved also to go thither. He sailed in the spring of 987. For a time fair weather attended him. But soon a persistent spell of rain set in, rendering worthless the directions he had received. So it came about that the land which at length he sighted was not the rugged coast he had been led to expect, with ice-clad mountains towering above it, but a low, flat country. Seeing that he had been carried from his course, the Norseman did not trouble to investigate this shore. He turned his prow northward and, favoured by a clear sky and southerly breeze, came at last to his father's house.

Bjarni's story of land to the south does not appear to have excited immediate curiosity in Greenland. Thirteen years elapsed before Leif, Eric the Red's eldest son, "a large man and strong, of noble aspect, prudent and moderate in all things," determined to verify it.

Leif sailed from Greenland in the year 1000, and, sure enough, came in the fullness of time to the land which Bjarni had described. Helluland ("Slate land") he called it. We call it Labrador. Continuing his voyage southward, Leif next came to a wooded country which he named Markland (it was that same Newfoundland rediscovered by Cabot some five centuries afterward), and then to his much-debated Vinland. There, near a place where "a river, flowing from a lake, fell into the sea," he and his men put up huts and spent the winter.

Where was this place? In the south of Nova Scotia, or on the coast of Maine? One or the other, without a doubt. Upon that the experts are in agreement, though it seems likely they will go on arguing the exact locality until the crack of doom. The reader, who can afford to disregard unimportant detail, may be tempted to vote for Maine. So can he allow himself the satisfaction of reflecting that the first of the American states to adopt prohibition was known as "the wine country" to its first white tenants. The Norsemen so named it on account of the vines growing luxuriantly near the shore.

Leif returned to Greenland in the summer of 1001. There he found his father dead, and he himself the heir to his wealth and dignities. The further exploration of Vinland, therefore, he left to his brothers Thorvald and Thorstein.

Thorvald Ericsson, borrowing Leif's old ship and crew, sailed to that country in 1002, and spent nearly two years exploring its coast. He may have made his way as far south as Long Island. But in 1004 he and a number of his followers were killed in a fight with the natives, the Skraelings (*i.e.*, "inferior people"), as old Hauk termed them. Having thus lost their leader, the survivors straightway returned to Greenland.

Next year Thorstein Ericsson sailed for Vinland in the same ship, accompanied by Gudrid his wife. This expedition accomplished nothing. Thorstein died on the voyage, and the widowed Gudrid was constrained to go home without having even sighted the American coast. Two years later she made another venture.

In 1006 there came to Greenland a certain Thorfinn Karlsefni. This wealthy Icelandic trader fell a victim to the charms of the adventurous widow, wedded her, and at her persuasion undertook not merely to explore Vinland, but to colonize it. For the purpose he fitted out four ships, and sailed in the spring of 1007 with 160 men, a score or more of women, a great many cattle, and everything needful for the establishment of a permanent settlement.

The expedition came without misadventure to its destination. There, a few weeks afterward, it was reinforced by the first child born of a European mother in the New World—Snorro, the son of Thorfinn and Gudrid.

Hauk Erlendsson was directly descended from him. Him, too,

THE OSEBERG SHIP SET UP IN THE MUSEUM AT OSLO
Photo Norwegian State Railways

several proud houses of modern Norway claim as their common ancestor. Little Snorro passed only three years of his life in America. In 1010 natives in great strength attacked Thorfinn's colony and utterly destroyed it. The survivors were scarcely numerous enough to man the one ship which finally struggled back to Greenland.

Two years later yet another attempt was made to plant a colony in Vinland—this time by Freydis, a daughter of Eric the Red, and her husband Thorvard. Their venture also ended in disaster. Contact between the Old World and the New then was severed, and was not renewed till 1492. On this account the unbelieving doubt if it were ever established by Vikings.

Why, they ask, did the Norsemen, if they discovered the coasts of Maine and Nova Scotia, not abandon their Greenland settlement and migrate in a body to the pleasanter places in the south? The question is easily answered. Greenland was relatively near to the parent colony of Iceland, and, "in colonizing," it has been pointed out, "as in campaigning, distance from one's base is sometimes the supreme circumstance." In Greenland, again, the Norsemen had no native opposition to contend with till the fourteenth century. The hostility of the natives rendered it impossible for

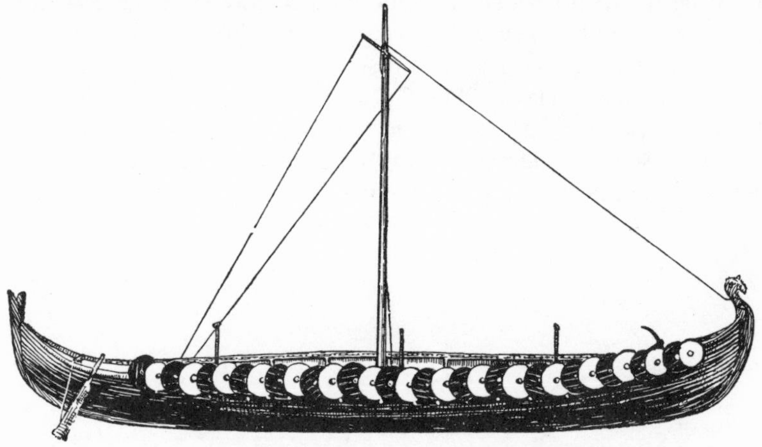

RECONSTRUCTED MODEL OF THE GOKSTAD SHIP
South Kensington Museum

them to maintain themselves in Vinland. Even in the sixteenth and seventeenth centuries European pioneers, possessed of firearms, had as much as they could do to hold their own. The Norsemen did not stand a chance.

So, before the end of the eleventh century, the very existence of Vinland became a mere tradition, known only to a few scholars. Outside Icelandic sagas one may search in vain through mediæval literature for references to the New World. Columbus, the Cabots, and the other navigators of the Age of Discovery had no knowledge of what the Norsemen had achieved before them. Europe in the eleventh century was not ripe for expansion. Still, the adventures of Leif Ericsson and his fellows, though they are without political or geographical significance, form an intensely interesting chapter in the history of navigation.

In the Oslo Museum are preserved the remains of a Viking

merchantman which was unearthed some years ago at Oseberg, in Norway. The Gokstad ship, of which a model may be seen in the Science Museum, South Kensington, was found at Gokstad, deeply embedded in blue clay and remarkably well preserved. It was built just about the time of the Norsemen's discovery of America, and was one of the smaller fighting vessels of the period, belonging to the so-called "Serpent" class. Made of oak, clinker built, and caulked with cow's hair spun in a sort of cord, such a ship would have been much stronger and more seaworthy than the Spanish ships of Columbus's time, and very much swifter.

For their long voyages the Norsemen usually employed vessels of the "Dragon" class. The Gokstad ship was propelled by sixteen oars on each side, and carried a single square sail amidships. The vessels of the "Dragon" class had as many as thirty oars a side. King Canute boasted a super-Dragon, with sixty oars a side.

III. MARCO POLO

Born 1254; *died* 1323

IN 1298, off the island of Curzola, on the Dalmatian coast, a battle was fought between the fleets of Venice and Genoa. The Venetians suffered defeat, losing most of their ships and some 7000 prisoners. Among the latter was a certain Marco Polo, a citizen of high standing, facetiously styled by his compatriots *il Milone* (" the Man of Millions ").

Marco Polo had spent many years in the Far East, in regions unknown to other Europeans of that time. For this reason contemporaries sprinkled his descriptions of what he had seen with more than the customary grain of salt. To them, indeed, his tales of the "constant succession of cities and boroughs" through which he had passed in China, India, and Burma, and of the "excellent hostelries" they provided; his tales of " fine vineyards, fields and gardens," of "many abbeys," and of manufactures of "cloth of silk and gold, and fine taffetas"—to say nothing of his more wondrous tales—were utterly incredible. The nickname which a wit applied to him, the man who was always talking of millions of people and millions of ducats, seemed to them to fit. Therefore it stuck.

But Marco Polo, though he despaired of convincing his own generation, did not despair of persuading posterity to believe him. So it came about that, while lying in gaol at Genoa, he beguiled his tedium by dictating (in French) to a fellow-prisoner, a Pisan named Rusticiano, a record of his adventures. Rusticiano's *The Travels of Marco Polo* is, perhaps, the greatest travel book ever written; it is also one of the greatest of history books, and a mine of information regarding the ethnography and the manners and customs of Asia. Incidentally, its publication resulted in the rediscovery of America. But of that more anon. First let us retell the story of its hero.

In the year 1260 two Venetian merchants, Nicolo Polo and his brother Maffeo, went on a trading expedition to the Crimea. Having completed their business in that quarter they ventured northward, up the valley of the Volga, until at length, greatly daring, they came to Kazan, the capital of Barka Khan, a grandson of the famous and mighty Zenghis.

Barka Khan received them with every mark of favour. As his guests they stayed at Kazan for several weeks. Then a neighbouring Tartar prince made war on their host, and the latter was soundly beaten. In the circumstances the Venetians deemed it prudent to return home forthwith, and to return by a circuitous route. This brought them to Bokhara. There they fell in with ambassadors returning from Persia to the Court of Kublai Khan, the Great Khan in China. The ambassadors urged the Polos to accompany them. Their royal master, they said, had never held converse with men of the Latin race, and was desirous of doing so. The adventurers were easily prevailed upon, and, in due course, arrived at Cambulac (Pekin).

Kublai Khan, an enlightened and progressive despot, was deeply impressed by what they had to tell him of Christendom; and at length, having loaded them with gifts and furnished them with "golden tablets"—passports which ensured them a safe passage through all parts of his dominions—he sent them to Europe with letters to the Pope. The letters requested that the Venetians might be allowed to return to China accompanied by a hundred learned teachers, "intelligent men acquainted with the Seven Arts, able to enter into controversy, and able clearly to prove to idolators and other kinds of folk that the Law of Christ was best."

In 1269, after a nine years' absence, the brothers Polo got back to Venice. There Nicolo was delighted to find his son Marco, whom he had last seen as a six-year-old child, a fine, well-grown lad, filled with his own adventuresome spirit. Yielding readily to entreaties he at once promised to show the boy the wonders of China so soon as he had mustered his hundred missionaries.

The task presented unexpected difficulties. In 1268, a few months before the Polos landed at Venice, Pope Clement IV died. Some two years elapsed ere a successor was appointed. During the interregnum the Vatican authorities—engrossed in more immediate problems—would not give serious attention to Kublai Khan's request. Even in 1271, when Cardinal Theobald of Piacenza was raised to the papal chair as Gregory X, the Polos, so far from being offered the services of a hundred learned teachers, were given only two youthful, inexperienced Dominicans. And these young men had but little interest in their mission; when it came to the point, no arguments could induce them to move beyond

CHURCH OF THE HOLY SEPULCHRE, JERUSALEM
Photo E. N. A.

Palestine. So Nicolo and his brother were constrained to continue their journey to Kublai's Court with young Marco as their sole attendant.

They started the journey by way of Palestine, because they had promised the Great Khan some oil from the lamp which burned in the Holy Sepulchre at Jerusalem. This they duly obtained. They then made their way to Jaffa and took ship to Mersina, on the coast of Cilicia, going thus far northward in order to avoid molestation at the hands of the Sultan of Egypt's forces, which were then raiding Syria. From Cilicia they advanced into Armenia. Thence they dropped down through Mesopotamia to Basra, where they secured passages in an Arab vessel which took them to Ormuz.

AN ARAB DHOW

Their intention was to complete the journey by sea. At Ormuz, however, they met with merchants who undertook to guide them overland. Accordingly they changed their plans and, escorted by their new companions, struck northward across the Persian deserts to Damghan. There they turned to the east, and, having passed through Khorassan and northern Afghanistan, came to the Pamir. Thence they descended into Eastern Turkestan, and so on to Campichu, by way of Kashgar, Khotan, and Lob Nor.

From Campichu they made a purely sightseeing digression—an expedition of several hundreds of miles over the Gobi Desert—in order that they might visit Karakoran, "the first city that the Tartars possessed after they had issued from their own country."

Karakoran, now only a vast extent of sandswept ruins, was in those days a military centre of much importance, the most populous town in China.

Having returned to Campichu, the travellers resumed their easterly course, and, following the line of the Great Wall, were brought at length, three and a half years after their departure from Venice, to

A STRETCH OF THE GREAT WALL OF CHINA
Photo E. N. A.

the Court of Kublai Khan. That potentate received his old friends with sincere delight, even though they failed to bring with them those masters of 'the Seven Arts' whose presence he had desired.

Young Marco also was given a cordial welcome. According to Rusticiano's narrative,

> His Majesty . . . entertained him with a friendly countenance, and taught him to write among other of his honourable courtiers; whereupon he was much esteemed of all the Court, and in a little space learned the customs of all the Tartars, and four languages, being able to read and write them all.

C

Thus the boy rose to a high position at Pekin, and soon came to be entrusted with important diplomatic missions. As the Great Khan's envoy, he went to Burma and India, to Tibet and to Japan.

To India he travelled by sea. His enterprise in piloting a Tartar fleet thither made him famous throughout China. Kublai Khan, in recognition of the exploit, bestowed on him the governorship of

MARCO POLO

the city of Yang-chow, a post which for several years he filled with conspicuous success. The Emperor also heaped many other dignities on him.

Critics have laboured to show that the uncorroborated testimony of Rusticiano's narrative is insufficient proof of these statements. It so happens, however, that the testimony in question is not uncorroborated. In Chinese official records the Venetian is mentioned by name as having been a member of the Imperial Council in 1277.

After they had sojourned in China for sixteen years the Polos began to feel homesick. Also they began to be conscious of the insecurity of their position. As *protégés* of Kublai, they had incurred the enmity of many nobles who were jealous of favours showered upon foreigners; and Kublai was growing old. What would be their status, they asked themselves, when their patron was no more? In 1291, therefore, they sought permission to return to Europe. The Great Khan would not hear of the suggestion. Why, said he, should they engage in so arduous and dangerous a venture? Did they desire riches? If so, he would gladly double the amount of their possessions. In any case, he declared, affection forbade him to let them go.

Just at this time ambassadors from Persia chanced to arrive at Pekin. Kublai's nephew, Argon, the Khan of Persia, had lately lost his favourite wife, and the latter, as she lay on her deathbed, had made her lord promise that none should take her place save a woman belonging to her own tribe. The ambassadors had come in quest of a suitable princess.

At Pekin they found one. Then arose the question: how was the lady to be conveyed to Persia? A land journey must involve many perils and much hardship. A sea journey, on the other hand, seemed to be quite impracticable, for among the Tartars there were no navigators capable of piloting a fleet to Ormuz. Then it was suggested that one of the Polos might be given the command. Had not Marco already navigated Tartar ships to India? Thereupon, to quote Rusticiano's narrative, "the ambassadors . . . conferred with the Venetians and agreed that they, with the Queen, should go to the Great Khan and desire leave to return by sea and to have the three Latins, men skilled in sea affairs, with them to the country of King Argon." Kublai, we are told, "was much displeased with their request. Yet upon hearing their petition he granted it. Then he caused Nicolo, Maffeo, and Marco to come into his presence, and, after much demonstration of his love, would have them promise to return after they had spent some time in Christendom." So were they sent upon their way, laden with presents and bearing letters to the principal rulers of Europe, including the King of England (Edward I).

For the accommodation of the Princess and her suite a fleet of fourteen five-masted vessels had been fitted out. This, with Marco Polo in command, sailed from Chin-chew in the early part of 1292, and, proceeding by way of the Malacca Strait, round the south of Ceylon, and up the Malabar coast, arrived at Ormuz after a two years' voyage. Whether the Princess—"the Lady Kokachin," as Marco styled her—fared better in thus travelling by sea than she would have on land is open to question. The hardship endured by those who took part in the expedition may be gauged by the fact that six hundred of the sailors, two of the Persian ambassadors, and some twenty members of the royal suite died on the voyage.

On reaching Ormuz, Marco learned that Argon Khan was dead. He delivered his charge, therefore, to the deceased monarch's

MARCO POLO ARRIVES AT ORMUZ

son and successor. Then, accompanied by his father and his uncle, he set out from Persia and made his way overland to the Black Sea.

At Trebizond the Venetians again took ship. So in 1295, having been away for twenty-four years, they at last got back to their native city. Friends and relatives had long ago given them up for dead; and, clad in their Tartar garments, they found it no easy matter to establish their identity. Even after they had contrived to do this they were still generally regarded as vagabonds, disreputable wanderers.

With a view to dispelling such suspicions they resolved to give a great banquet. To this they invited all their former acquaintances. The majority, impelled by curiosity, accepted; and, at the conclusion of the feast, we are told,

> when the cloth had been drawn and all the servants had been bidden to withdraw from the dining-hall, Messer Marco, as the youngest of the three, rose from the table, and, going into another chamber, brought forth the three shabby dresses of coarse stuff which they had worn when they first arrived. Straightway they took sharp knives and began to rip up some of the seams and welts, and to take out from them jewels of the greatest value in vast quantities—such as rubies, sapphires, carbuncles, diamonds, and emeralds—which had all been stitched up in these dresses in so artful a fashion that nobody could have suspected the fact.

MARCO POLO RETURNS TO VENICE

Wealth made the Polos important and influential men at Venice. But it did not gain credence for the story of their adventures.

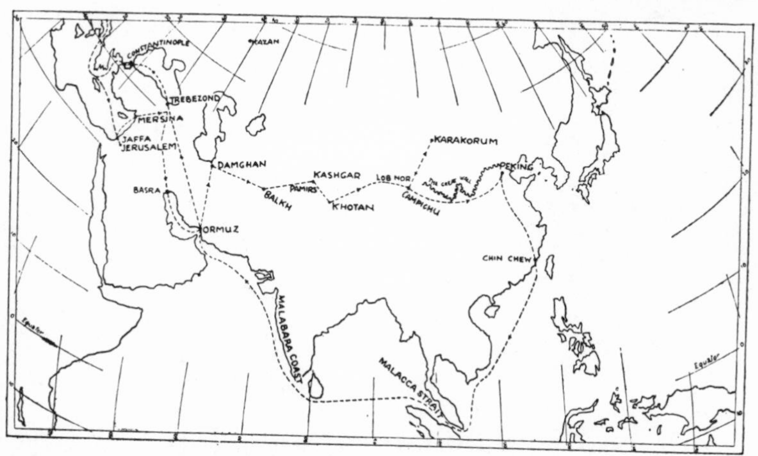

SKETCH MAP OF MARCO POLO'S WANDERINGS

Pious and incredulous friends, indeed, went so far as to urge Marco openly to confess the fraud which, they alleged, he had tried to perpetrate in his book; they professed to be anxious that he should die with a clear conscience. Marco refused to alter a word. His refusal has been commended by the verdict of history. *The Travels of Marco Polo*, though not free from exaggeration and error (what travel book is?), is a model of its kind, the work of one who by the light of present-day knowledge is shown to have been a remarkably keen and truthful observer. The picture it contains, John Masefield has written,

> is the picture we all make in our minds when we repeat to ourselves those two strange words, 'the East,' and give ourselves up to the image which that symbol evokes. It may be that the Western mind will turn to Marco Polo for a conception of Asia long after 'Cathay' has become an American colony.

But what had the book to do with the discovery of America? Simply this: it was largely a greedy desire to verify its extravagant estimate of the wealth of Zipangu (Japan), and to find a direct Western route to the "land of gold," that led Christopher Columbus, on August 3, 1492, to set sail from Palos on his first and memorable voyage across the Atlantic.

IV. PRINCE HENRY THE NAVIGATOR

Born 1394; *died* 1460

It is strange, perhaps, that a man who did not make even one notable voyage should have been singled out from all other men to receive the title of "The Navigator." Stranger still is it that such a man should have deserved the title. Yet the claim advanced on behalf of Prince Henry of Portugal, *alias* Prince Henry the Navigator, can hardly be disputed. The Prince was no seaman. Eulogists, moreover, by ascribing to him intentions which he did not entertain, have exaggerated his achievements. Despite this, the fact remains that he was the pioneer of modern maritime enterprise and of scientific navigation.

About 1420 the Prince, a son of King John I of Portugal, built an observatory on the headland of Sagres, one of the promontories which terminate at Cape St Vincent, the extreme south-west point of Europe. There he established a school of seamanship; and there for forty years he devoted himself to geographical research, and to the equipping and organizing of expeditions of discovery. At the designing of ships, at the preparing of maps, at the making and improving of nautical instruments, he laboured with unflagging zeal; and though—in the strict mediæval sense—he was an uncompromising champion of the Church, he did not hesitate to employ Arab cartographers and pilots, and Jewish astronomers, to instruct his captains.

At the beginning of the fifteenth century the peoples of Europe knew little of the world which lay beyond their continent. Even the sailor-folk of Genoa and Venice rarely ventured far from their accustomed routes, rarely lost sight of the friendly shore; and the ocean which stretched out to the west was still generally regarded as "the green sea of darkness," wherein the unwary mariner might expect to be lured to his doom by watchful sirens, or by unicorns and other fabulous creatures. Ere the middle years of the century came, such phantoms had ceased to terrify. Prince Henry had robbed them of their power.

The Portuguese of that time were hardy and resourceful sailors, skilled in the handling of ships. They were skilled, too, in the building of ships; and their three-masted caravels—similar in rig and design to the Mediterranean felucca of to-day—were the fastest sailing vessels afloat. But Portuguese mariners, fishermen, and

THE HEREFORD MAP, 1280

traders alike were steeped in superstition, and they had no knowledge of the deeper mysteries of their calling. Had they not been urged on by the scholar at Sagres it is improbable that they would have led the way into the unknown, that they would have inaugurated "the Age of Discovery."

The results of Prince Henry's labours are writ large in history. In 1420 Portugal, one of several petty Iberian principalities, was a country of little account. Fifty years later the Portuguese were the foremost maritime people in Europe, and had already laid the foundations of their once vast empire. Under the direction of

Prince Henry they had colonized Porto Santo and Madeira, had discovered the Azores and the Cape Verde Islands, and had crept down the African coast nearly to the Equator. Further, there is reason to believe that in 1448 they actually crossed the Atlantic,[1]

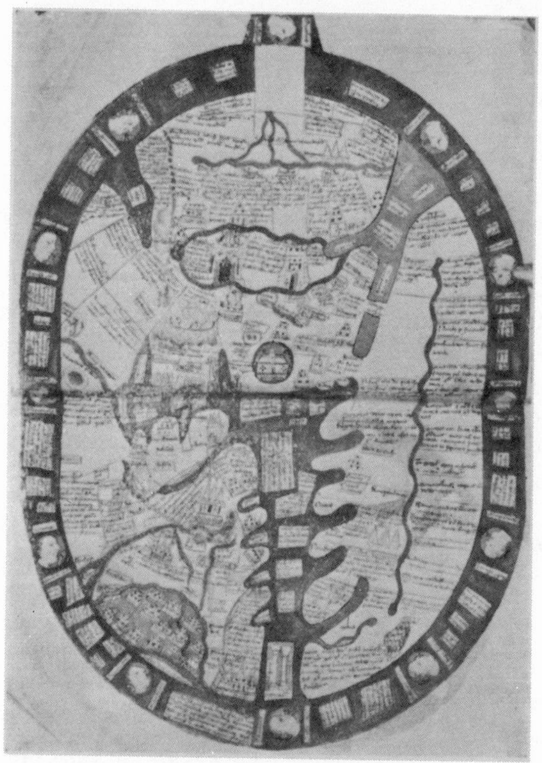

THE WORLD, DRAWN IN THE LATTER HALF OF THE FOURTEENTH CENTURY
The East with Paradise is at the top, Jerusalem near the centre, and the Pillars of Hercules at the bottom.
British Museum

and that the subsequent discovery of Brazil by Cabral was made to seem fortuitous as a means of circumventing Pope Alexander VI's division of the world between themselves and the Spaniards.

The movement thus started quickly gained impetus. Ere the close of another half-century Portugal had become the centre of an empire which extended from the region of the Amazon to the

[1] The evidence is reviewed in *The Geographical Journal*, vol. v, p. 221 *seq.*, and vol. ix, p. 185 *seq.*

islands of the far Pacific. Other states, moreover, had entered the race for dominion overseas, and most of the main ocean tracks had been explored. These, it is sometimes said, were the results which Prince Henry aimed at. Really they were results he never even contemplated.

Though one of the great figures in the history of modern times, the Prince was also one of the great figures in the history of the Middle Ages. A child of the New Learning, he was equally a child of Chivalry. He was, in fact, the last of the Crusaders; and the secret of his character and aims may be found in his will. Therein he wrote: "I humbly beseech my Lord Saint Louis, to whom I have been dedicated from my birth, that he and all Saints and Angels will pray God to grant me salvation."

Louis IX, better known as St Louis, King of France from 1226 to 1270, having learned from disastrous experience the impracticability of expelling the Saracens from the Holy Land, made it his mission to gain Egypt and Tunis from the infidel. But in northern Africa the knights of Christendom fared hardly better than in Palestine; St Louis's exploits, though they constitute one of the most romantic stories in the epic of the Crusades, accomplished nothing. That he might succeed where the sainted Louis had failed was the pious hope which inspired Henry the Navigator. In 1415—the year of the battle of Agincourt—the Prince took the first step toward its achievement. He then led a Portuguese force to Morocco and wrested Ceuta from the grip of the Mussulman. Thereafter he directed all his energies, and all the resources of the great Order of which he became the head, to this object.

Portugal owed its liberation from Moorish domination largely to the activities of three religious Orders of Chivalry—the Orders of Crato, St Benedict of Aviz, and Santiago of the Sword. To these Orders—akin in origin to the Hospitallers, the Templars, and the Teutonic Knights—a fourth subsequently was added. In 1312 the Templars were suppressed by Papal decree, and in all lands save Portugal were deprived of their estates. In Portugal the knights were exonerated by the commissioners who had been appointed to inquire into their alleged misdeeds. In that country, therefore, in 1319, the Vatican consented to the refounding of the Order under a new name—the "Order of Chivalry of Our Lord Jesus Christ"—"for the defence of the faith, the discomfiture of the Moors, and the extension of the Portuguese monarchy."

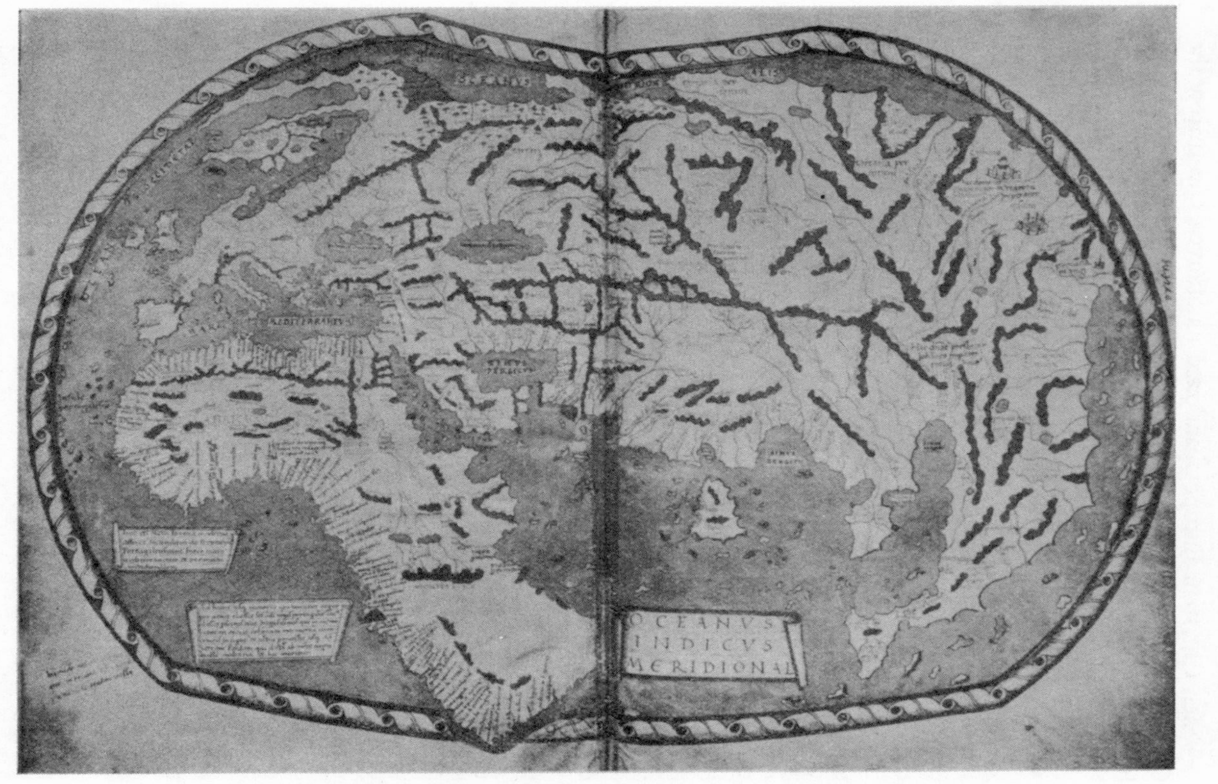

THE WORLD, DRAWN IN 1492 BY HENRICUS MARTELLUS GERMANUS

Giving a view of the Portuguese discoveries along the west coast of Africa and just beyond the Cape of Good Hope, rounded in 1487.

From a beautifully illustrated MS. copy in the British Museum

When Christian Europe abandoned its efforts to overthrow the Crescent in the Holy Land, the Teutonic Knights looked about for other occupation, and eventually undertook the conversion of the heathen tribes of Prussia.[1] Similarly, after the expulsion of the Moors from Portugal the Knights of Christ, under the Grand Mastership of Henry the Navigator, undertook to establish the Cross in northern Africa. To encourage them in their work the Papacy granted them spiritual jurisdiction of the lands they might discover, and comprehensively absolved all who should perish in the cause; while Pope Alexander VI—"somewhat superfluously," it has been remarked—released them from their vows of chastity and poverty.

Thus the popular conception of Prince Henry as the genius who planned the circumnavigation of Africa, with a view to the opening up of direct sea communication between Europe and the East, is largely illusory. It may be doubted, indeed, if the idea of rounding the Cape ever entered his mind. His purpose was to penetrate Africa, and to defeat the ends of the Mussulman by bringing about an alliance between the princes of Europe and Prester John, that elusive Christian potentate dear to mediæval tradition.

Commonly identified with the apostle John—who, it was believed, had escaped death in fulfilment of the words in St John xxi, 22 and 23—Prester John was said to be the sovereign lord of seventy-two kings and to rule over a great empire wherein crime and vice were unknown. For this reason, chronicles tell us, he styled himself "Prester"—that is, presbyter or priest; as in the case of the Pope, *servus servorum*, a high-sounding title would have been a wholly inadequate expression of his majesty and power.

In the fourteenth century the kingdom of Prester John had been definitely located in the upper regions of the Nile—to wit, in Abyssinia. The waters of the Nile, moreover, so geographers affirmed, found their way to the sea through two channels—the eastern, which bore them to the Mediterranean, and the western, which bore them to the Atlantic. Prince Henry aspired to dis-

[1] In the sixteenth century the Knights adopted the teaching of Luther. Their Order was then abolished, and a certain Albert Hohenzollern, who happened to be Grand Master at the time, assumed, and made hereditary in his family, the title of Duke in East Prussia. He and his descendants ruled as dukes in East Prussia till 1618, when their line died out. The duchy then passed to the last duke's next-of-kin, John Sigismund of Hohenzollern, Elector of Brandenburg.

cover the western mouth, and then, by gradually conquering the lands toward the source, to join hands with Prester John, and so to enable Christianity to outflank Islam. The course of the "Western Nile" is shown on mediæval Arab maps; and Bilad Ghana, "the wealthy land"—Senegal we call it now—which lay round the mouth, was well known to mediæval Arab traders. The latter journeyed thither from Egypt by overland routes across the desert.

Prince Henry's quest proved long and arduous. Portuguese captains deemed the dreary Sahara coast to be interminable; many despaired of ever reaching the fertile regions which were said to lie beyond it. In 1445, however, one of them, a certain Diniz Dias, sighted to the south of the desert a headland green with luxuriant vegetation—Cabo Verde (the Green Cape) he called it—and, pushing on, came at last to the promised land, to Bilad Ghana, a name subsequently corrupted by the Portuguese to Guinea. He dropped anchor in the mouth of the Senegal river, believing he had found the long-sought approach to Prester John's realm.

Wrote a contemporary chronicler:

> Those who were present said afterwards that it was clear from the smell that came off that land how good must be the fruits of that country, for it was so delicious from the point they reached, though they were on the sea, it seemed to them that they stood in some gracious fruit garden ordained for the sole end of their delight. . . . And so, as they were going scanning the coast to see if they could discern the river, they perceived before them, as it might be about two leagues of land measure, a certain colour in the water of the sea which was different from the rest, for this was of the colour of mud. . . . And it happened that one of those who were throwing in the sounding lead, by chance and without any certain knowledge, put his hand to his mouth and found the water sweet. . . . "Of a surety," said they, "we are near the river of the Nile, for it seemeth that this water belongeth to the same, and by its great might the water doth cut through the sea and so entereth into it." Thereat they made signs to the other caravels, and all of them began to coast in and look for the river, and they were not very long in arriving at the estuary.

The success of this venture did not lead to the results anticipated by Prince Henry. Its immediate results were the voyages of Bartholomew Dias and Vasco da Gama, and the voyages of

Columbus and the Cabots. Another of its results was the slave trade.

Portugal, wasted by Moors, had much need of labour in the fifteenth century. By shipping negroes from the Guinea coast to the slave-market at Lagos Prince Henry sought to supply this want

PRINCE HENRY OF PORTUGAL
From a print in the British Museum

and, at the same time, to regain the money he had spent on discovery and to reward his captains for dangers braved. For the subsequent shame of the slave trade he cannot fairly be held to blame. In his time Aristotle's comforting doctrine that some men were born for servitude was universally accepted by the thought and conscience of Europe, and at first negroes were sent only to Portugal, where generally they were well treated by the people. Wrote a chronicler:

As our people did not find them hardened in the belief of the other Moors, and saw how they came into the law of Christ with a good will, they made no difference between them and their free servants, born in our own country.

Nor need we doubt—again to quote the chronicler—the sincerity of Prince Henry's "great joy because of their salvation, who otherwise would have been destined to perdition."

Dreamer and man of action, ascetic and scholar, an idealist endowed with a business brain and a consummate gift of leadership, the Navigator is one of the most interesting characters in history. He lived at a point of time where two ages met, and in him the highest qualities of the old may be seen blended with the highest qualities of the new. Though rightly esteemed as a national hero by the Portuguese, good English blood flowed in his veins. His mother was a daughter of "Old John of Gaunt, time-honour'd Lancaster"; and in 1446, in recognition of his English ancestry and great achievements, King Henry VI admitted him to the illustrious fellowship of the Knights of the Most Noble Order of the Garter.

Prince Henry died at his post on November 13, 1460, worn out by his labours, and was buried in the church of St Mary at Lagos, the little seaport whence had sailed the many expeditions which he fitted out. In the following year his bones were moved to the famous monastery at Batalha. There they still rest, beside those of his father.

The last of the expeditions which he actually arranged was that undertaken by Diego Gomez in 1458. Gomez on this occasion rounded Cape Verde and reached the mouth of the river which he named the Rio Grande. This point on the Senegambian coast was the farthest south that had yet been attained by a Portuguese captain.

V. CHRISTOPHER COLUMBUS

Born c. 1451; *died* 1506

AROUND the identity of the discoverer of the New World there threatens to rage as pretty a controversy as around the authorship of Shakespeare's plays. Attempts are being made to show that Christopher Columbus was of Spanish, not of Italian, birth, and we are bidden to dismiss as romance, based on forgery and other spurious evidence, the long-accepted stories of his youth. The day may come when we shall have to do this. The day may come

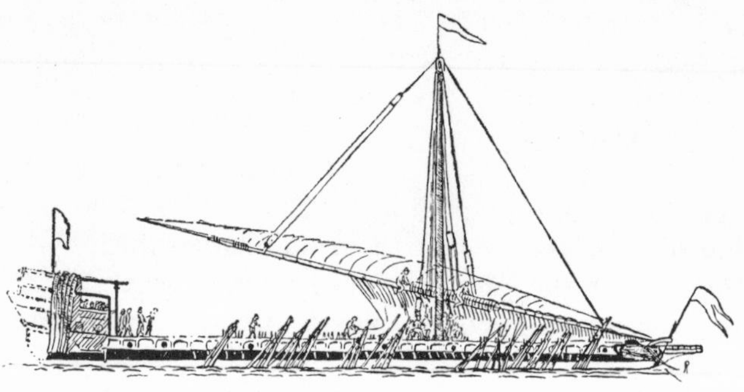

A VENETIAN GALLEY
From *The Sailing Ship*, by Romola and R. C. Anderson

(who can tell?) when the Baconians will prove their theory. Neither day would seem to be imminent. In the meantime, let us cling contentedly to old beliefs.

In any case, whether he were Cristofero Colombo of Genoa or Cristobal Colon of Galicia, in Spain, the navigator who crossed the Atlantic in 1492 can still be known to us by his popular Latinized name. It is tolerably certain, moreover, that in 1470, some six miles off the coast of Portugal, a Venetian galley attacked and sank the ship which he (aged nineteen) was then commanding.

A strong swimmer, he contrived to reach the shore, and so cordially was he received by the sailor-folk of Lisbon that he decided to throw in his lot with them. The enterprising merchants of Portugal seemed likely to offer wider opportunities to an ambitious mariner than the Genoese masters whom he had hitherto served. In 1474 he married one of their daughters.

His wife, a lady of some fortune, owned an estate on the Madeiras. Thither he repaired after his marriage, and there for several years he lived, quietly elaborating the scheme which had already taken shape in his mind. Portuguese seamen were then

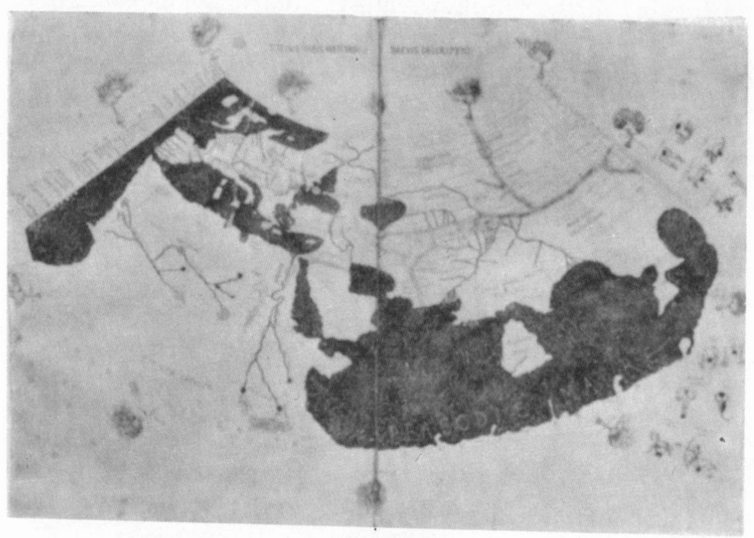

THE WORLD, DRAWN *c.* 140 A.D. BY PTOLEMY (CLAUDIUS PTOLEMÆUS) OF ALEXANDRIA
British Museum

steadily advancing toward the East along the coast of Africa. Columbus believed that by sailing westward he could find a shorter route. A careful comparison of the writings of Marco Polo with the theories of Ptolemy, an astronomer who lived at Alexandria in the second century A.D., turned belief into conviction.

Ptolemy's notion of a globular earth had been rejected as heretical by the mediæval Church. It continued, none the less, to be accepted by many thinking men. For fifteen hundred years, indeed, Ptolemy remained the leading authority on the world's size and shape. He had reckoned the globe, however, to be smaller by one-sixth than it really is.[1] Marco Polo, for his part, consider-

[1] Ptolemy calculated the equatorial circumference of the earth to be 20,400 miles.

ably overestimated the distance he travelled eastward across Asia. Thus, working from false data and having no reason to suspect the existence of an intervening continent, Columbus arrived at the conclusion that a straight course of 2500 miles due west from Lisbon would bring him to Asia—to Zipangu (Japan), Marco Polo's "land of gold."

A voyage of 2500 miles across an unknown sea was a formidable undertaking in the fifteenth century. But it was not one from which an experienced navigator need shrink. The compass and other nautical instruments — the astrolabe, quadrant, and log-line—were sufficiently reliable to encourage sailors to laugh at the old practice of creeping along coasts. Given a well-equipped fleet, Columbus had no doubt as to his ability to execute his project. By 1482 his plan was complete. He had but to find the means to carry it out. His search for a patron took him ten years. It was not, however, as is sometimes suggested, simply crass stupidity on the part of the powers-that-were that forced him thus to hawk about his scheme.

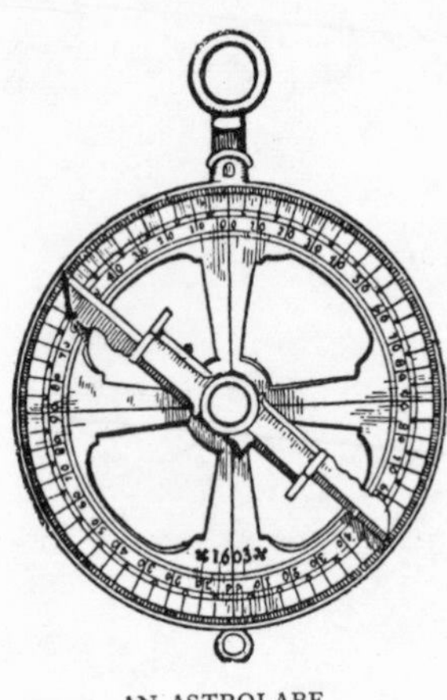

AN ASTROLABE

First, he submitted it to King John II of Portugal. That monarch and his advisers were much too well informed on matters nautical to condemn it as impracticable. They turned it down because their hopes were centred in the circumnavigation of Africa, then nearly completed. The discovery of a westward route to the East was the last thing they wished. The Portuguese, they saw, could not monopolize it; its discovery must ultimately benefit other maritime nations.

Columbus next tried to enlist the support of Genoa. There, too, he was frustrated by political considerations. Though the spread of Turkish power in the Mediterranean was making it increasingly difficult for Italian merchants to do business in Syria, the old trade routes between Europe and the East were not entirely closed. Alexandria was still an open port. The Genoese maintained that it was in their interests to keep trade in the existing channel. The Venetians shared this view.

Columbus went from Venice to Spain. His scheme appealed to "the Catholic Sovereigns," Ferdinand and Isabella, for the very reason that it did not appeal to the King of Portugal. But in 1487, when he arrived at their Court, they were deeply involved in their final struggle with the Moors; with that conflict in progress they would not commit themselves to a definite promise of support. Disheartened by delays Columbus journeyed to Paris, hoping to persuade the French king, Charles VIII, to fit out an expedition. At the same time he sent his brother Bartholomew to England.

In English seafaring circles at that time there was an almost uncanny pre-knowledge of the existence of the New World. As early as 1480 we learn from William of Worcester's *Annals of England*, 1324–1491, two ships sailed from Bristol to find "the island of Brazil," and were out eight weeks before storms turned them back. Nor was this an isolated venture. During the ensuing ten years several similar attempts were made.

In England, Bartholomew Columbus almost certainly would have secured the assistance he sought. As chance would have it, however, he fell in with pirates in the Channel. He was thus delayed in reaching London, and in January 1492, before he could be given an answer, and while the king of France—a country hardly yet infected with the maritime fever—was considering the matter, Christopher received a summons to Madrid. Granada had just fallen, and Queen Isabella had decided to take up his scheme.

Given a well-equipped fleet, we have said, Columbus had no doubt as to his ability to accomplish the voyage. That he should have attempted it with the expedition furnished by the Spanish Queen is proof of his confidence. One of the three ships provided, the *Santa Maria*, was a vessel of 100 tons burthen, but the two other, the *Nina* and the *Pinta*, were little more than open boats, and, save for the traitorous Pinzon and a few others, the fleet was manned almost entirely by gaol-birds unwillingly pressed into service. Even lavish promises of reward would not induce the required number of volunteers to enlist under a foreign leader in so desperate a venture.

The *Santa Maria* and her consorts sailed from Palos on August 3, 1492, and shaped a course toward the Canaries. Thence Columbus purposed to steer due west, along the 28th parallel, till he came to Zipangu. At Teneriffe he was delayed for three weeks. The *Pinta* had broken her rudder; till a new one had been fitted the fleet could not proceed. On September 2 the ships again weighed anchor, Columbus assuring his followers that ere another three weeks should pass they would find themselves in Asia.

Three weeks passed. Yet, though conditions had been consistently favourable, land was nowhere to be seen. The crews began to murmur. The very steadiness of the prevailing 'trades' dismayed them; on the homeward voyage, they asked, would they

THE "SANTA MARIA"
From a model in South Kensington Museum

have to battle continuously with adverse winds? The behaviour of the compass alarmed them yet more. As they advanced they noticed that the needle, which in Spain pointed just to the east of the pole star, shifted farther and farther to the west; were they sailing, they wondered, across a limitless ocean into regions where the very laws of nature were strange?

Columbus, too, was perplexed by the variation of the compass. But he refused to give way to his fears, and, in the hope of reassuring those whom he led, invented a full but fantastic explanation of the phenomenon. By such means, and by tempering threats with cajolery, he contrived to keep his followers steadfast.

During the morning of October 7 the cry "Land ahead!" was raised on one of the ships. The gloom which had settled on the crews instantly vanished. Buoyed up by extravagant visions of riches to be gained, the men's enthusiasm now exceeded that of their chief, and the latter fondly imagined he had overcome the

CHRISTOPHER COLUMBUS
The oldest authentic portrait, from a copy made by order of the Duke of Tuscany in 1568, now in the Uffizi Gallery, Florence.

worst of the difficulties which he had to surmount. But when evening fell, and it was found that a deluding cloud had given rise to false hopes, a violent reaction set in. Murmurings developed into threats of mutiny. "Wait but three days," pleaded Columbus; "if in three days land does not appear, then will I myself put my ship about and return."

The three days passed. Not yet was land to be seen. Signs,

however, were not wanting to suggest its nearness—land birds flying round the ships, reeds and timber drifting in the sea. Presently someone observed a carved stick floating on the water, and

LANDING OF COLUMBUS
From a drawing by Stephen Reid

someone else a branch bearing fresh berries. With one accord the men consented to go on—for a few more days at any rate.

At last, during the night of October 11-12, Columbus standing on the poop of the *Santa Maria* detected the sign which he had long and often sought—a light, or what appeared to be a light, twinkling faintly in the distance. In anxious suspense he waited for day to break. The night seemed interminable. But dawn, when at length it came, showed that this time hope had not deceived him. Along the horizon stretched a misty brown line, which, as the day wore on, was seen to be the coast of a green island.

On the following morning, clad in full armour, Columbus went ashore and took possession of the island on behalf of his royal masters, while his attendants—to the astonishment of the simple, naked natives who crowded round—unfurled the gorgeous standard of Spain. The island was one of the Bahamas group. Columbus piously called it San Salvador. To-day it is known as Watling Island. So it is made to honour a seventeenth-century English buccaneer rather than the man who, by discovering it, brought the Old and New Worlds into contact.

Not until 1819, when, on the break-up of Spain's empire in the West, the republic of Colombia came into being, did even a variation of Columbus's name appear upon maps. Amerigo Vespucci lent his to the American continent, and for doing so has been most unjustly blamed. He himself was in no way responsible. Martin Waldseemüller, a German cosmographer, first made the suggestion in his *Cosmographiæ Introductio*, published in 1507.

At one time Vespucci served under Columbus in the capacity of victualling officer. Subsequently he undertook voyages on his own account—very notable voyages, too—and rose to the high office of grand-pilot of Spain. Emerson's oft-quoted statement that "broad America must bear the name of a . . . pickle-dealer of Seville . . . whose highest naval rank was boatswain's mate in an expedition that never sailed," and who "managed . . . to supplant Columbus, and to baptize half the world with his dishonest name," is wholly false.

Columbus did not tarry among the Bahamas. The natives gave him to understand that if he sailed to the south-west he would come to gold-producing lands. On October 22, therefore, he bore off toward them, and in due course sighted the coast of Cuba, or, as he thought, of China. On the way he touched at other islands. The inhabitants, he has told us, were shy, but friendly and willing to trade, and from their language he picked up words—*tobacco* and *hammock*, for example—which, in slightly varying forms, have passed into the common speech of Europe. From Cuba he proceeded to Haiti. This island he named Hispaniola; and though he failed to find there the cities described by Marco Polo, he believed he had reached an outlying region of Japan.

Toward the end of November he had the misfortune to be deprived of one of his ships. Martin Pinzon, whom he had looked on as his most trustworthy lieutenant, deserted with the *Pinta* and made for Europe. A few weeks later the expedition suffered a heavier loss. On Christmas Eve, owing to carelessness on the part of the officer in charge, the *Santa Maria* was wrecked on a sand-bank. Thus left with only the *Niña*, a craft of 40 tons burden, Columbus decided to return to Spain, having first built a fort for the wrecked ship's crew. He set sail on January 4, 1493, taking with him five natives and at least enough gold to excite the greed of his Spanish employers.

On her eastward voyage the *Niña* encountered tremendous seas. Time after time it seemed that the little vessel must perish. But the *Pinta* fared even worse. The *Niña*, indeed, overhauled her in mid-Atlantic. Columbus himself, therefore, despite the treacherous purpose of Pinzon, brought the news of his discoveries to Europe. The *Niña* arrived at Palos on March 15.

In all, Columbus led four expeditions to the West, and the third, that of 1498, reached the mouth of the Orinoco river. In the preceding year, however, John Cabot, an Italian in the service of the English king, Henry VII, touched the Labrador coast. Thus, though the credit of having discovered—or, rather, of having rediscovered—America belongs to Columbus and Spain, the Cross of St George was the European flag first to be unfurled on the mainland of the continent.

Columbus to the end of his days did not doubt that the West Indies—so called—formed a part of Asia. Men generally shared his conviction. In 1513 Nuñez de Balboa crossed the isthmus of Darien and gazed on the ocean beyond. Faith in the Columbian hypothesis, however, remained still unshaken; the Pacific was held to be an inland sea. This notion was finally exploded as a result of the Portuguese advance in the East.

In 1517 traders from Lisbon arrived at Canton, and so gained fuller knowledge of the waters which lie to the east of China. Portuguese sailors then began to guess at the truth: that the Indies, which Columbus discovered, had been wrongly named, and that a western sea-route to Asia had yet to be found. Ferdinand Magellan at once determined to renew the quest. Refused an

RETURN OF COLUMBUS TO SPAIN
From the painting by R. Balaca
Photo J. Roig

increase of pay by the Portuguese Government, he entered the service of the Emperor Charles V (who was also king of Spain), and in September 1519 set out on the voyage which showed the New World to be 'new' in a sense which, up to that time, only he and a few others had suspected.

As governor of Spain's American empire, Columbus soon—and perhaps inevitably—fell out with his grandee colleagues. In 1500 intriguers at Court contrived to drive him from office. One Francisco de Bobadilla was then appointed viceroy in his stead. By Bobadilla's orders, the ex-governor was sent back to Spain in chains, and, though the king and queen readily found him guiltless of the charges brought against him, he was never really restored to favour. The words put into his mouth by Tennyson well express the regrets which embittered the close of his life:

> Cast off, put by, scouted by court and king—
> The first discoverer starves—his followers, all
> Flower into fortune—our world's way—and I,
> Without a roof that I can call mine own,
> With scarce a coin to buy a meal withal,
> And seeing what a door for scoundrel scum
> I open'd to the West, . . . I
> Could sometimes wish I had never led the way.

Broken in health and spirit, and almost penniless, he died at Valladolid in 1506. Several years elapsed ere the Spanish authorities, "slowly wise and meanly just," sought to atone for their neglect of him by showering honours on his descendants. Restless while alive, the great navigator could not rest even when dead. His bones continued to travel for nearly four centuries. In 1513 they were moved from Valladolid to Seville. In 1536 they were sent to Hispaniola, and thence, in 1797, to Havana. Finally, in 1898, after the Spanish-American War, they were brought back to Seville.

In 1492, when he sailed from Palos, Columbus made straight for the Canaries, so that he might be borne thence across the Atlantic by the prevailing trade winds. Ten years earlier he had intended to sail due west from Lisbon. Say he had carried out that intention in 1492. He would then have struck the American continent somewhere in the vicinity of Long Island. In that case, instead of a New Amsterdam (later renamed 'New York'), would

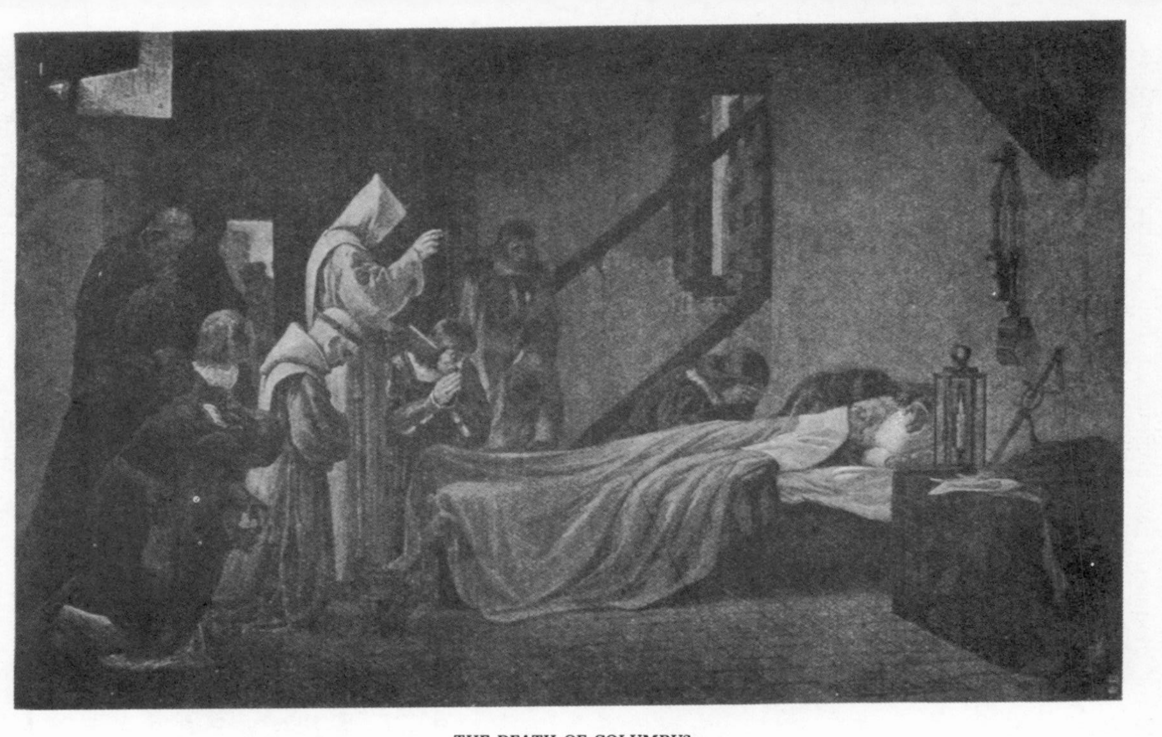

THE DEATH OF COLUMBUS
From the painting by F. Ortego
Photo J. Roig

a New Madrid have arisen at the mouth of the Hudson River? Or would the Spaniards have abandoned their enterprise toward the West?

Within twenty years of Columbus's death Spanish conquerors had annexed the greater part of Central and South America. In North America the first permanent European settlement was planted in 1607. Chile, Mexico, and Peru happened to produce those metals which sixteenth-century economists held to be wealth in its most desirable form. In North America gold and silver were not to be found. North America, therefore, was long looked on merely as a gateway to better lands. Explorers came and went. Fisherfolk visited the waters off Newfoundland. Settlers did not arrive till the glamour of the Age of Discovery had faded, till sober-minded men began to see that agriculture and industry were, after all, the surest sources of wealth, and that colonies were of value not merely for what could be got out of them, but for what could be sold to them; that by planting settlers overseas they were creating new markets.

HOUSE AT VALLADOLID WHERE COLUMBUS DIED

The Spaniards of the sixteenth century, by seizing treasure which the natives of their empire had been accumulating for hundreds of years, provided themselves and the other peoples of Europe with convenient instruments of exchange, and placed commerce on a new basis. But they did their own country more harm than good. American gold proved the ruin of Spain. Meanwhile, on the Newfoundland fisheries were being laid the foundations of Britain's imperial greatness.

How far have accidents determined the course of history? An interesting book might be written on the subject. Not the least provoking chapter would deal with the chance which led Columbus to the Bahamas and John Cabot to the Gulf of St Lawrence.

VI. VASCO DA GAMA

Born c. 1460; *died* 1524

THE Portuguese of the fifteenth century owed their maritime ascendancy in no small measure to the efforts of Prince Henry the Navigator. The main motive which inspired that practical visionary was a desire to locate the capital of Prester John, and so, by bringing the fabled Christian potentate of the East into alliance with the Christian rulers of the West, to stem the tide of Mohammedan conquest. If also he could open a direct sea-route between Europe and the spice-producing lands of Asia, so much the better. In 1460, when he died, this ambition was far from attainment. Yet the Navigator had not laboured in vain. Others faithfully carried on the work which he had begun, and in 1481, on the accession of King John II, their endeavours received a fresh and powerful stimulus.

John II steadfastly championed the cause of discovery, sparing neither pains nor money in his encouragement of enterprise. In 1487, in pursuit of Prince Henry's objects, he sent out three expeditions. Two of them were land expeditions, the leaders, Pedro Covilham and Alfonso de Payva, being instructed to traverse Africa from west to east. Meanwhile, the third, a fleet under Bartholomew Dias, sought to circumnavigate the continent. Neither of the land leaders returned to Europe. Covilham, however, who got to Christian Abyssinia, contrived to send back a report which not only lent colour to the Prester John tradition, but definitely asserted that ships, by sailing down the Guinea coast, could reach the southern extremity of Africa. Between that point and India, the writer added, lay open sea. Shortly afterward Dias arrived at Lisbon, and in part, at any rate, confirmed this statement.

In latitude 20° S., Dias related, he encountered a tremendous storm. To avoid, therefore, the danger of shipwreck on an unknown shore he stood well out to sea. When calmer weather set in he again turned south-eastward and made for the coast. But presently, since he did not sight land as soon as he had anticipated, his crews began to murmur. Finally, they prevailed upon him to bear northward. So at length he came to an inlet which he named Cowherd's (*dos Vaqueiros*) Bay,[1] the inlet now known as Algoa Bay.

Seeing that the coast still tended to the east he assumed that he had not yet reached the extremity of Africa. But neither threats nor entreaties would induce his sorely tried followers to pursue the quest farther. Reluctantly, therefore, he agreed to shape a course toward home. Not many days later, while sailing westward, he beheld a great headland looming ahead; the Stormy Cape (*Cabo Tormentoso*) he named it, because a tempest nearly overwhelmed his ships as he was rounding it. Having rounded it, he forgot in a moment its inhospitable greeting. He then saw that the coast turned sharply to the north, and realized that he had accomplished his mission after all—that the headland was the southernmost point of Africa, and that he had passed to the east of it. On his return to Portugal he changed its name, at King John's insistence, to 'the Cape of Good Hope' (*Cabo de Boa Esperança*).

> "Thou southernmost point," the joyful King exclaimed,
> "Cape of Good Hope be thou for ever named."

Elated by hopes of extending his sovereignty to eastern lands, King John straightway laid plans for sending out another expedition. Political troubles for some time delayed the execution of the scheme. Not until 1497, two years after the accession of King Manoel I, were the arrangements—expedited latterly by the news of Columbus's discoveries—finally made. Vasco da Gama was entrusted with the command.

Born at Sines about 1460, while his father was acting as governor of the Province of Alemtejo, Gama had as a young man fought with distinction in his country's service, and had proved himself an intrepid and skilful mariner, animated by an indomitable perseverance. His demeanour, we are told, was generally stern and cold, though he would sometimes relax so far as to dance a hornpipe with his sailors; and, if an iron disciplinarian, he was scrupulously just to those who served under him, holding neither birth nor fortune, but merit only, to be the road to promotion. Wrote

[1] Dias so named it by reason of the cattle he found browsing near the shore, guarded by their herds. 'Algoa,' the name subsequently given to the bay, is a corruption of *à la Goa*. Just as Delagoa Bay became a regular port of call for homeward-bound East Indiamen, so Algoa Bay became a regular port of call for vessels outward bound.

his biographer, Gaspar Correa: He "ever preferred a low man who had won honour with his right arm to a gentleman." A better leader could hardly have been found.

The fleet placed at his disposal comprised four ships. Two of them, the *São Raphael* and the *São Gabriel*, were built specially for the purpose under the direction of Bartholomew Dias, who freely gave Gama the benefit of his wide experience. Roomy craft

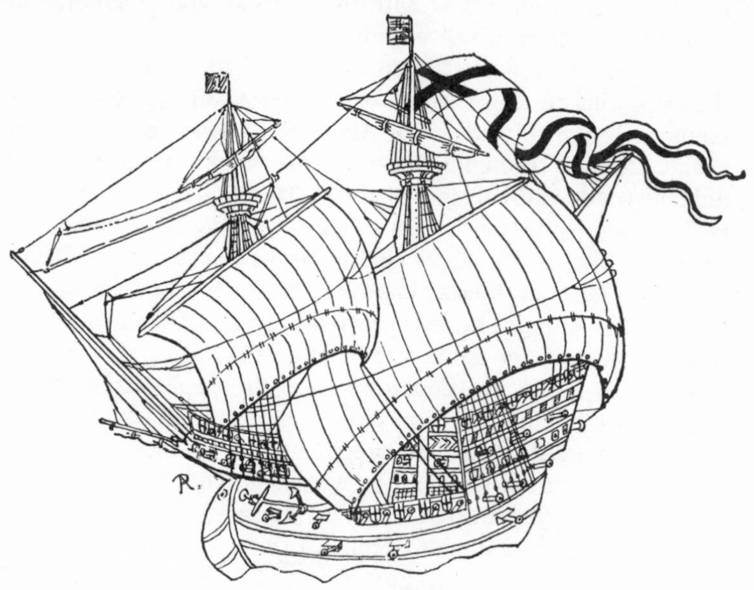

AN ENGLISH SHIP OF THE FIFTEENTH CENTURY
From *The Sailing Ship*, by Romola and R. C. Anderson

of about 120 tons burden, broad abeam and low amidships, with lofty 'castles' fore and aft, they proved to be much better adapted for voyages in stormy latitudes than the vessels of the caravel type, which the Portuguese had hitherto employed. Each had three masts, the fore and main carrying two square sails, and the mizzen a single lateen.

Gama chose the *São Gabriel* as his flagship. His brother, Paulo, he made captain of the *São Raphael*. The other two vessels—the *Berrio*, a 50-ton caravel, and a small store-ship—were commanded, respectively, by a certain Nicolau Coelho and by an old retainer of the Gama family, Goncala Nunes by name. To take part in the expedition a hundred and seventy men were mustered in all, the post of chief pilot being allotted to Pedro de Alemquer, who, in 1487, had accompanied Dias in a similar capacity.

On the evening of Friday, July 7, 1497, everything being ready for a start, the admiral and his captains repaired to a chapel which Prince Henry the Navigator had provided at Belem [1] for the use of seafaring folk. There they kept solemn vigil throughout the night. Next morning, in the presence of the king and Court, they and their crews embarked with much pomp and ceremony, and set forth on their great adventure.

On July 27 the fleet reached the Cape Verde Islands. Thence it ran parallel to the African coast as far as lat. 10° N. At this point, acting on the advice of Alemquer, Gama decided to fetch a wide compass through the South Atlantic in order to escape the difficult winds and currents of the Gulf of Guinea. Accordingly he bore south-westward, continuing on that course until he was within six hundred miles of the mainland of America. Then he turned to the south-east, and, beating slowly back against the trade winds, brought his fleet, on November 7, into the anchorage to which he gave the name of St Helena Bay.

Since the day of his departure from the Cape Verdes he had sailed four thousand five hundred miles without sighting land. Such an achievement had no precedent. Columbus, in 1492, on his voyage from the Canaries to Watling Island, his first landfall in the New World, covered only two thousand six hundred miles.

The Hottentot natives of South Africa were disposed at first to be friendly to the men from Portugal. Their friendship, however, soon turned to enmity. But though, during a skirmish, Gama was struck by a spear, the adventurers suffered no serious hurt at their hands, and on November 16 they resumed their voyage. Six days later they dropped anchor in Mossel Bay. There Gama had his store-ship, which had become unseaworthy, broken up, and her crew and contents transferred to the other vessels. This done, he again set sail, and, having passed on Christmas Day along the coast of the land which—in honour of the season—he named Natal (Latin *Dies Natalis*), he came without further misadventure to the mouth of the Zambesi, which, on learning that not far to the north lay very rich lands, he called the River of Good Tokens (*Rio dos Bons Signaes*).

[1] Now a suburb of Lisbon. The church of St Maria, built to commemorate Gama's voyage, stands on the site of this chapel.

There he decided to stay for some time in order to repair his ships and allow a spell of much-needed rest to his men. Many of the latter, we learn from the *Roteiro*,[1] a log or journal kept by a member of the expedition, had lately fallen sick, "their feet and hands swelling, and their gums growing over their teeth, so that they could not eat." At that time European sailors were strangers to scurvy. Ere long they came to know the disease only too well.

On February 24 Gama again set sail, and on March 2 he arrived at Mozambique, a trading centre much frequented by Arabs. Lying in the harbour, he found many merchant vessels—large ships and decked, though badly designed and constructed. To the surprise of his followers, however, all were provided with 'Genoese needles,' quadrants, and navigating charts, and all were laden with rich merchandize—gold and silver, pepper, cloves, and cloth.

The Portuguese, continuing northward, next touched at Mombasa, another important commercial centre of Arab Africa. Thence they made their way to Malindi. By the Mohammedan rulers of Mozambique and Mombasa the "dogs of Christians" had been received with scant courtesy. The Raja of Malindi, on the other hand, proved himself a true and loyal friend to them. For nine days, April 15–23, he entertained them royally, loading them with gifts and favours. Thanks to his good offices, moreover, their leader secured the services of a pilot who undertook to guide him to India.

On April 24, therefore, Gama once more weighed anchor, and, instead of pursuing his original plan of coasting to Abyssinia, put out to sea. For twenty-three days, favoured by a steady breeze from the south-west (the herald of monsoon rains), he held on a straight course north-east. Then, on May 18, after skirting the northern islands of the Laccadive group, the pilot turned due east. Four days later—ten months and two weeks after their departure from Lisbon—the Portuguese ships rode at anchor in the harbour of Calicut on the Malabar coast.

Calicut is now a place of little importance. At that time it was a busy and populous centre, famous for the manufacture of the fabric still known as calico. But, though a Hindu city, ruled by a Hindu *zamorin*, Moplahs—fanatical Mohammedan immigrants from Arabia—controlled its industries. These people, anxious to

[1] A translation of the *Roteiro*, edited by E. G. Ravenstein, is to be found among the publications of the Hakluyt Society.

keep trade between Europe and the East in the existing channel, lost no opportunity of inciting the natives against the new-comers. By adopting a conciliatory policy, and at the same time spreading abroad a report that his small squadron was the advance guard of a fleet of fifty vessels, Gama gained for his followers a promise of protection from the *zamorin*. That ruler, indeed, "determined in

LANDING-PLACE, CALICUT
Photo E. N. A.

his heart to establish with the Portuguese all the peace and friendship that was possible." The Moplahs, however, won the support of his chamberlain, and contrived to kidnap Gama one day as he was leaving the palace.

Had not his brother acted promptly the admiral would probably have lost his life. On hearing of what had happened, Paulo da Gama at once seized six leading *nairs*, or nobles. By holding these men to ransom, he eventually secured an exchange of prisoners. Next day, vowing a bloody vengeance on the city, the Portuguese left Calicut. Thence they proceeded to Cannanore. Afterward they went to Cochin. Then, early in August, satisfied that rumour had not exaggerated the wealth of India, their leader determined to make for home.

On the return journey across the Arabian Sea his fleet was much delayed by calms and contrary winds. Scurvy, moreover, again broke out on board, and took so deadly a toll of his crews that at Malindi he was compelled to abandon the *São Raphael*; he no longer had hands enough to work her. Wrote the author of the *Roteiro*:

> Thirty of our men died in this manner—an equal number having died previously—and those able to navigate our ships were only seven or eight; and even then were not so well as they ought to have been.

With his two remaining ships, the *São Gabriel* and the *Berrio*, Gama departed from Malindi early in January 1499. On the voyage home sickness and bad weather dogged him persistently; not until September 5 did he at length enter the Tagus. At Lisbon, however, he and his devoted followers received a welcome which amply compensated them for all the hardship they had borne, and their sovereign heaped rewards upon them. Had they not found the long-sought route to the East? The King straightway styled himself 'Lord of the Conquest, Navigation and Commerce of Ethiopia, Arabia, Persia, and India,' [1] and in the follow ing March sent out the senior admiral in his service, Pedro Alvares Cabral, with a fleet of thirteen ships, to make good his claim to the title.

Borrowing a leaf from Gama's book, Cabral, on his voyage southward, gave a wide berth to the coast of Africa. But he bore farther to the west, and on April 22—by chance, or, as some say, by design—discovered Brazil. In due course, however, he arrived at India, and forcibly established factories at Calicut and Cochin.

A few months later, at the instigation of Moplah merchants, Hindus attacked and destroyed the factory at Calicut. King Manoel, thus afforded a pretext for making a more definite assertion of his authority, forthwith put in hand the equipping of a punitive expedition. At first he gave the command to Bartholomew Dias. Subsequently, in response to earnest entreaties, he transferred it to Gama. "Sire," said that dour old seaman, "the king of Calicut arrested me and treated me with contumely; and I did not return to avenge the injury. Therefore he has committed a greater one. On this account, I feel in my heart a strong desire and inclination to go and make havoc of him."

[1] The title was first used by King Manoel in a letter dated September 1499; it was confirmed by Pope Alexander VI in 1502.

He duly carried out his purpose. Calicut he reduced to a shambles. He then sailed southward to Cochin, "doing"—as he boasted—"all the harm that he could on the way to all that he found on the sea." So, by ruthless means, he laid the foundations upon which his successors, the famous viceroys Almeida and Albuquerque, built—likewise by ruthless means—Portugal's proud but short-lived empire in the East.

Almeida acquired footholds for his countrymen at a number of points on the Indian coast, notably at Goa, and in 1505 trading fleets bearing cargoes of spices and other oriental produce began to appear regularly at Lisbon. By shipping them direct the Portuguese were able to sell these things at a much lower rate than could the merchants of Italy. The Venetians and Genoese thus lost such of their trade as the Turks had not already taken from them.

Since the Syrian ports had been closed to Christians, Alexandria was the only market open to them, and the conveyance of merchandize thither from Calicut was a costly business. Goods had first to be sent by ship to Jidda on the Red Sea, and then by smaller craft to the head of the Gulf of Suez. There they were loaded on camels and so brought to Cairo. From Cairo they were carried down the Nile in barges to Rosetta, and thence sent by camel transport to the coast. At Jidda, at the head of the Gulf of Suez, and again at Cairo and Rosetta, the local authorities demanded heavy dues. These charges, which the Portuguese avoided, very greatly increased the prices which Italian buyers had to pay.

At length, finding their European trade seriously threatened, the Arab dealers in the East organized a league against Portugal. The Venetians lent them aid. But, when it came to fighting, the ships of the Arabs were no match for those of their rivals. In February 1509, off Diu, near Bombay, Almeida won a decisive victory. After that the Portuguese rapidly extended their influence. Albuquerque, who took office as viceroy in 1510, gained territories not only in India but in Arabia, Persia, and Ceylon; also in Borneo and, most important of all, in the Moluccas, "the Spice Islands." He even opened up trade with China and Japan.

In 1580 the old ruling house of Portugal died out. King Philip II of Spain, who was related by marriage to the last native king, then seized the throne. The Portuguese accepted the Spanish yoke very unwillingly, and in 1640, under a new royal house (the house of Braganza), they reasserted their independence.

For sixty years, however, they were constrained to follow the fortunes of Spain. During that time they lost nearly all their eastern possessions.

In 1584 King Philip vented his spleen on the Dutch by closing Lisbon harbour against them. The merchants of Amsterdam were not the men to be dismayed by a move of this kind. Barred from getting in Portugal the spices which they had long made it their business to distribute in northern Europe, they resolved to ship them direct, and so, incidentally, to cut out the middleman's profits. In these circumstances was formed the Netherlands East India Company.

The Dutch secured their first footing in the East on Amboyna, a small island in the Moluccas group. Supported by the natives, whom they treated with a fairness the Portuguese had never shown, they quickly widened their sphere of influence, and by the middle of the seventeenth century—when they captured Malacca,[1] their rivals' chief stronghold—they had reduced Portugal's empire in Asia practically to its present dimensions.

That empire comprises to-day three small districts in India, a part of Timor, and the island of Macao. The rest passed almost entirely into the hands of the Dutch, who now own in and around the Malay archipelago wealthy and populous lands with a total area of some 800,000 square miles. Numerous ruined buildings, such as the old cathedral at Malacca, and the many people partly of Portuguese descent and bearing Portuguese names who are to be found in every Malayan seaport, alone remain to testify that Portugal was once a great power in those seas.

The British empire in Asia had an origin somewhat similar to that of the Dutch. The merchants of Amsterdam, having gained practically a monopoly of the spice trade, elected in 1599 to raise the price of pepper from 3s. to 8s. a pound. London merchants refused to pay this price. Certain of them, therefore, banded together, and, following the precedent created by the Dutch, decided to send their own ships to the spice lands. To this "Company of Merchants of London trading into the East Indies" Queen Elizabeth gave a royal charter in December 1600, and early in the next year the directors sent out a fleet, commanded by Captain James Lancaster, to open up trade with Java.

[1] Malacca is now a British possession. The Dutch ceded it in 1825 in exchange for Bencoolen in Sumatra.

Lancaster founded a factory at Bantam. Other factories were soon established elsewhere. The company's enterprise, however, at once excited the jealousy of the Dutch, who, securely planted in the Malay archipelago, began to treat the British in very much the same way that they had treated the Portuguese. So keen became the rivalry between the two nations that, in 1623, Dutchmen at Amboyna had no compunction in brutally murdering the English factor and his assistants simply because the latter commanded trade facilities they coveted. After this the London merchants, while stubbornly maintaining a hold on the spice lands, resolved to concentrate their attention on India. During the seventeenth century they established factories all round the coast.

Meanwhile a French East India Company, too, came into being.

In 1580 the Spanish Government indignantly protested against Drake's trespassings in Spanish seas. Queen Elizabeth retorted: "Neither can a title to the ocean belong to any people or private persons; forasmuch as neither nature nor public use and custom permitteth any possession thereof." Other rulers tacitly endorsed the English Queen's words. Following the lead of the sea-dogs of Devon, Frenchmen and Dutchmen, Danes, Germans, and Swedes jostled and fought through the door to the West which Columbus had opened. Likewise, through the door opened by Bartholomew Dias and Vasco da Gama, men of all European nations, heedless of warnings to trespassers, rudely pressed into Asia.

Gama returned to Europe from his second expedition in 1503, and in recognition of his services was forthwith created Count of Vidigueira. Other "great favours" also were bestowed upon him, a new office, the Admiralty of India, being specially set up for his benefit. The royal rescript is still extant. In it "D. Vasco da Gama, a Gentleman of the King's Household," is named as "Admiral of the aforesaid India, with all the pre-eminences, liberties, power, jurisdiction, revenues, privileges and rights which, as appertaining to the aforesaid Admiralty, our Admiral of those realms ought by right to possess, and does hereby possess." Nor was this an empty form. From harbour dues alone Gama derived so large an income that, according to the Venetian ambassador, there was not in all Portugal a nobleman, or even a prince of the Church, so wealthy. The next twenty years, therefore, he passed in leisured ease on his estates at Vidigueira.

Yet the old seaman did not allow himself to lose interest in the profession to which he had devoted his life, and in 1524, when given the offer, he readily emerged from retirement to take up the

VASCO DA GAMA
From an old engraving

post of Viceroy in the East. But he was then in his sixty-fourth year; his constitution could not stand the strain of office in the climate of India. Within two months of his arrival he was stricken down with fever, and at Cochin, on Christmas Eve, he died.

VII. FERDINAND MAGELLAN

Born c. 1470; *died* 1521

COLUMBUS returned to Spain in 1493, having found, so he thought, a western sea route between Europe and Asia. King Ferdinand straightway sent an embassy to Rome to petition for a share of the Indies which Papal decree had conferred on the crown of Portugal. Pope Alexander VI (Rodrigo Borgia), anxious to promote peace in Christendom, acceded to the request. On May 4 he issued a Bull which divided the world into two parts by a line drawn from pole to pole, and passing through a point 100 leagues to the west of the Azores. The eastern half he assigned to Portugal, the western half to Spain; and neither Power, he ordained, might encroach upon the other's sphere of influence.

King Ferdinand was well satisfied with the arrangement. Not so the King of Portugal, John II (1481–95). Recent research suggests that a ship fitted out by Prince Henry the Navigator crossed the Atlantic in 1448, and that the existence of Brazil was a secret in the possession of the Portuguese Government long before Columbus 'discovered' America. King John II, it would seem, had no intention of renouncing his claim to this known but unexplored land.

At any rate, without disclosing the reason for his demand, he urged that the line of demarcation between the Spanish and Portuguese spheres should be moved 270 leagues farther to the west. The Pope obligingly agreed. On June 7, 1494, he issued a second Bull. This secured for Portugal a large part of Brazil, which Cabral officially discovered and annexed in 1500. On the other hand, it brought a part of the former Portuguese Indies within the Spanish sphere.

Early in the following century it became apparent that the Indies discovered by Columbus had no connexion with the Portuguese Indies; that between the two lay an impassable barrier of land, and an ocean of unmeasured extent. Spanish empire builders were thus presented with a perplexing problem. How, without trespassing on Portugal's preserves, could they send ships to those spice-producing eastern lands which rightly belonged to Spain?

Balboa and other explorers dreamed of finding a western approach by way of a channel through the isthmus of Darien. Such a channel was not to be found. The Cabots, meanwhile, sailing under the English flag, were equally unsuccessful in their search for a north-west passage. Thus Spain seemed to be completely cut off from the East. Then, in 1516, there arrived at the Court of Charles I,[1] King Ferdinand's successor, a navigator, Magellan by name, who undertook to open to Spanish commerce a practicable south-west passage.

Fernão de Magalhães, *alias* Ferdinand Magellan, belonged to one of the noblest families of Portugal. He was born, probably, in 1470, at Villa de Sabrosa in the district of Villa Real, Traz-os-Montes. As a young man he served with distinction under Almeida and the great Albuquerque, and played a notable part in the building up of the Portuguese empire in the East. But King Emmanuel, John II's successor, we are told, "always loathed him." In consequence he was denied rewards and honours which he deemed to be his due. At length, much angered by the treatment accorded him, he shook from his feet the dust of Portugal, and, crossing the Spanish frontier, resolved to offer his services to King Charles, his own ungrateful sovereign's chief rival in the field of maritime endeavour. In Spain he contrived to enlist the support of Juan Rodriguez de Fonseca, bishop of Burgos and president of the so-called "Council of the Indies," which was responsible for the management of colonial affairs. He had little difficulty, therefore, in gaining the ear of the King. Charles and he, in the manner of those days, then entered into a formal agreement.

The navigator undertook to assert the King's sovereignty in such East Indian lands as the Bull of 1494 had brought within the Spanish sphere. The King undertook to furnish the navigator with a fleet, and to allow him not only one-twentieth part of the profits of the expedition, but, in perpetuity, one-fifteenth part of the profits accruing from any two of the islands he might annex. Upon Magellan also was conferred the hereditary title of

[1] Better known as the Emperor Charles V. Ferdinand's daughter Joanna (the elder sister of Catherine of Aragon, Henry VIII of England's first queen) married Philip, only son of the Emperor Maximilian I. Philip died in 1506, and Joanna became insane. Thus their son Charles in 1516, on Ferdinand's death, inherited the throne of Spain. In 1519, on the death of Maximilian, he was elected Holy Roman Emperor.

'Governor' over all lands he should discover, together with a substantial pension.

The fleet entrusted to his command comprised five vessels—the *Conception*, *Santiago*, *Santo Antonio*, *Trinidad*, and *Victoria*, ranging in burden from 75 tons to 120 tons. The crews numbered 270 persons. Much time and trouble were spent in fitting out the ships, and the expedition, which sailed from Seville on August 10, 1519, was the best equipped that had ever left Spain. The arma-

MAGELLAN'S SHIP "VICTORIA"

ment included 62 culverins, 10 falconets, 10 bombards or mortars, and 50 harquebuses; also 5600 lbs. of gunpowder. In the list of navigating appliances appear 21 wooden quadrants, 12 compasses, 7 astrolabes, 23 charts, and 18 hourglasses. A considerable cargo also was carried. This was made up mostly of mirrors, glass beads, and quicksilver—commodities likely to find a ready market in savage lands.

From Seville the fleet headed for the Canaries, which were reached after twelve days' sailing. Teneriffe's volcano chanced to be in eruption. Terrified by the spectacle, as the followers of Columbus had been terrified before them, Magellan's men for some time refused point-blank to continue the voyage.

On leaving Teneriffe the five vessels ran parallel to the African coast as far as Cape Verde. Thence Magellan bore across the

Atlantic to Cape St Roque, in Brazil, and from there he slowly coasted southward till he came to the Rio de la Plata. This estuary he explored for many miles in the belief that it was the passage he sought. Resuming his southward course, he arrived at length, a few days after Christmas, at Port St Julian, in lat. 49½° S. There he decided to anchor for the winter.

The adventurers while cruising down the coast of Brazil had been favoured by good weather. This and the friendliness of the natives made progress easy and comfortable. They found the natives to be simple souls. Antonio Pigafetta, a knight of Vicenza, who accompanied Magellan, recorded with glee in his punctiliously kept *Journal* [1] how some of them in exchange for the king of a pack of playing-cards gave him five fat fowls; "and," he added, "they thought they had cheated me."

Off Patagonia conditions were less pleasant, and the dreary weeks spent at Port St Julian, where the natives were hostile and provisions scarce, provoked grave discontent among the crews. The men openly scoffed at the possibility of rounding the American continent, and day by day demanded of their admiral, more and more insistently, that he should return to Europe. On Easter Day 1520 discontent developed into mutiny. Heavily Magellan's hand fell on the leaders of the revolt. Several, including Quesada, captain of the *Conception*, were put to death; others were marooned. These stern measures served at least to muzzle dissatisfaction.

On August 24 the fleet—reduced to four vessels, the *Santiago* having run on a sandbank while reconnoitring in June—left Port St Julian, and on October 21 at last was sighted what proved to be the most southerly point of the American mainland. That day was St Ursula's Day. Therefore, St Ursula being the patron saint of maidens, Magellan named the headland the 'Cape of the Virgins.' Next day he rounded it, and passed into the channel he had come so far to find.

The dangerous passage of Magellan's Strait—a tortuous waterway 400 miles in length, in places not two miles wide, and flanked by snow-capped cliffs rising to 7000 feet in height—occupied thirty-eight days, but was accomplished without mishap, save that at Cape Froward, half-way through, the captain of the *Santo Antonio* turned his ship about and made off during the night for Spain.

[1] Lord Stanley's *First Voyage round the World*, 1874 (Hakluyt Society's Publications, vol. lii), contains an English translation.

On November 28 the three remaining vessels sailed into the ocean beyond. Magellan named this ocean 'the Pacific'; his ships while crossing it did not encounter a single storm.

The crossing, none the less, was fraught with peril. The Spaniards, as America receded behind them, little guessed how far they would have to travel ere again they came to land. Their provisions—their supplies of water, too—were almost exhausted when but half the distance had been traversed. The privation they endured may be gauged by the following entry in Pigafetta's *Journal*: "We ate biscuit reduced to powder and full of grubs, and we drank water that was yellow and stinking. We also ate the ox-hides which were under the main-yard, so that the yard should not break the rigging; they were very hard on account of the sun, rain, and wind, and we left them for four or five days in the sun, and then we put them a little on the embers and so ate them; also the saw dust of wood, and rats." In the circumstances, it is surprising, perhaps, that only nineteen men died of scurvy.

The first land touched by the starving mariners was the group of islands known to us as the Ladrones (*i.e.*, 'Robbers').[1] The Spaniards so named the islands on account of the thieving propensities of the natives. From those same natives, however, they obtained much-needed fruit and vegetables.

The next place of call was Zebu, an island of the Philippine group. The fleet arrived there on April 7. The King of Zebu, who had already heard of Portuguese conquests in the East, hastened to make terms with the Spanish strangers. Not only did he acknowledge the King of Spain as his suzerain, but allowed himself and all his leading subjects to be baptized. The ruler of Mactan, a neighbouring and vassal island, proved less submissive. Magellan determined to teach him a lesson. Accordingly, at the head of sixty followers, he landed on the island. But the natives fought with unexpected resolution, and the Spanish force, hopelessly outnumbered, was cut down almost to a man. Pigafetta, who escaped, thus described how his leader fell:

> He, with a few of us, like a good knight, remained at his post, without choosing to retreat farther. Thus we fought for more than an hour, until the Indians succeeded in thrusting a cane lance into

[1] Annexed by Magellan, the Ladrones remained in Spanish hands till 1899. They were then bought by Germany. The Treaty of Versailles (1919) allocated them to Japan.

the captain's face. He then, being irritated, pierced the Indian's breast with his lance, and left it in his body. . . . The enemies,

FERDINAND MAGELLAN
From an old print

seeing this, all rushed upon him, and one of them with a great sword, like a scimitar, gave him a great blow on the left leg, and brought the captain down on his face; then the Indians threw themselves upon him, and ran him through with lances and scimitars and all the other arms which they had, so that they deprived of life our mirror, light, comfort, and true guide.

This disaster encouraged the King of Zebu to reassert his independence. In the circumstances, the captain of the *Victoria*, Sebastian Del Cano, upon whom the command of the expedition had devolved, deemed it prudent hastily to depart from the Philippines. So, having abandoned the *Conception*, which he was no longer able to man, he gave orders for the *Victoria* and *Trinidad* (Captain Espinosa) to weigh anchor, and sailed southward to Borneo. Thence he made his way to Brunei, and so to Tidor, one of the Molucca Islands. There, having secured a rich cargo of spices, he announced his intention of returning to Europe round the Cape of Good Hope. Espinosa would not agree to the proposal; he insisted on retracing his course. The two captains, therefore, parted company.

The *Victoria* sailed from Tidor on November 20, thus narrowly escaping a Portuguese fleet which put in there a few days afterward and seized the *Trinidad*. Skilfully piloted by Del Cano, the little vessel—though buffeted by almost continuous storms, though undermanned by a scurvy-stricken crew, and assailed several times by Portuguese merchantmen—struggled back to Spain. She anchored in the River Guadalquivir, near the Mole of Seville, on September 9, 1522, after an absence of nearly three years—the first ship to circumnavigate the world. On board were 18 men, all that remained of the 270 who had set out under Magellan's leadership.

The survivors included Pigafetta. Barefoot and clad only in a shirt, that brave knight, on landing, repaired straight to the shrine of St Mary of Victory to render thanks for his deliverance. "Then," he wrote, "leaving Seville, I went to Valladolid, where I presented to his sacred Majesty, Don Carlos, neither gold nor silver, but things more precious in the eyes of so great a sovereign. I presented to him, among other things, a book written by my own hand of all the things that had occurred day by day in the voyage."

Pigafetta was not a keen or accurate observer. The stormy petrel, for example, he described as a "bird of such a nature that when the female wishes to lay her eggs she goes and lays them on the back of the male, and there it is that the eggs are hatched." Again, he described a Patagonian native as "so tall that the tallest of us only came up to his waist." His *Journal*, however, is a lively and worthy record of a memorable venture. The voyage finally dispelled all lingering doubts as to the world's shape. Incidentally, it proved that a vessel sailing westward round the globe must lose a day. The *Victoria*, we have said, arrived at Seville on September 9. According to her log-book the date was September 8. For some time mathematicians were much puzzled by the discrepancy.

Del Cano brought back spices which realized a sum more than sufficient to pay the cost of the expedition. King Charles, therefore, in recognition of his achievement, granted him as a coat-of-arms a globe displaying cloves and nutmegs, and bearing the motto *Primus circumdedisti me*. Magellan did not leave an heir who could be honoured. His wife and infant son both died before the *Victoria* returned. His other relatives owed allegiance to a rival crown.

VIII. SEBASTIAN CABOT

Born c. 1474; *died* 1557

On August 3, 1492, Christopher Columbus crossed Palos Bar and shaped a course toward the West, convinced that he was about to effect a revolution in the history of man. A revolution he effected, but it did not assume quite the form he expected. The immediate and most striking result of his voyage (and of the voyage to India accomplished by Vasco da Gama in 1498) was a shifting of the commercial centres of Europe from the ports of Mediterranean and Baltic states to those of countries whose shores were washed by the Atlantic.

The Spaniards and the Portuguese reaped the first-fruits of the Age of Discovery. Yet Englishmen, fated to garner the rich, ripened crop, were already astir. Had not chance ordained otherwise even Columbus himself might have sailed under the Cross of St George. In 1485 he sent his brother, Bartholomew, to England to seek the patronage of King Henry VII. Bartholomew fell in with pirates and was delayed on his journey. Christopher, meanwhile, gained the support of Spain. "So," in the words of Francis Bacon, "the West Indies by Providence were then reserved for the crown of Castilia."

That Henry VII would have backed Columbus's scheme can hardly be doubted. In English maritime circles—at Bristol in particular—schemes of a like nature were at that time being actively mooted. As far back as 1480, according to the chronicle of William of Worcester, two ships were sent out by John Jay, a wealthy Bristol merchant, to find "the islands of Brazil and Antilia to the west of Ireland." [1] Their commander, Thomas Lloyd, "the most scientific mariner in all England," cruised in the Atlantic for eight weeks ere storms compelled him to return. For several years Bristol seamen spasmodically continued the quest. John Cabot then took it up.

[1] These fabled lands, a creation of Arabic tradition, are shown in the maps of several mediæval cartographers.

John Cabot—Giovanni Caboto, to give his name its Italian form —was born about 1425, and belonged, like Columbus (or was the latter a Spaniard?), to a Genoese family. In 1460 he moved to

JOHN CABOT
From the painting attributed to James Herring. Bristol Museum and Art Gallery

Venice, and as a merchant adventurer was admitted to full rights of citizenship. He settled at Bristol in 1489.

Of his early career little is known. It is recorded, however, that on one occasion, while journeying to Arabia, he met a spice caravan and made of the drivers close inquiry regarding the lands whence their merchandise came. So it is probable that, by following a line of thought similar to that pursued by Columbus, he arrived independently at the conclusion that the East could be reached by way of the West; the more northerly the course taken, he reasoned, the shorter must be the sea-passage between Europe and Asia, the two continents "being in the shape and making of them broad towards the north and pointed towards the south."

From a letter addressed in 1498 to King Ferdinand by Pedro de Ayala, a member of the Spanish embassy in London, we learn that from 1490 onward expedition after expedition went forth from Bristol at the instigation of Cabot with a view to solving the riddle of the Atlantic. "The people of Bristol," wrote Ayala, "have, for the last seven years, every year sent out two, three, or four light ships in search of the island of Brazil . . . according to the fancy of this Genoese." Cabot in person led several of these ventures, and there is reason to think that in 1494 he may actually have sighted the North American coast. Be this as it may, in December 1495, roused to emulation by the news of Columbus's success, he made his way to London in order that, as Puebla, the Spanish ambassador, reported to Madrid, he might "propose to the King of England an enterprise like that of the Indies."

On receiving Puebla's despatch the Spanish authorities sent a remonstrance to England, pointing out that the undertaking, if put in hand, would be a violation of the Bull of 1494, by which the Pope had divided the world beyond Europe between Spain and Portugal. The warning arrived too late. Henry VII had already issued letters patent, authorizing Cabot and his three sons, Lewis, Sebastian, and Sancius, "to sail to all places, lands and seas, of the East, West, or North."

The charter required that the navigators should depart from Bristol, and that they should return only to that port. Also it laid down that they should pay to the King a fifth share of the profits of their venture. Incidentally, it stipulated—tacitly, at any rate—that they should abstain from sailing to the South. This provision, no doubt, was made by the politic Henry with the view to avoiding conflict with Spain.

It is not known if Lewis and Sancius took part in the voyage. John Cabot and his other son, however, accompanied by a crew of eighteen English sailors, left Bristol in the *Matthew* [1] on May 2,

[1] At least one other ship started from Bristol. In some accounts four others are mentioned. Only the *Matthew* seems to have completed the crossing of the Atlantic.

1497, and on June 24, having pursued a straight course to the west, they reached what they imagined to be their goal, or, to quote Hakluyt, "discovered that land which no man had before attempted." They found it inhabited by savages [1] clad in skins.

THE "MATTHEW" OF BRISTOL
From a drawing by Ellis Silas

Three of these they captured and took with them to England as a gift to their patron.

Whence hailed those men? The question is likely to be long debated. If reliance can be placed on Sebastian's map of 1544 (preserved in the Imperial Library at Paris) the *Matthew's* landfall must have been either Nova Scotia or Cape Breton Island. Other evidence supports the more widely accepted opinion that

[1] Probably Beothics. Never a numerous people, the Beothics, or aboriginal inhabitants of Newfoundland, fled before the advance of civilization into the interior, and, like the white bears and the great auks which once haunted the island, have long been extinct.

the ship first struck Newfoundland—probably in Bonavista Bay. Recording John Cabot's return, in a letter addressed to the Duke of Milan from London, and dated December 18, 1497, the Arch-priest of Soncino wrote:

> The sea is full of fish which are taken not only with a net but also with a basket in which a stone is put, so that the basket may plunge into the water. . . . The Englishmen, his partners, say that they can bring so many fish that the kingdom will have no more business with Islande (Iceland).

From Newfoundland the Cabots seem to have ranged up the Labrador coast to Cape Chudleigh. At this point, according to a statement ascribed to Sebastian, the sight of "monstrous great lumps of ice swimming in the sea, and continual daylight," drove their followers to mutiny. So were they forced to abandon their enterprise. They arrived back at Bristol toward the end of July.

What country they had discovered—whether "the island of Brazil," or some outlying part of "the territories of the Great Khan"—they could not say. At Bristol, nevertheless, they received a tremendous ovation. Wrote Lorenze Pasqualigo, a Venetian gentleman resident in the city: "Honours are heaped upon John Cabot. He is called Grand Admiral; he is dressed in silk; and the English run after him like madmen."

Royal recognition was meted out less lavishly. In the Privy Purse expenses, under the date of August 10, 1497, appears the following entry: "To him that found the new isle, £10." The King, it is true, also allowed the discoverer an annual pension of £20; and a pound sterling was then worth at least fifteen times as much as it is worth to-day. The pension, however, was to be paid from the receipts of the customs-house at Bristol. Henry had hoped for gold. What use had he for barbarous islanders and fish? His royal bounty may be taken as the measure of his disappointment.

Yet to the King—and to England as well—the fish which the Cabots found proved a source of greater wealth than the "spoils of Mexico" laid by Columbus at the feet of Ferdinand of Spain. From 1501 onward fleets from the south-western ports—Barnstaple, Bristol, and Bideford, Fowey, Dartmouth, Plymouth, Weymouth, and Poole—regularly visited Newfoundland, and year by year the product of the fishery increased. In 1615 it was sold in England for £200,000. By 1640 its annual value had risen to

£700,000; by 1670 to £800,000. Compare these figures with Spain's yearly return of American treasure. For the year 1521 it has been estimated at £52,000; for the year 1545 at £630,000. That was the maximum. By 1575 it had fallen to £440,000, and by the end of the century to £280,000. The rate of decline then became rapid.

For a long time, on the other hand, the Newfoundland fishery continued to be one of the principal industries of the British realm. Moreover, from among fisherfolk trained on "the banks" were largely recruited not only the men who beat the Spaniards in 1588, but the men who afterward made all the seven seas owe allegiance to the English flag. To encourage the industry, in the interest of the State but without cost to herself, Elizabeth, the most sagacious and most parsimonious of queens, ordained political fasts—days on which her faithful lieges were required by the law to eat cod.

In 1498 the stout-hearted Cabots, John and Sebastian, though justly indignant at Henry's meanness, accepted a second patent at his hands, and, sailing from Bristol on April 5 with a fleet of six ships, recrossed the Atlantic. Details of the voyage are wanting. In a despatch dated July 25, Ayala reported to the Spanish Government that the ships were expected back in September, and in that month one of them, much battered by storms, is known to have put in at an Irish port. Regarding the return of the others, history is silent. Nor has history anything further to say of John Cabot. Biographers incline to the belief that the gallant old sailor died at sea in 1498, leaving the command to his son.

The Cabots, it would seem, planned the expedition with the intention of colonizing newly found regions, and took with them from Bristol upward of three hundred emigrants. What happened to these people can only be conjectured. Thevet, the French cosmographer, relates how they were left at a place where they perished of hunger and cold. The story lacks confirmation.

In 1499 Sebastian again sailed to the West. But again he failed to achieve any tangible success. Shortly afterward, deprived of English patronage, he transferred his allegiance to Spain. Between 1507 and 1515 he led several ventures under the flag of King Ferdinand—some to the Gulf of Mexico, some to South America. But he appears to have found the Spanish service as unremunerative as the English. At any rate in 1516 he returned to Bristol.

The people of that city made him welcome; and in the following year Henry VIII employed him, in conjunction with Sir Thomas Perte, to attempt a north-west passage to the East. This was the most notable, perhaps, of all his exploits at sea.

Having crossed the Atlantic, Perte and his Italian colleague sailed northward till they reached latitude $67\frac{1}{2}°$. Then, according to one account of the voyage, they entered Hudson's Bay, giving "English names to sundry places therein," and "still finding the open sea . . . thought verily to have passed on to Cathay." Their crews, however, mutinied. They themselves, moreover, became involved in a bitter feud. So was their fond hope dashed; and their enterprise brought to an untimely end.

In 1518—probably as a consequence of his quarrel with Perte—Sebastian once more repaired to Madrid. There, at last, his ambitions met with encouragement. Indeed, the young King Charles—who in the following year, as Charles V, became the head also of the Holy Roman Empire—forthwith appointed him Pilot-Major of Spain. For thirty years he performed the duties of this important office. Yet his affections remained in England; and in 1548, on receiving an invitation from the Duke of Somerset, who was acting as regent on behalf of King Edward VI, he straightway went to London.

Ignoring Spanish protests, Somerset, always eager to develop English commerce, promised the veteran sailor his support and created for him an office similar to that which he had held in Spain. In the pension grant the office is described as that of "Grand Pilot of England." It carried a salary of £166 13s. 4d. a year.

Sir Clements Markham has written:

> At this time there was no one in Europe who could be compared with Cabot, either as a practical explorer or as a scientific navigator. With an experience extending over nearly half a century, he had commanded expeditions alike in the far North and in the far South. He had been for years at the head of the hydrographical department of Spain. . . . He was a man of vast knowledge, a very able and judicious councillor, of a very kindly and generous disposition.

Despite his seventy-four years, an officer better qualified to direct the maritime affairs of England could hardly have been found.

The close monopoly enjoyed by settlers from the Hanse towns

DEPARTURE OF JOHN AND SEBASTIAN CABOT FROM BRISTOL
From the picture by Ernest Board, R.W.A., in the Bristol Museum and Art Gallery
By permission of the Artist

—the merchants of the Steelyard [1]—had long exercised a strangling influence on the activities of English traders. Cabot made it his first business to break the monopoly. This done, he set himself

OLD HANSEATIC WAREHOUSES, HAMBURG
Photo E. N. A.

to open up for the people of his adopted country an exclusive route to the East such as the Portuguese and the Spaniards could claim —the former by way of the Cape, the latter by way of the Strait of Magellan. Experience had shown him the difficulty of finding a north-west passage. He concentrated his energies, therefore, on

[1] The Steelyard, the headquarters of the Hanse merchants in London, stood on the site now occupied by Cannon Street Station.

the quest for a north-east passage. This he believed would prove shorter and easier than the other.

The most notable of the expeditions he organized were those undertaken, in 1553, by Sir Hugh Willoughby and Richard Chancellor, and, in 1556, by Stephen Burrough. These ventures did not achieve their object. They resulted, however, in much valuable exploration. Also they led to the establishment of trading relations between England and Russia. In 1557, for the first time on record, the Czar sent an embassy to London.

In 1555 was incorporated the Muscovy Company, with Cabot as its governor. This corporation was the parent of the East India, the Hudson Bay, and the other famous companies which made England the leading colonial and commercial Power. From its inception may be dated the continuous history of British oversea expansion and of the British mercantile marine.

The rules (preserved in the pages of Hakluyt) which Cabot laid down for the guidance of his captains are full of sound wisdom. One of them calls for particular mention. Logs, it ordained, must be kept in every vessel, and in them were to be recorded such matters as the course, the altitude of the sun, observations on winds and tides, descriptions of lands, and notes on the variation of the compass. Hitherto no regular logs had been kept. Lead sheathing, as a protection from the ravages of worms, was another of the Grand Pilot's innovations. Sir Hugh Willoughby's ship, the *Bona Esperanza* (120 tons), was the first English vessel thus to be treated.

In 1556, on the eve of his departure from the Thames, Stephen Burrough drew a delightful portrait of his chief. He wrote:

> On the 27th of April Sebastian Cabota came on board our pinnace at Gravesend, accompanied with divers gentlemen and gentlewomen, who, after they had viewed our pinnace and tasted of such cheer as we could give them on board, they went on shore, giving to our mariners right liberal rewards; and the good old gentleman, Master Cabota, gave to the poor most liberal alms, wishing them to pray for the good fortune and prosperous success of our vessel, the *Serchethrift*. And then, at the sign of the 'Christopher,' he and his friends banketted, and made me and them that were in the company great cheer; and for very joy that he had to see the towardness of our intended discovery, he entered the dance himself among the rest of the young and lusty company; which being ended, he and his friends departed, most gently commending us to the governance of Almighty God.

This picture of the fine old man, brimming, Polonius-like, with the energy of second childhood, is confirmed by a friend's description of his last hours. As he lay dying, wrote Richard Eden, he solemnly affirmed "that he had the knowledge of finding the longitude by Divine revelation, yet so that he might not teach any man." From this Eden concluded he "was in that extreme age somewhat doted, and had not yet, even in the article of death, utterly shaken off all worldly-vain glory." He died in 1557, aged eighty-three. Neither the place of his death nor the exact date is known. The place and date of his birth are also disputed. He was born probably in 1474, and probably at Bristol. "A Genoas son, borne in Bristowe," so he is described in Stow's *Annals* under the date 1498.

SEBASTIAN CABOT

Seeing how big a part he played in our national history, it is strange that so few details of his exploits have come down to us. The explanation is stranger still. In 1555 a man named Worthington was made his partner in office. This was done ostensibly on the plea of his age. It seems, however, that Queen Mary did it at the insistence of her husband, King Philip of Spain, and that Worthington was really a Spanish agent. At any rate, after Cabot's death he disappeared, and with him disappeared most of the great navigator's documents and maps. Perhaps these records will yet be found in some obscure depository at Seville or Madrid.

IX. RICHARD CHANCELLOR

Died 1556

IN 1548 the Duke of Somerset, while acting as regent on behalf of his nephew, King Edward VI, appointed Sebastian Cabot, a veteran of seventy-four summers, to the office of Grand Pilot of England, and entrusted him with the task of developing the country's sea-borne trade. As a means to this end Cabot first made it his business to break down the monopoly long enjoyed by the German merchants of the Steelyard. He next set about, in conjunction with "certain grave Citizens of London," to open to English traders a north-east passage to Asia.

From Clement Adams's account of "The new navigation and discovery of the kingdom of Moscovia," preserved in the pages of Hakluyt, we learn that the aforesaid citizens, perceiving

> the commodities and wares of England to be in small request with the countries and people about us . . . began to think with themselves how this mischief might be remedied. Neither was a remedy (as it then appeared) wanting to their desires. . . .
>
> Seeing that the wealth of the Spaniards and Portingales, by the discovery and search of new trades and countries, was marvellously increased . . . they thereupon resolved upon a new and a strange navigation. And whereas . . . Sebastian Cabota . . . happened to be in London, they began first of all to deal and consult diligently with him, and after much speech and conference together, it was at last concluded that three ships should be prepared and furnished out for the search and discovery of the northern part of the world, to open a way and passage to our men for travel to new and unknown kingdoms.

The ships in question were the *Bona Esperanza* (120 tons), the *Edward Bonaventure* (160 tons), and the *Bona Confidentia* (90 tons). Commanded respectively by Sir Hugh Willoughby, the leader of the expedition, Captain Richard Chancellor, and Captain Cornelius Durfoorth, they carried crews of thirty-five, fifty, and twenty-two souls. Accommodation was also provided on board for eighteen merchants.

Cabot undertook to supervise the arrangements, and as a result of his vigilance and wide knowledge, the fleet was far better equipped than any that had yet sailed from England. The device adopted to render the vessels "staunch and firm" calls for particular mention. "In certain parts of the ocean"—to continue our chronicler's narrative—

> a kind of worm is bred, which many times pierceth and eateth through the stoutest oak that is. Therefore, that the mariners, and the rest to be employed in this voyage, might be free and safe from this danger, they (the shipwrights) cover a piece of the keel of the ship with thin sheets of lead.

Lead-sheathing had been practised in Spain for half a century. The *Bona Esperanza* and her consorts were the first English vessels thus to be treated.

Having regard to the length of the intended voyage, the fleet was victualled for eighteen months. With a view, moreover, to obtaining all possible information "concerning the Easterly part or tract of the world," Cabot sent for "two Tartarians which were then of the king's stable, . . . and an interpreter was gotten to be present, by whom they were demanded touching their country and the manners of their nation." The men were found, however, to be "more acquainted (as one there merrily and openly said) to toss pots than to learn the states and dispositions of people."

When selecting Sir Hugh Willoughby for the leadership the promoters of the venture unanimously invited Richard Chancellor to act as pilot-major. The latter, like Humphrey Gilbert, Martin Frobisher, and other illustrious English navigators of that time, was a *protégé* of Sir Henry Sidney, father of the famous Sir Philip, and sometime Lord Deputy of Ireland. A speech delivered by his patron on the occasion of his appointment deserves to be quoted. Said Sir Henry, addressing the assembled merchants:

"My very worshipful friends, I cannot but greatly commend your present godly and virtuous intention, in the serious enterprising (for the singular love you bear to your Country) a matter, which (I hope) will prove profitable for this nation, and honourable to this our land. Which intention of yours we also of the Nobility are ready to our power to help and further; neither do we hold any thing so dear and precious unto us, which we will not willingly forgo, and lay out in so commendable a cause. But principally I rejoice in my self that I have nourished and maintained that wight which is like, by some means and in some measure, to profit and stead you in this worthy action.

"But yet I would not have you ignorant of this one thing: that I do now part with Chancellor, not because I make little reckoning

SIR HUGH WILLOUGHBY
Reproduced, by permission of Lord Middleton, from the painting at Wollaton Hall

of the man, or that his maintenance is burdenous and chargeable unto me, but that you might conceive and understand my good will, and promptitude for the furtherance of this business, and that the authority and estimation which he deserveth may be given him. You know the man by report, I by experience; you by words, I by deeds; you by speech and company, but I by the daily trial of his life have a full and perfect knowledge of him.

"And you are also to remember into how many perils for your sakes, and for his country's love, he is now to run: whereof it is requisite that we be not unmindful, if it please God to send him good success. We commit a little money to the chance and hazard of Fortune. He commits his life (a thing to a man of all things most dear) to the raging sea, and to the uncertainties of many dangers. We shall here live and rest at home quietly with our friends and acquaintance: but he in the meantime, labouring to keep the ignorant and unruly mariners in good order and obedience, with how many cares shall he trouble and vex himself? with how many troubles shall he break himself? and how many disquietings shall he be forced to sustain? We shall keep our own coasts and country. He shall seek strange and unknown kingdoms. He shall commit his safety to barbarous and cruel people, and shall hazard his life amongst the monstrous and terrible beasts of the sea. Wherefore, in respect of the greatness of the dangers, and the excellence of his charge, you are to favour and love the man thus departing from us: and, if fall out so happily that he return again, it is your part and duty also liberally to reward him."

A MONSTROUS AND TERRIBLE BEAST OF THE SEA
From an old manuscript

The preparations for the voyage were completed in May 1553, and on the 20th of that month Willoughby and his followers—the latter all "apparelled in Watchet or sky-coloured cloth"—set out from Ratcliffe, near the present London Docks. As they approached Greenwich,[1] "where the Court then lay, . . . the courtiers," we read, "came running out, and the common people flocked together, standing very thick upon the shore: the Privy Council, they looked out at the windows of the Court, and the rest ran up to the tops of the towers." The ships thereupon fired a salute, shooting "their pieces after the manner of war, and of the

[1] The Palace of Greenwich, a favourite residence of royalty in Tudor and Stuart times, stood on the site now occupied by the Hospital. William and Mary founded the Hospital in 1694.

sea, insomuch that the tops of the hills sounded therewith and . . . the sky rang again with the noise thereof."

Wrote Clement Adams:

> It was a very triumph . . . to the beholders. But, alas, the good King Edward—in respect of whom principally all this was prepared—he only by reason of his sickness was absent . . . and not long after . . . the lamentable and most sorrowful accident of his death followed.

From Greenwich the fleet proceeded to Harwich. There it lay for a week. Then, the wind being favourable, the adventurers "committed themselves to the sea." After many days' sailing, they at length sighted land. This proved to be Rose Island. Continuing their course northward up the Norwegian coast, they next touched at a group which they named the Cross of Islands. There, being "a man of good foresight," Willoughby called his captains together and bade them, in the event of a storm scattering the fleet, each to "endeavour his best to go to Wardhouse (Vardö) . . . in the kingdom of Norway, and . . . there . . . stay and expect the coming of the rest."

On that very day, it so happened, a tempest did suddenly arise, causing seas "so outrageous that the ships could not keep their intended course." Willoughby "with his loudest voice" cried out to Richard Chancellor, and earnestly requested him not to go far from him. But the pilot-major could not comply. The *Bona Esperanza*, being a faster vessel than the *Edward Bonaventure*, was soon swept "quite out of sight, and the third ship also."

The *Bona Confidentia* was never seen again. Willoughby, however, after beating about for six weeks in the Arctic Seas in a vain attempt to make Vardö, contrived, on September 18, to bring his ship to the mouth of the Arzina River, on the Murmansk coast. There he resolved to pass the winter. "Wherefore," as he recorded in his *Journal*, a document which was happily recovered,

> we sent out three men south-south-west, to search if they could find people, who went three days' journey, but could find none: after that, we sent out other three westward four days' journey, which also returned without finding any people. Then sent we three men south-east three days' journey, who in like sort returned without finding of people, or any similitude of habitation.

The sequel can be briefly told. Some of the ship's company were still alive in January 1554. A will bearing that date was found on board, a few weeks later, by Russian fisherfolk. The testator, however, and his companions—the earliest of England's martyrs to the cause of discovery—had by that time all perished of cold and hunger.

Chancellor, when separated from his chief, duly made his way to Vardö. There he waited a week. Then, despairing of being joined by Willoughby or Durfoorth, he determined to proceed alone. Some Scottish fishermen, with whom he chanced to fall in, tried to dissuade him. But, "holding . . . that a man of valour could not commit a more dishonourable part than for fear of danger to avoid and shun great attempts," he remained steadfast in his resolution "either to bring that to pass which was intended, or else to die the death." His crew likewise were "prepared, under his direction and government, to make proof and trial of all dangers." With his single ship, therefore, he resumed the voyage, holding "on his course towards that unknown part of the world" until he came to "a place where he found no night at all, but a continual light and brightness of the Sun shining upon a huge and mighty sea."

At length, the *Edward Bonaventure* entered the White Sea—"a certain great bay, which was one hundred miles or thereabouts over." On its shore, not far from the spot where Archangel now stands, her company landed. Just then Chancellor espied a fishing boat in the distance. He at once made toward it, while the fishermen, "amazed at the strange greatness of his ship," rowed away in terror. Presently he overtook them; and when

> they (being in great fear, as men half dead) prostrated themselves before him,

he looked

> pleasantly upon them, comforting them by signs and gestures. And . . . this humanity of his did purchase to himself. For they being dismissed, spread by and by a report abroad of the arrival of a strange nation, of a singular gentleness and courtesy: whereupon the common people came together offering to these new-come guests victuals freely, and not refusing to traffic with them,

provided they would wait till leave had been obtained from the Czar.

The famous monarch known to history as Ivan the Terrible was then ruler of Russia. An energetic reformer, eager to bring his realm into touch with Western Europe, he welcomed the news that Englishmen had found their way to its coasts, and at once sent an envoy to conduct them to Court. But communication between Moscow and Archangel was slow and difficult, and, pending instructions from the Czar, the authorities at the latter place refused to commit themselves. Chancellor, therefore, not understanding

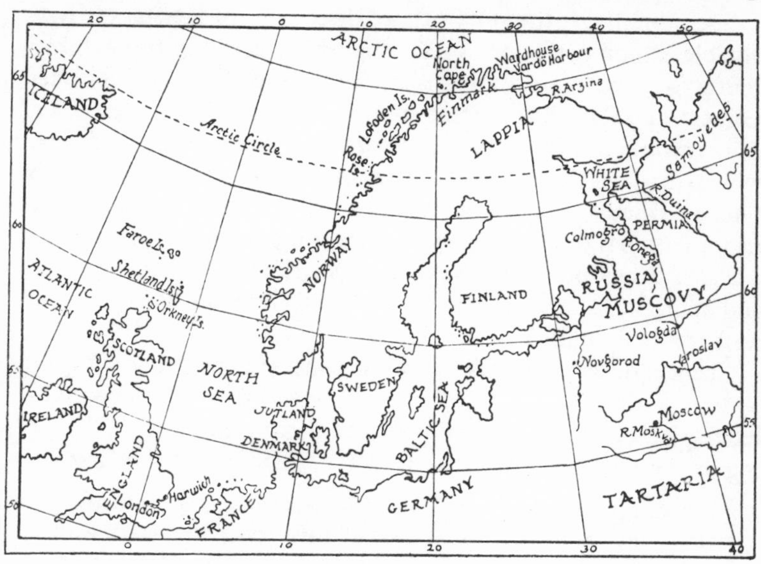

WILLOUGHBY AND CHANCELLOR'S DISCOVERY OF THE WHITE SEA AND MUSCOVY

the delay and thinking that an attempt was being made to delude him, determined to follow up his voyage by an even more daring venture overland to the Russian capital. Accordingly, having induced the "Muscovites," by means of threats, to furnish him "with all things necessary," he began the journey, using "certain sleds, which in that country are very common—the people almost not knowing any other manner of carriage—because of the exceeding hardness of the ground."

Fortune favoured him. Before he had gone many days he met with the "sledderman" sent by the Czar. This messenger, "who by some ill hap had lost his way," handed him letters written "with all courtesy and in the most loving manner that could be: wherein express commandment was given that post-horses should be gotten for him and the rest of his company without any money." This thing, we are told, was "of all the Russes . . . so willingly done that they began to quarrel, yea, and to fight also, in striving and contending which of them should put their post-horses to the sled." So, "after much ado and great pains . . . (for they had travelled very nearly fifteen hundred miles), Master Chancellor at last came to Moscow."

Such, briefly, is the story of the 'discovery' of Russia, the most notable exploit performed by an English navigator in the sixteenth century. The more daring achievements of Drake, Frobisher, Gilbert, and Ralegh are better known. The voyage of the *Edward Bonaventure*, however, may be regarded as the pioneer movement which marked the real beginning of the continuous history of Greater Britain. It was not a haphazard venture. Its promoters had a national object in view—to win for England a place in the world such as Columbus had given to Spain and Gama to Portugal; and upon the foundations which they well and truly laid other men well and truly built.

Chancellor arrived back at London in 1554, bringing with him —despite the protests of the Hansa merchants of Novgorod— letters, addressed to "the most excellent King Edward VI," offering liberal facilities to English traders. "If," wrote the Czar,

> you will send one of your Majesty's council to treat with us, . . . your country's merchants . . . shall have their free mart with all free liberties through my whole dominions . . . to come and go at their pleasure, without any let, damage, or impediment.

The letters—"written in the Moscovian tongue," in characters "much like to the Greek . . . very fair written in paper, with a broad seal hanging at the same"—came, of course, not to King Edward, but to his half-sister Mary. That much-maligned Queen, though wedded to Philip of Spain, forthwith "disannulled Pope Alexander's division"—the Bull of 1494, which gave the unexplored world to the Spanish and Portuguese crowns—and, by conferring a royal charter on the body of merchant adventurers who had promoted Willoughby's expedition, brought into being the Muscovy Company.

Members of the earlier associations of Merchant Adventurers had traded each at his own risk and on his own resources, and, for the most part, with lands near at hand. The Muscovy Company was a joint-stock concern. As such, though it actually achieved very little, it was the forerunner of the great trading corporations which, during the seventeenth and eighteenth centuries, carried the flag of England to the ends of the earth.

On May 1, 1555, while the Company's first fleet was being fitted out in the Thames, Chancellor re-embarked in his old ship, the *Edward Bonaventure*, and again made his way to the White Sea, with a view to establishing marts in the Czar's dominions. He reached Moscow early in October, and on July 20 in the following year, having transacted his business, he set out from Archangel on his voyage home. With him sailed a Russian ambassador, the first sent to England.

On November 10, after "traversing the sea four months," the *Edward Bonaventure* arrived "within the Scottish coast in a Bay named Pettislego."[1] That night, as she lay at anchor, she was suddenly caught by a storm, and, "beaten from her ground tackles," was driven upon rocks. There she quickly "brake and split in pieces." Chancellor, meanwhile, abandoned the doomed vessel, and made a brave effort to pilot the ambassador and his suite to shore in a small boat. But "the same boat by rigorous waves of the seas was by dark night overwhelmed." Her company, including Chancellor, perished to a man, also the ambassador's attendants. Only the ambassador was saved.

He owed his life to the exertions of a party of Scottish wreckers. These men, however, elected to hold him to ransom; and he remained a prisoner in their hands till February 1557. Then he was escorted

> by the merchants adventuring for Russia, to the number of one hundred and forty persons, towards the city of London, where by the way he had not only the hunting of the fox and such like sports showed him, but also by the Queen's commandment was received and embraced by the right honourable Viscount Montague, sent by her grace for his entertainment.

He entered the capital through Smithfield Bars and, on "the five and twentieth of March . . . (the day twelvemonth he took his leave from the Emperor his master), was most honourably brought to the King and Queen's court at Westminster."

For some thirty years after this the merchants of London continued to direct their energies largely to the Russian trade, and,

[1] Pitsligo.

despite the difficulties of the voyage to Archangel, they were amply repaid for their labours. The more direct route to the Czar's dominions was barred against them; the hostility of the Hanseatic League rendered the Baltic a *mare clausum* to English shipping.

After 1584, when Ivan the Terrible died, the Russian trade declined. Ivan's successor did not look on Englishmen with favour. Englishmen, moreover, were then finding markets elsewhere. Yet they long pursued the quest of the North-East Passage. This was at length navigated by Baron Nordenskjöld, the Swedish explorer. Sailing from Stockholm in the *Vega* in 1878, the baron for the first time brought a ship round the north coast of the Old World. He found the passage to be just practicable, but utterly useless.

For the account rendered by Chancellor to Queen Mary "concerning the state of Muscovy," the reader must turn to the "larger discourse" handed down to us by Hakluyt. It is an extraordinarily interesting document. Space allows us here to give only one or two extracts.

Current reports regarding the intense cold of Northern Russia —such "cold that the very ice or water which distilleth out of the moist wood which they lay upon the fire is presently congealed and frozen"—the scrupulous captain of the *Edward Bonaventure* could not confirm. Yet, he wrote, the

> mariners which we left in the ship . . . in their going up only from their cabins to the hatches, had their breath oftentimes so suddenly taken away that they eftsoons fell down as men very near dead, so great is the sharpness of that cold climate.

Moscow, he tells us, was "in bigness as great as the City of London, with the suburbs thereof." But, though it contained "many and great buildings," its streets, he added, were "for beauty and fairness nothing comparable to ours." Likewise he found the other towns which he visited to be

> built out of order, and with no handsomeness: their streets and ways are not paved as ours; the walls of their houses are of wood; the roofs for the most part are covered with shingle boards.

The following is his description of the Kremlin:

> There is hard by the city a very fair Castle, strong and furnished with artillery, whereunto the Castle is joined directly towards the North with a brick wall. The walls also of the Castle are built with

brick, and are in breadth or thickness eighteen foot. This Castle hath on the one side a dry ditch, on the other the river Moscua, whereby it is made almost inexpugnable.

In the Castle aforesaid, there are in number nine churches, or chapels, not altogether unhandsome, which are used and kept by certain religious men . . . all which for the greater part dwell within

THE SACRED GATE OF THE KREMLIN
Photo E. N. A.

the Castle. As for the king's Court and Palace, it is not of the neatest, only in form it is four square, and of low building, much surpassed and excelled by the beauty and elegance of the houses of the kings of England. The windows are very narrowly built, and some of them by glass, some other by lattices admit the light. And whereas the palaces of our princes are decked and adorned with hangings of cloth of gold, there is none such there.

On the possibilities of trade with Russia, Chancellor reported in glowing terms. He was impressed in particular by the richness of the corn crops: "Such store of corn that, in conveying it towards Moscow, sometimes in a forenoon a man shall see seven to eight hundred sleds laden with it."

X. SIR WALTER RALEGH

Born 1552; *died* 1618

SOLDIER, sailor, and explorer, courtier and statesman, scholar and scientist, poet and man of letters, Sir Walter Ralegh stands out a conspicuous figure on the crowded Tudor stage. Of the man himself, however, the father of the British Empire, strangely little is known. Though he passed his manhood in the glare of a searching publicity, though contemporaries eagerly watched and made note of his actions, his character is shrouded in controversy, even simple points of fact and chronology remain in dispute.

The inscriptions on two portraits painted by Zuccaro assign his birth to the year 1554. Tradition assigns it to 1552. Tradition is probably right; and it is almost certain that he was a native of East Budleigh, in Devon. About a mile from the church stands Hayes Barton, a sixteenth-century farmstead. His father, unable to afford the upkeep of the family home, Fardell, near Ivybridge, rented this house from a certain Richard Duke. The son subsequently tried to buy it. "Being born in that house," he wrote, "I had rather seat myself there than anywhere else."

The father married three times. His first wife, a daughter of John Drake, of Exmouth, bore him two sons, John and George. The second wife added a girl to the family. This Mrs Ralegh was the daughter of one Giacomo de Ponte, a Genoese merchant with shipping interests in west country ports; and her marriage seems to have cemented some business arrangement. At all events, improved financial circumstances enabled the impoverished squire whom she wedded to aspire to a more distinguished alliance when contemplating his next matrimonial venture. The third Mrs Ralegh, Elizabeth, the widow of Otho Gilbert, of Compton, was a daughter of Sir Philip Champernoun. Already the mother of three children, John, Humphrey, and Adrian Gilbert—names writ large in the sea-history of Britain—she became in due season the mother of three more—Carew, Walter, and Margaret.

Otho Gilbert provided for his son Humphrey to be educated

at Eton. His other sons were brought up with the younger Raleghs at Hayes Barton. But the boys were not allowed to neglect their studies, and all of them—Walter in particular—developed into finished scholars. Passing their days, moreover, within easy reach of the busy ports of Exmouth and Budleigh Salterton they acquired a deal of miscellaneous lore which in after years stood them, and their country, in good stead. Among their playmates may be mentioned one John Davis, a fisher-lad whose humble parents lived near by at Sandridge. Davis's personality had a determining influence on their lives.

In 1567, at the age of fifteen, Walter Ralegh went to Oxford—to Oriel, a college which can also claim Cecil Rhodes, the greatest of modern imperialists, among its sons. There he remained till the spring of 1569, when he enlisted in a band of volunteers, raised by his cousin, Henry Champernoun, and crossed the Channel to succour the persecuted Huguenots. Four years elapsed ere he returned to England. How he was employed during these years we do not know. Though tradition tells of gallant deeds performed by him at Jarnac and other battles, and of how he—and with him Sir Philip Sidney—narrowly escaped death at Paris on the night of St Bartholomew (August 23-24, 1572), the details are obscure. Yet a curious fact emerges. He went to France a soldier; he returned to England a sailor. Somehow during his sojourn abroad he contrived to gain a practical experience of navigation.

Shortly after his return he repaired to London, ostensibly to study law. But legal pursuits did not appeal to him. In 1575 the discovery of new lands was his consuming ambition. In 1578 he made his first essay to achieve it. In that year Humphrey Gilbert, who stood in high favour at Court, was granted letters patent authorizing him to verify his theories on the possibility of a north-west passage to the Indies,[1] and straightway began to fit out an expedition. His half-brother joined him in the enterprise.

During the summer eleven ships were assembled at Plymouth. The fleet, however, did not sail until November. Dissension among the captains delayed its departure, and, in the end, only seven vessels put to sea. Meanwhile, King Philip of Spain got wind of the project, and, rendered suspicious by Drake's exploits, sent out a force to intercept the English adventurers. Where the

[1] Humphrey Gilbert's *Discourse for a Discoverie of a New Passage to Cataia* (China) was published in 1576.

fleets met we do not know; nor do we know exactly what happened at the meeting. But on this occasion, it would seem, the Spaniards had the better of an encounter with their northern rivals. Gilbert, at any rate, lost one of his ships, and when, early in 1579, the others, war-worn and weather-worn, returned to Plymouth, he had nothing but failure to report. He and Ralegh at once set about to organize another expedition. But Queen Elizabeth was anxious just then to avoid occasion for conflict with Spain. In the circumstances, the scheme had to be shelved.

In the next year, through the good offices of one of his mother's influential relatives, Ralegh secured the command of a "foot-band" of a hundred men, and went to Ireland to assist in the suppression of the Desmond rebellion in Munster. A Puritan at heart, convinced that Popery and Spanish intrigue lay at the root of the Irish trouble, he found this work wholly to his liking, and threw himself into it with an enthusiasm which soon brought him to the notice of his superiors. In December 1581 Lord Grey, the commander of the royal forces, entrusted him—as a mark of favour—with the conveyance of despatches to the Queen.

His appearance, when he arrived at Court, bore out all that report had said about him. Indeed, six feet in height and massively built, with blue eyes, dark hair, and thick, curly beard, the young warrior presented a striking figure. Unusually observant, he was quick to note the impression he made. Inordinately ambitious, he was quick to take advantage of it. Elizabeth to the end of her reign delighted in allowing herself to be caressed by the attentions of youthful gallants. Few such men knew better than Ralegh how to feign the adoration she demanded. So it came about that a formal visit to Greenwich ripened into a stay of indefinite duration, a stay which involved the Queen in no small amount of scandal, though generally—as the staid Bacon wrote, in an attempt to defend Elizabeth's eccentric amours—"gratifications of this sort did not much hurt her reputation, and not at all her Majesty."

Privileges and favours were heaped on the new favourite. In 1584 Elizabeth granted him a patent for exporting cloth. Shortly afterward she granted him a patent for licensing the sale of wine. In 1585 as Lord Warden of the Stannaries he acquired control of the mining industry in Devon and Cornwall. In the next year he was created Vice-Admiral of those two counties and, in 1587, Captain of the Guard. Meanwhile, by the award of confiscated

Desmond lands, he became one of the territorial magnates of the realm. Knighthood was conferred on him in 1584, and in that same year he acquired a suitable town residence—Durham House, in the Strand, the bishop's London palace, which the Crown had lately appropriated. Subsequently the manor of Sherborne was added to his estates.

But Ralegh, though avaricious, could not content himself with

SIR WALTER RALEGH
From the portrait by Zuccaro in the National Gallery

a mere quest for private fortune. When, therefore, in 1583, Humphrey Gilbert, eager to plant an English colony in America, invited him to co-operate in another voyage to the West, he not only offered his services, but undertook to bear a large part of the cost, and had a ship, the *Ark Ralegh*, specially built for the purpose. This famous four-master, renamed the *Ark Royal*, served as the flagship of Lord Howard of Effingham during the stirring days in 1588 when the might of Spain bore down on England. In 1583 Ralegh intended to command her in person. But, in laying his plans, he reckoned without the Queen. When the time came for the expedition to start, Elizabeth point-blank refused him leave to accompany it: she would not hear of her favourite braving the perils of uncharted oceans. So Gilbert had to sail without him.

He left Plymouth on June 11, 1583, with five ships and everything he deemed needful for his purpose—even "music in good variety, for solace of our people and allurement of savages, not omitting the least toys, as Morris dancers, hobby-horses, and May-like conceits to delight the savage people"; and on August 3 he reached Newfoundland. There for eleven days he ruled as governor. His followers then rebelled, and insisted on returning to England. They complained of the fogs and cold, and of the absence of precious metals; they had been brought out, they said, under false pretences.

On the homeward voyage the fleet encountered a terrific storm. Only one of the ships, the *Golden Hind* (40 tons), survived the buffeting of the waves. Gilbert was among the number of the drowned. As the sea devoured the *Squirrel*, the 10-ton bark that carried him, the crew of the *Golden Hind* could hear his voice above the roar of the tempest. "Courage, brothers!" it cried, "remember we are as near heaven by water as by land."

Ralegh, profoundly moved by the news of the tragic ending of this adventure, was roused from idle dalliance. He at once hastened to the royal presence and, finally, persuaded Elizabeth to transfer to him the patent she had granted to Humphrey Gilbert. In conjunction with Adrian Gilbert, William Saunderson, and others, he then founded a "fellowship" for the discovery of the North-West Passage and the planting of colonies overseas. In April 1584 the Fellowship sent out its first expedition—"two barks well furnished with men and victuals," in the command of Arthur Barlow and Philip Amadas.

Humphrey Gilbert in the preceding year had crossed the North Atlantic, intending to work southward down the American coast. Barlow and Amadas were instructed to cross to the West Indies by way of the Canaries, and then to work northward.

After sixty-five days' sailing they sighted the "main of Florida." Thence they pursued their appointed course till they came to a sound [1] in which lay an island, called "Roan Oke" by the inhabitants. On this island they landed; and a pleasant spot they found

[1] Albemarle Sound.

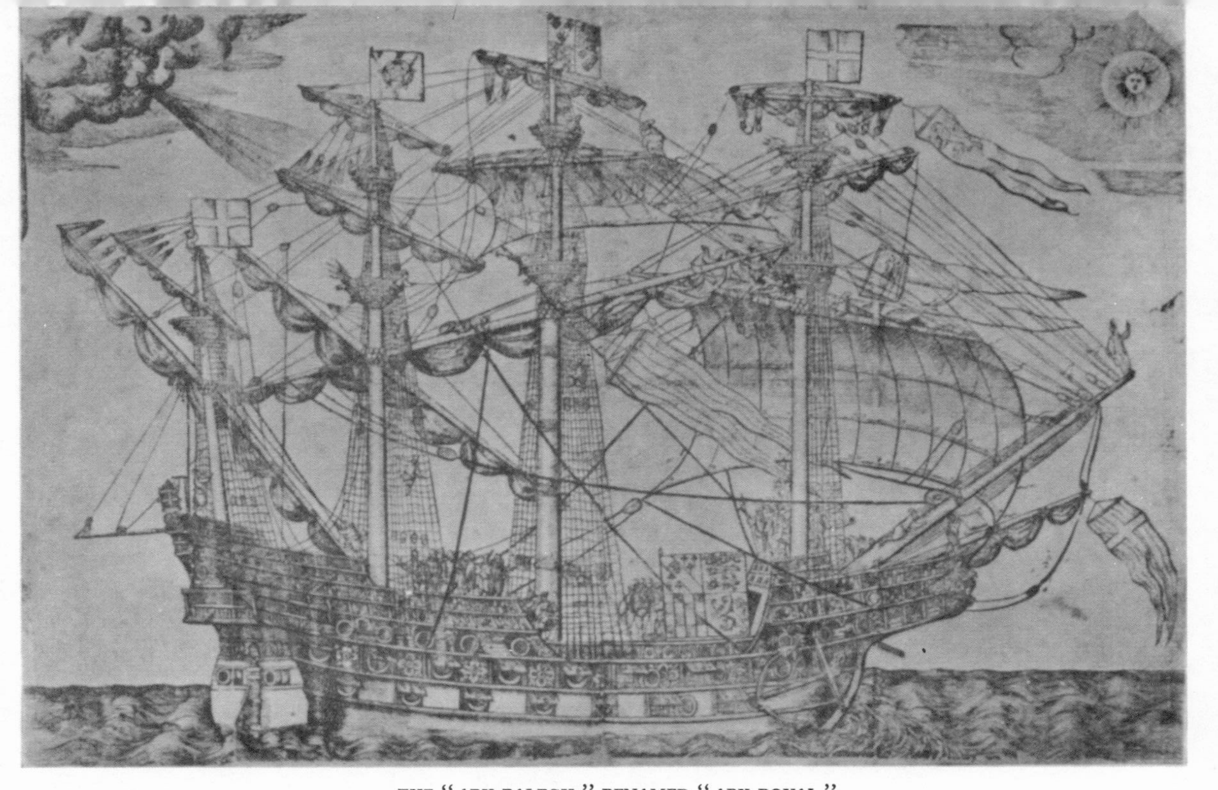

THE "ARK RALEGH," RENAMED "ARK ROYAL"
Flagship of Lord Howard of Effingham at the defeat of the Armada, 1588.

it, rich in timber and fruit-laden vines, and with "deer, conies, hares, and fowl" in abundance. For six weeks they traded with the islanders, bartering European baubles for pearls and furs. Then they returned to England, taking with them two natives—Manteo and Wanchese by name—to substantiate their story. Ralegh was delighted with their report, and his enthusiasm

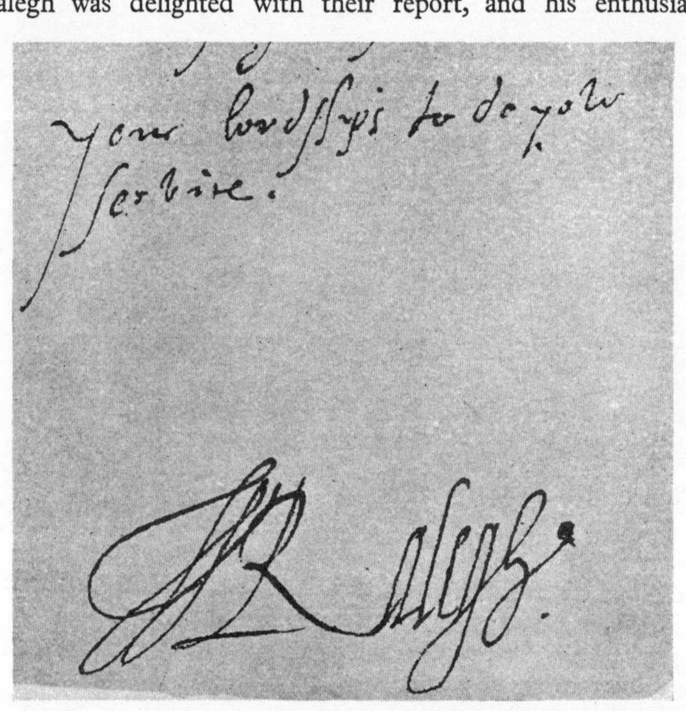

SIGNATURE OF SIR WALTER RALEGH, 1586

infected the Queen. Elizabeth promptly ordered that the new country should be known as Virginia.

In the following April Ralegh sent out seven ships, under Sir Richard Grenville, with the object of forming "the first colony." The ships were pitifully small, the largest, the *Roe Buck* and the *Tyger*, being only of 140 tons burden. Yet, in addition to the crews, they carried 108 prospective settlers, including Sir Ralph Lane, governor-designate of the colony.

Grenville arrived at Virginia on July 27 and duly planted a settlement. Then, toward the end of August, he set sail for England, having first pledged himself to return in the next year with stock and further supplies. In the meanwhile things went ill with the colonists. Instead of clearing land, Lane and his fellow pioneers sought to get rich quickly by Spanish methods, wasting their energy on futile quests for precious metals, and incurring the bitter enmity of the Indians. Soon they found themselves, with their supplies exhausted, in imminent danger of annihilation.

SIR RICHARD GRENVILLE

A strange chance delivered them from this perilous situation. In March 1586 there appeared on the scene an English fleet under Drake, whom curiosity had led to visit the colony. Yielding to entreaties, Drake agreed to ship the settlers to England. Barely had they gone when Grenville, true to his promise, returned. Unable to make out why the settlement had been abandoned, Sir Richard decided to leave fifteen of his men to keep the flag flying while he himself hastened home for further instructions. The indomitable Ralegh at once organized another expedition, entrusting the command to Captain John White.

This fresh band of emigrants, who included among their number seventeen women and nine children, sailed from Portsmouth on

May 8, 1587. But when they arrived at Roanoke, the only trace they could find of Grenville's men was the skull of one who had evidently been murdered. Mindful of the grim warning, Governor White prudently insisted on building a fort, and there, on August 18, his daughter Eleanor, the wife of Ananias Dare, gave birth to Elizabeth Dare, the first child of English parents to be born on American soil.

A few days afterwards White and some of his company set sail for Europe to recruit additional settlers, the rest undertaking, meanwhile, to build huts and clear land. Just then, however, seafaring England was occupied preparing for the pending conflict with Spain. Two years elapsed before the governor could get a relief expedition fitted out. By that time his garrison, victims of the deadly tomahawk, had suffered a fate similar to Grenville's. When he landed at Roanoke on August 16, 1590, he found his fort deserted and "no man nor sign" anywhere.

For three centuries White's fort lay neglected. At length, in 1896, historical enthusiasts, the Roanoke Colony Memorial Association, took steps to preserve the remains, erecting a small monument on the spot. Subsequently—though not until 1927—they persuaded the Congress of the United States to appropriate a sum of money in order that the site of the "Lost Colony" might be maintained as a public park.

Ralegh while striving to establish an English settlement in North America did not neglect the quest for a north-west passage. In 1585 he sent out John Davis in command of the *Sunshine* and *Moonshine*, barks of fifty and thirty-five tons respectively, with instructions to follow the track of Martin Frobisher into the frozen north. In 1586, and again in 1587, Davis led similar expeditions. Meanwhile, at his own cost, Ralegh kept numerous privateers at sea; nor did he waver in his determination to give his queen "a better Indies than the King of Spain hath any." Between 1590 and 1602 he sent at least two expeditions to Roanoke. Yet he failed to establish a colony; and in 1603, in consequence of his attainder, he was forced to surrender his interests to the Crown. But he had not laboured in vain. Of Virginia he wrote in a letter which he addressed to Cecil from his prison: "I shall yet live to see it an English nation." This vision he was spared to see realized—in part, at any rate. The colony founded in 1607 was the work of other men, and it was founded on the banks of the James River, not at Roanoke. None the less, it was a direct outcome of his enterprise.

Ralegh held many public offices under Queen Elizabeth. His royal mistress, however, refused to make him a Privy Councillor. She preferred that he should remain her private counsellor. Only once, in 1587, did he receive an important civil appointment. He then served on the committee nominated by the Council to organize

JAMESTOWN IN 1622

national resistance to Spain, and was largely responsible for the plan of campaign finally adopted.

The part he played in the actual defeat of the Armada is still debated. While the Spanish fleet was pursuing its course up the Channel, his duties as Vice-Admiral of Devon and Cornwall seem to have kept him on shore. He must have put to sea, however, as soon as the danger of a landing had passed. At any rate, we hear of him performing prodigies of valour in the engagement which took place off Gravelines on July 29.

In the next year Drake and Norris, hoping still further to embarrass King Philip, attempted to set on the Portuguese throne a pretender hostile to Spain.[1] Ralegh, as a humble volunteer, accompanied them on this abortive expedition; just then he had strong reasons for wishing to absent himself from England. Toward the end of 1588 a new star, in the person of the young Earl of Essex, had appeared in the firmament of Elizabeth's favour. Loath to be outshone, the old favourite impetuously challenged his

[1] Portugal came under the rule of King Philip II in 1580, and was constrained to follow the fortunes of Spain till 1640.

rival to combat. The sagacious Burghley contrived to prevent the duel. But a report of the quarrel, despite Burghley's efforts to "bury it in silence," reached the ears of the Queen. Ralegh, in consequence, was heavily censured. Nor did he find forgiveness awaiting him on his return from Portugal. In dudgeon, therefore, he crossed to Ireland, and, as the guest of a neighbouring landlord, his old friend Edmund Spenser, busied himself with schemes for improving his estates.

THE GREAT ARMADA IN THE CHANNEL
From an engraving after a tapestry made for Lord Howard of Effingham

Spenser, like Ralegh, had distinguished himself in arms during the suppression of the Desmond rising, and also had been rewarded with a grant of confiscated lands. The poet then elected to make Ireland his home; and in 1589, when Ralegh visited him, he was living at Kilcolman Castle, industriously translating into allegory his knowledge of affairs and men. He had already written three books of the *Faerie Queene*.

The day's work done, host and guest passed many a happy evening together. Spenser in pastoral language has told the story—how Ralegh, "the Shepherd of the Ocean," came to him "from the Main-sea deep," provoking him "to play some pleasant fit";

> And, when he heard the music which I made,
> He found himself full greatly pleased at it :
> Yet, emuling my pipe, he took in hond
> My pipe—before that emuled of many—
> And played thereon (for well that skill he conned) ;
> Himself as skilful in that art as any.
> He piped, I sung ; and, when he sung, I piped ;
> By change of turns, each making other merry.

The guest's song was largely

> a lamentable lay
> Of great unkindness and of usage hard,
> Of Cynthia, the Lady of the Sea,
> Which from her presence faultless him debarred.

But he also sang "Cynthia's" praises; and, wrote the host, he presently began

> to cast great liking to my lore,
> And great disliking to my luckless lot
> That banished had myself, like wight forlore,
> Into that waste, where I was quite forgot,
> The which to leave thenceforth he counselled me,
> Unmeet for man in whom was aught regardful,
> And wend with him, his Cynthia to see,
> Whose grace was great, and bounty most rewardful.

So it happened that, early in 1590, Ralegh returned to Court, accompanied by his friend. Tidings had lately reached him of the marriage between Essex and Walsingham's daughter, Frances, the widow of Sir Philip Sidney; and, knowing that the Queen would not suffer the attentions she demanded of a favourite to be tempered by true affection for another woman, he deemed that an opportunity had come for him to regain his old position. Nor was he wrong in his surmise.

To his companion also Elizabeth extended a gracious welcome. Not only did she insist that the completed portion of the *Faerie Queene* should be given to the world at once, but, moved to unwonted liberality, conferred upon the poet an annual pension of £50. "What!" exclaimed her astonished Treasurer, "all this for a song?"

Some two years later, in circumstances similar to those which had brought disgrace to Essex, Ralegh again fell from favour. Hitherto impervious to feminine charms, he became attached to the beautiful Elizabeth Throgmorton, one of the Queen's maids-in-waiting. This lady he secretly married. But murder will out. Early in 1592 the Queen learned the truth. Forthwith she banished the bride from Court. Ralegh she sent to the Tower, and—without even troubling to invent a pretext to justify her action—kept him a captive for several months. Only by playing on her incorrigible greed was he able to secure his release.

When thrown into prison, he had been about to take command

of a fleet of privateers which, in the intervals of love-making, he had fitted out for service against Spain. Though the Queen refused to set him at liberty on that account, the ships duly put to sea and met with remarkable success. Prize after prize they captured; and, when finally they returned to Plymouth, they brought back with them the great *Madre de Dios*, the most heavily laden treasure-galleon that had yet fallen into English hands.

Burghley then intervened on behalf of the prisoner in the Tower, and prevailed upon Elizabeth to allow him to go to Devonshire, in charge of a gaoler, to supervise the division of the spoil. Of this concession Ralegh took full advantage. By transferring the greater part of his share to the Queen, he once more won his way to the royal autocrat's good graces. So at last he found himself free to engage in a project he had long been turning over in his mind—his romantic, if mistaken, quest for El Dorado.

In the days of the conquest of Peru many of the Inca's subjects migrated eastward. These people, according to Spanish tradition, finally settled in Guiana, and there established an empire even wealthier than that which the Pizarros had overthrown. Its capital, a city called Manoa, was believed to be paved literally with gold.

In 1594, buoyed up by dreams of discovering this new Peru, Ralegh sent Captain Whiddon to reconnoitre. Early in the next year he himself followed with a fleet of five ships. Toward the end of March he arrived at Trinidad. There, having reduced the Spanish authorities to submission, he spent some time collecting information regarding the object of his quest. Then in sundry small craft—the bottom of an old gallego which he "caused to be fashioned like a galley," a barge, two wherries, and a ship's boat—he embarked an exploring party of a hundred men and, leaving his fleet at anchor near Los Gallos, set out for "Manoa the golden."

He hoped to reach the phantom city by way of the Orinoco; and at Trinidad he had enlisted the services of an Indian, Ferdinando by name, who undertook to pilot him through the tortuous channels of that river's vast delta. The man, however, played false, or had professed knowledge he did not possess. "At any rate," wrote Ralegh, "if God had not sent us another help, we might have wandered a whole year in that labyrinth of rivers." The other help was a " natural of those rivers." Ralegh espied him one day at a distance paddling a small canoe. He at once gave chase; and, after a long, hard pull—"by the swiftness of my barge rowing with eight oars"—he overtook and captured him.

XIII.
GVALTHERVS RALEGH,
EXPVRGATA CIVITATE, HISPANVM
Gubernatorem captiuum abducit.

CVm Gualtherus Ralegh, nauibus suis ad Insulam TRINI-DAD appulisset, Hispanos in PVERTO DE LOS ESPAN-NOLES, blandis verbis gestibusq; ad se inuitauit, & nõ tan-tum Insularum statum, sed & Hispanorum vires atque po-tentiam ab eis explorauit, postea vero cognitis rebus omni-bus, Capitaneum CALFIELD cum 100 armatis sibi adiunxit, & circa ve-speram ciuitatem S. JOSEPHI, in qua regius Gubernator DON ANTHO-NIO de BERREO erat, oppugnatam facile superauit. Quo facto, dimisit o-mnes qui in ciuitate erant, excepto solo BERREO quem cum sociis captiuum abduxit.

d 2

SIR WALTER RALEGH AT TRINIDAD, 1594

From a contemporary engraving in the Macpherson Collection

The Indian proved to be an intelligent and friendly fellow who knew the channels well. Under his guidance the English adventurers quickly came to the main stream.

Up this they rowed nearly four hundred miles, marvelling, as we may read in Ralegh's delightful description of the journey,[1] at the tropical glories of the country—the grass, the trees, the birds,

[1] Ralegh's *The Discoverie of Guiana*, published in 1597.

the deer—all so beautiful that it was a "good passing of the time" simply to see them. But they could find no trace of the empire they were seeking. Meanwhile the current, against which they had to pull, hour by hour became stronger. At length, having

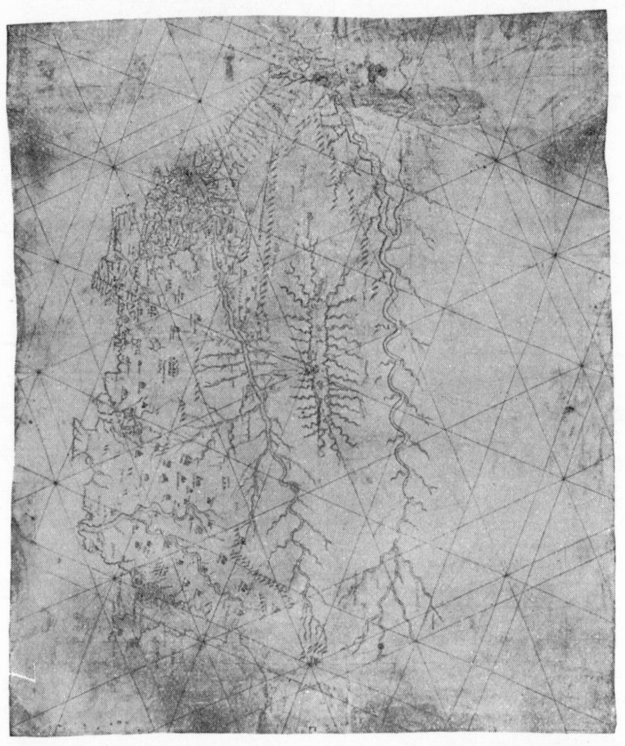

GUIANA, SHOWING THE SITE OF EL DORADO ON THE MYTHICAL LAKE OF MANOA (IN THE CENTRE OF THE MAP)

Drawn by or for Sir Walter Ralegh about 1595. The top is the south, the upper river being the Amazon, the lower the Orinoco.

British Museum

come to the point where, with a mighty rush of water, the Caroni joins the Orinoco, they implored their leader to turn back. He yielded to their entreaties. Even his heart had grown "cold to behold the great rage and increase of the river."

Ralegh, when he thus agreed to abandon the enterprise, did not despair of a future attempt. On his return to England he forthwith laid plans to renew the quest. Not till long afterward, however, could he carry them into effect. For the present he had to be content with sending out Captain Keymis to extend his knowledge of Guiana. He himself was required for duty nearer home.

In 1596 King Philip of Spain, eager to avenge the loss of his "invincible armada," again threatened England with invasion. Lord Howard of Effingham, therefore, purposed to singe his beard as Drake had singed it in 1587, and, with this object in view, a fleet was assembled at Plymouth. The Lord High Admiral appointed Essex to the command of one squadron. Ralegh, who had patched up his quarrel with his former rival, was given the command of another.

LORD HOWARD OF EFFINGHAM
From the painting in the National Portrait Gallery

The fleet set sail on June 1. Ten weeks later it came back, having achieved a feat unequalled in the annals of war; and to Ralegh, who, like Nelson at Copenhagen, overrode the prudence of his commanding officer and boldly led his squadron into the enemy's harbour, the success of the venture was largely due. In the next year, Essex and Ralegh, as joint commanders, led another expedition against Spain. This, the so-called "Island Voyage," proved a less glorious affair. Yet it served its purpose; it finally laid the invasion bogey.

At home, meanwhile, the succession question had come to the fore. Ralegh professed himself to be a supporter of James of Scotland. He did not hasten, however, to give the Scottish king proof of his loyalty. So he brought himself under suspicion of double-dealing. The suspicion had no foundation. But James was a poor judge of men. In 1603, when he came to the throne, he not only dismissed Ralegh from Court, but stripped him of his offices, even his lands.

What happened then cannot be plumbed to the bottom. Ralegh may have said words which had better been left unspoken. That he actively engaged in the so-called Bye Plot, a conspiracy to overthrow James in favour of Arabella Stuart, is fantastically improbable. Anything that savoured of treason was wholly foreign to his nature; and in his eyes—the eyes of a Puritan—even a pacifist king was preferable to a Romanist queen. Yet such was the crime with which James elected to charge him.

While awaiting his trial he attempted suicide. Subsequently, however, on November 17, 1603, at Winchester Castle, he faced his accusers with unflinching courage. The bluster of the Attorney-General, Sir Edward Coke, raged round him without effect. Shouted Coke: "I want words to express thy viperous treasons!" "True," the prisoner quietly replied, "for you have spoken the same thing half a dozen times over already." But wit could not save him. The jury had been paid to convict, and the judge duly passed sentence of death.

In deference to public opinion, James commuted the sentence to one of imprisonment for life. But neither public opinion, nor the entreaties of the Queen and the Prince of Wales,[1] could persuade him to do justice to an innocent man. For nearly thirteen years he left Ralegh to lie in the Tower. The prisoner devoted much of this time to chemical experiments, vainly seeking to discover the philosophers' stone and an elixir that would cure all diseases. The rest of the time he devoted to more valuable work. His *History of the World*, and many of his other writings, both prose and verse, were produced within the dark walls of the Tower.

Meanwhile, he persistently pleaded with James to allow him to renew the quest of El Dorado. At last, in 1617, the King gave his consent to a modified scheme. A certain mine in Guiana, of which Keymis had heard, promised to solve his financial difficulties. So he sent Ralegh to find it, having first made him promise not to trespass on Spanish preserves.

Ralegh, aged sixty-five, valiantly went. Twelve months later he returned, having learned at last that the ideal city of the philosophers, like the philosophers' stone, did not necessarily exist just because "every child affirms the same." Moreover, since to fight

[1] Prince Henry, Charles I's elder brother, who died in 1611.

Spaniards and to seize Spanish lands was a tenet both of his religious and of his political creed, he returned, having broken his promise to James, and—the crowning misfortune—bereaved of his son, who had fallen in battle on a far-away shore. Thus he had not only failure to report, but disobedience to explain. He wrote to the King:

"If I have spent my poor Estate, lost my son, suffered by sickness and otherwise a world of miseries; if I have resisted with the manifest hazard of my life the robberies and spoils with which my companions would have made me rich; . . . if when I had gotten my liberty, which all men and Nature itself do much prize, I voluntarily lost it,—I beseech your Majesty to believe that all this I have done because it should not be said to your Majesty that your Majesty had given liberty and trust to a man whose end was but the recovering of his liberty, and who had betrayed your Majesty's trust.

"My mutineers told me that if I returned for England I should be undone, but I believed in your Majesty's goodness more than in all their arguments. So I am the first that being free and able to enrich myself, yet hath embraced poverty and peril. . . . But your Majesty's wisdom and goodness I have made my judges."

James was unmoved by this plea. In 1580 a Spanish ambassador demanded the head of the pirate Drake. Elizabeth replied by knighting the culprit. In 1618 the Spanish ambassador demanded the execution of the pirate Ralegh. The latter was forthwith sent to the scaffold. Drake, it is true, had brought his sovereign a shipload of gold; had Ralegh done likewise would James have given a different answer?

XI. SIR JOHN HAWKINS

Born 1532; *died* 1595

THE old town of Plymouth has come down in the world. It savours to-day of the squalid. In Elizabethan times, when the Hawkins family occupied a "tenement and garden in a certain venella on the east side of Kinterbury Street," it must have been a very pleasant place. A few Tudor houses still stand to suggest the charm which decay and industrialism have stolen from it.

The founder of the fortunes of the Hawkins family, Hakluyt's "old Master William Hawkyns" whom King Henry VIII "much esteemed," died just before Queen Elizabeth's accession. An astute business man, he amassed great riches as a merchant adventurer, and became the leading burgess of his town. Several times he held office as mayor. He also represented Plymouth in Parliament. Incidentally, he may be accounted the patriarch of the sea-dogs of Devon.

In 1528, Hakluyt tell us, "not contented with the short voyages commonly made then only to the known coast of Europe," he fitted out "a tall and goodly ship of his own of the burthen of 250 tons, called the *Paule of Plimmouth*," and made the first of "three long and famous voyages unto the coast of Brazil"; and in that country he "behaved himself so wisely with the savage people that he grew into great familiarity and friendship with them." Very profitable, therefore, his ventures proved. On each occasion he brought the *Paule* back to Plymouth, laden with "oliphants' teeth" and other rich merchandize.

His wife, the daughter and heiress of a Cornish knight, Sir John Trelawny, bore him two sons, William and John, who, on his death, succeeded to the business. The elder seems to have undertaken the work of management. The younger held himself responsible for the trading.

For some time John Hawkins stuck quietly to the task of swelling his own and his brother's fortune, and so well had he been trained that he was able to trade even at Spanish ports without coming into collision with officials. But at length, about 1560, "having made divers voyages to the Isles of the Canaries, and there, by his good and upright dealing, being grown in love and favour with the people," he bethought him of his father's voyages to the West, those voyages of which, as a boy, he had never wearied of hearing. His Spanish friends in the Canaries gave him to understand that in the New World he would find African negroes "very good merchandise." He decided, therefore, to turn his knowledge of the Guinea coast to account, and to try his hand at slave-running.

Writers, who persist in viewing the past through the eyes of the present, have unsparingly condemned the decision, and very unfairly. In the sixteenth century—and in the seventeenth and eighteenth as well—the employment of negro slaves in America was generally approved by the conscience of Europe. Hawkins would have been astonished had it been suggested to him that he might be transgressing a moral law. The only laws he knew he was breaking were the monopoly laws of a foreign state, and that was a consideration to which he attached little importance. For many years he had traded amicably at Spanish ports on the eastern side of the Atlantic. Why should he not be able to trade equally amicably at Spanish ports in America?

His brother William approved the project. His father-in-law, Benjamin Gonson,[1] Treasurer of the Navy, likewise approved it, and in Sir Lionel Ducket, an enterprising Father of the City of London, Sir William Winter, and Sir Thomas Lodge, a governor of the Muscovy Company, he found three other influential supporters. At Plymouth, therefore, during the summer of 1562, he fitted out three ships, the *Solomon* (120 tons), the *Swallow* (100 tons), and the *Jonas* (40 tons). In these little vessels, although he purposely overmanned them, "for fear of sickness and other inconveniences whereunto men in long voyages are commonly subject," he reckoned he could accommodate three hundred slaves.

The fleet sailed in October and made straight for the Canaries. Hawkins then went on to Sierra Leone, and at length, having procured the required number of blacks—"besides other merchandises which that country yieldeth"—he "sailed over the ocean sea unto the island of Hispaniola."

[1] John Hawkins married Gonson's daughter, Katherine, in 1558. His son, Richard, was born in 1560.

There everything fell out exactly as he had foreseen. At the port of Isabella the Spanish officials at first refused him permission to trade. But slaves were in great demand on the island. So the Englishman, by pretending that he was a mariner who had been driven from his course while making a voyage of discovery, soon overcame their scruples. Why, they asked themselves, should not this unfortunate stranger be allowed to dispose of a part of his cargo in order to supply his wants? After all, Spain and England were friendly powers, and had not King Philip been married to Queen Elizabeth's sister?

At Puerto Plata and elsewhere the performance was repeated. Thus Hawkins got rid of all his slaves, receiving "by way of exchange such a quantity of merchandise that he did not only lade his own three ships with hides, ginger, sugar, and some quantity of pearls, but he freighted also two other hulks with hides and other like commodities which he sent into Spain."

And that was the beginning of the quarrel which culminated in 1588 in the defeat of the Armada. The goods consigned to Spain were seized at Seville, and confiscated by order of the Government. Nor could the owner obtain compensation. He even went so far as to address a personal letter on the subject to the Spanish King whom he had helped to entertain at Plymouth in 1556. Philip did not deign to reply. Instead, terrified by Hawkins's impudent intrusion into his western dominions, he issued peremptory orders that foreigners must be strictly excluded from all Spanish ports.

Remonstrances made by the English Government proved equally unavailing. Not a hide, not a penny, would King Philip concede. Hawkins determined, therefore, to make good his losses—40,000 ducats forsooth—by further trading, and his Queen, satisfied that the traffic in slaves offered rich profits at very small risk, encouraged his purpose. When, on October 18, 1564, he set out on his second venture, his fleet of four ships included the *Jesus* (700 tons),[1] the pride of Elizabeth's Navy.

Having taken four hundred negroes on board, the ships left the African coast in January 1565. In mid-Atlantic, as ill-luck would have it, they fell in with calms and, while they drifted

[1] Purchased in 1544 by King Henry VIII from merchants of Lubeck, the *Jesus*, according to Hakluyt, "was the last great ship which was either builded or bought beyond the seas."

helplessly for twenty-eight days, Hawkins became alarmed lest, owing to shortness of water and food, he might lose much of his precious 'black ivory.' But, at length, wrote John Sparke, a fellow townsman who sailed with him in the *Jesus*, "the Almighty God, who never suffereth His elect to perish, sent us the 16th of February the ordinary breeze, which is the north-west wind, which never left us till we came to an island of the cannibals, called Dominica." There provisions were obtained in plenty.

Hawkins then began to consider what next he would do. In attempting to trade at Hispaniola he saw he would be asking for trouble. So he finally decided to strike across to Burboroata—the place now known as La Guayra, in Venezuela; on the Spanish Main he hoped he would find that nothing was known of him. In this he was wrong. The Governor had already received orders from Spain that he must not on any account grant a foreigner a licence to trade.

Hawkins spun his old story. "He was come thither," he said,[1] "in a ship of the Queen's Majesty of England, being bound to Guinea; and thither driven by wind and weather: so that being come thither, he had need of sundry necessaries for the reparation of the said Navy, and also great need of money for the payment of his soldiers, unto whom he had promised payment; and therefore although he would, yet would not they depart without it."

The recital of this fable did not have the desired effect. The Spanish settlers at Burboroata were willing, even eager, to buy. But the Governor stood firm; he still refused to give Hawkins leave to trade. Hawkins, therefore, not to be denied, "prepared 100 men, well armed with bows, arrows, harquebusses, and pikes; with the which he marched to the townwards." The Governor then changed his tone, and "straight, with all expedition, sent messengers," who asked the Englishman to restate his request. Hawkins restated it bluntly, adding that, unless it were granted at once, "he would displease" the Governor.

The Governor did not wish to be displeased. So he again sent messengers who assured Hawkins that "all things should be to his content." The Englishman demanded hostages as a pledge of good faith. These were given; and the traffic in negroes began. Two hundred slaves were disposed of at Burboroata. Hawkins sold the other two hundred at Rio de la Hache. And at

[1] Sparke's narrative.

each place he insisted on receiving payment in cash—in solid gold or silver.

Having thus completed his business he decided to attempt a survey of the Caribbean Sea. A fuller knowledge of secrets which the Spaniards jealously guarded might be useful, he thought, on future occasions. So he spent several weeks taking soundings, noting currents, and charting the coastlines of islands. He then made for Florida and, still surveying and charting, slowly followed the shore of the American mainland as far as Newfoundland.

On his way northward he succoured the struggling Huguenot colony which Laudonnière had lately planted in Florida, at the mouth of the May River.[1] At first he was regarded with suspicion by the Frenchman, who feared—perhaps not without reason—that he "would attempt something in Florida in the name of his mistress." The fear proved unfounded. Indeed, Laudonnière subsequently stated, the English commander

> gave divers presents to the principal officers of my company according to their qualities: so that I may say we received as many courtesies of the General as it was possible to receive of any man living. Wherein, doubtless, he hath won the reputation of a good and charitable man, deserving to be esteemed as much of us all as if he had saved our lives.

From Florida, it may be noted, Hawkins probably introduced tobacco[2] into England. "The Floridans," wrote Sparke,

> when they travel, have a kind of herb dried, who with a cane and an earthern cup in the end, with fire, and the dried herbs put together, do suck through the cane the smoke thereof; which smoke satisfieth their hunger, and therewith they live four or five days without meat or drink. And this all the Frenchmen used for this purpose; yet do they hold opinion withal, that it causeth water and phlegm to void from their stomachs.

William Harrison, writing in 1573, observed that "the taking in of the smoke of the Indian herb called tobacco by an instrument formed like a little ladle . . . is greatly taken up and used in England." Yet this tobacco cost 3s. an ounce, a sum equivalent to 30s. of our money. Tavern-keepers used to hire out pipes containing an adulterated mixture.

[1] Now known as St John's River.

[2] The practice of smoking was adopted in Spain in 1559. In that same year Jean Nicot (from whose name is derived the word 'nicotine') introduced it into France.

At Newfoundland, Hawkins allowed his men a spell of much needed rest and a change of diet. Then, "with a good large wind," he bore across the Atlantic; and on September 20, after an absence from England of nearly a year, he dropped anchor in the harbour of Padstow, on the north coast of Cornwall, "with a

SIR JOHN HAWKINS
From *Plymouth Armada Heroes*, by Mary W. S. Hawkins

loss of twenty persons in all the voyage, as with great profit to the venturers of the said voyage, so also to the whole realm, in bringing home both gold, silver, pearls, and other jewels in great store."

Queen Elizabeth was highly gratified by the success of the expedition. She summoned Hawkins to Greenwich, bade him dine at the palace, and—for sheer fun of the thing—invited the Spanish ambassador, Don Diego Guzman De Silva, to meet him. Hawkins treated the Spaniard to a full account of the voyage, concealing only the details of his little displays of force. De Silva did not know what to make of the story, or what action to take.

Wrote the puzzled ambassador to King Philip:

> He assured me that he had given the greatest satisfaction to all the Spaniards with whom he had had dealings, and had received full permission from the governors of the towns where he had been. The vast profits made by the voyage have excited other merchants to undertake similar expeditions. Hawkins himself is going out again next May, and the matter needs immediate attention. I might tell the Queen that, by his confession, he has traded in ports prohibited by your Majesty, and require her to punish him, but I must request your Majesty to give me full and clear instructions.

King Philip sent very emphatic instructions. The King of Portugal also made a formal complaint; Hawkins, he asserted, by raiding negroes on the Guinea coast, had violated Portuguese rights. But Elizabeth at that time felt reasonably secure on her throne. Despite the advice of the cautious Lord Burghley, she paid little heed to protests. Indeed, she granted Hawkins a coat of arms glorifying his deeds (sable, on a point wavy a lion passant or, in three chief bezants; and for a crest, a demi-Moor, proper, in chains); and in 1567, when he set forth again on a slave-trading venture, she lent him not only the *Jesus* but another of her ships as well, the *Minion* (360 tons), commanded by Captain John Hampton.

For this expedition Hawkins also secured the services of one Captain Francis Drake. Drake sailed with him as owner and master of the *Judith*, a small but well-equipped vessel of 50 tons burden. Therefore, since he himself and his brother fitted out three other ships, the *Swallow*, the *Angel*, and the *William and John*, he left Plymouth on October 2 in command of a fleet of six sail.

In due course he appeared off the Spanish Main with five hundred slaves for the Spaniards to buy. Some he sold at Burboroata. The rest, as before, he disposed of at Rio de la Hache. The governors of those places did everything they could to obstruct his activities. But he—to use his own phrase—"forced them to friendly commerce"; and he got away in the end with treasure to the value of about £150,000 of our money stowed away in the *Jesus*. This was in August 1568. He had anticipated finishing his trading earlier in the year. Seeing, therefore, that the hurricane season was at hand, he resolved to make forthwith for England.

But he had already tarried too long. As he was working along the west coast of Cuba a hurricane swept down upon him, and his ships—their bottoms foul as a result of ten months at sea—could not make way against it. Spars got broken, and much rigging was lost. In the circumstances, Hawkins prudently decided to abandon the struggle, and to run before the wind. He finally found shelter, at the head of the Gulf of Mexico, in the harbour of San Juan d'Ulloa.

It has been suggested that his story of the storm was largely fictitious—an invention designed to justify an inquisitive desire to explore the "treasure house" of Mexico, a place which no English captain had yet seen. Be this as it may, he could hardly have chosen a less propitious time. He arrived at San Juan on September 16. On the very next morning there appeared off the coast a Spanish fleet of "thirteen great ships," under Admiral Alvarez de Baçan, whom King Philip had sent out expressly to deal with him. What was Hawkins to do?

Having regard to the harbour's very narrow mouth, he might, had he chosen, have prevented De Baçan entering. In that case the Spaniard must either have sought out some other port or, should a gale have arisen, have suffered his ships to be driven ashore and wrecked. But to deny a Spanish fleet admission to a Spanish port would have been an act of war which even Hawkins, fearing "the Queen's indignation in so weighty a matter," shrank from committing. So, to quote his own words, "I thought it rather better to abide the jutt of the uncertainty than the certainty. The uncertain doubt, I accounted, was their treason, which by good policy I hoped might be prevented; and, therefore, as choosing the least mischief, I proceeded to conditions."

The negotiations lasted three days. Meanwhile, we may be sure, Hawkins looked anxiously for the gale which, at that season, he had good reason to expect. But the gale did not come. In the end, therefore, De Baçan sailed into the harbour, having first agreed that the Englishmen should stay there, with free permission to buy and to sell, until they had repaired their ships, and that they should then be allowed to depart unmolested. But De Baçan had no intention of respecting the terms of a treaty which he had signed under duress. The man whom he had been sent out to seize now lay in his power, caught like a rat in a trap. He did not mean to let Hawkins escape; Hawkins knew that well enough.

Such accounts as have come down to us of the affair at San Juan d'Ulloa represent De Baçan as a base, treacherous knave. Those accounts, it must be remembered, are all English accounts, heavily biased. Despite the undertaking he had given, the Spaniard, it is true, on the morning of September 24 suddenly fell on the English ships. But what provocation had he received? May he

THE "REVENGE"
Redrawn from an old print
From *Twenty Famous Naval Battles* (Crowell)

not have been forestalling some subtle move on Hawkins's part? We are not told.

The English fleet, outnumbered, out-gunned and with no space in which to manœuvre, did not stand a chance in the fight. Captains Hampton and Drake, by masterly seamanship, got the *Minion* and the *Judith* away from the harbour. The treasure-laden *Jesus* and all the other vessels were lost. Of the ships in Queen Elizabeth's navy, only the *Jesus* and Sir Richard Grenville's *Revenge* ever fell into Spanish hands. Hawkins himself and a number of the *Jesus's* crew contrived to put out to sea in small boats, and were picked up by the *Minion*. Their position, however, and that of their comrades, was still fraught with peril. Badly battered, overcrowded, and lacking both water and food, the *Minion* and the *Judith* could not have offered resistance had De Baçan pursued them. Happily, the Spaniard was content to leave well alone.

Even so, Hawkins had troubles enough to contend with. To procure provisions was his most pressing need. With this object in view, he made for the west coast of Florida. But he could not find food enough there to take all his company across the Atlantic. Therefore, seeing no other solution of the problem, he put a hundred volunteers on shore, and bade them fend for themselves till he could return and rescue them. Then he set sail for Europe.

Drake, as a result of the "troublesome voyage" of 1567–68, became filled with an undying hatred of Spain and everything Spanish. When he returned to England, he solemnly declared war on King Philip, and he gave up the rest of his life to harassing and robbing that monarch. Hawkins, an older man and perhaps more level-headed, took a broader view of the matter. While Drake strove to avenge private wrongs, he—as Comptroller and Treasurer of the Navy—made it his business to ensure that England should be ready to engage in the national struggle with Spain which he saw soon must begin.

But first a sense of loyalty to subordinates, one of the most pleasing characteristics of sixteenth-century seamen, required him to rescue the comrades whom he had left in Florida. After his departure many of them had found their way to Spanish plantations, and had been taken on as foremen. For a time they did fairly well for themselves; but in 1572 they were brought over to Spain and thrown into the prison of the Inquisition at Seville. To save them from death at the stake, Hawkins finally had to enter into a conspiracy worthy of King Philip himself.

One day, with the full knowledge of Queen Elizabeth and Lord Burghley, he went to the Spanish ambassador and represented himself as a captain who was dissatisfied with the English service. Would King Philip, he asked, take him into his pay? The ambassador swallowed the bait. King Philip, ever suspicious, did not bite so readily. He demanded proof. But, in the end, Hawkins managed to convince him, and so—to cut a long story short—to secure the release of his men. King Philip ordered them to be set at liberty, each with ten dollars in his pocket; whilst to his new admiral, from whom he expected much, he gave a title of nobility and £40,000 in cash. Further, he confided in Hawkins the details of the so-called Ridolfi Plot, which was then being hatched in Spain against Queen Elizabeth's life. Thus a shameless intrigue was justified after all. "The story," Professor Froude has written, "reads like a chapter from *Monte Cristo*, and yet it is literally true."

The ships which King Philip sent against England in 1588 were, according to a contemporary writer, "so huge that the ocean groaned beneath their weight," and so numerous that "the sea was invisible." The facts, perhaps, hardly bear out these statements. Yet the Armada unquestionably was a very formidable force. But for Hawkins's work at the Admiralty, it might well have vanquished the English fleet. Queen Elizabeth inherited only the ruin of her father's Navy. During the early years of her reign, moreover, it was very ill managed and hopelessly inefficient. Hawkins, when he undertook the duties of Comptroller and Treasurer, found himself confronted by a Herculean task. He stuck to it with grim determination, and from 1573 down to the year of his death he toiled almost continuously in his office at Deptford.

The administrative reforms he carried through during that time were many and far-reaching. But what in the end gave England her commanding advantage at sea were the changes he effected in *matériel*. By cutting down cumbersome upper works, by lengthening keels and drawing finer lines, and by improving rigging, he made English ships the best and fastest sailers in the world. He also enormously increased armaments.

The *Ark Royal* (800 tons), which in 1588 carried the flag of Lord Howard of Effingham, fired a broadside of 377 lbs. Few Spanish ships could throw one-half of this weight of metal. The broadside of the *Nuestra Señora del Rosario* (1150 tons) amounted to 198 lbs.; that of the *Anunciada*, a vessel of about the same size as Howard's, amounted only to 67 lbs. The Spaniards, we read, considered "the cannon . . . to be an ignoble weapon, good merely for the opening of the fray, and for trifling with until the arrival of the moment for engaging hand to hand." Hawkins relied on gunfire for victory—on gunfire and mobility. The event abundantly justified his theories.

To assist him in his work he was able to command the services of Peter Pett and other skilful designers. Many of his innovations, however, were actually his own inventions—the studded sail, for example, the use of a capstan for weighing anchor, and the jointed mast, which Sir Walter Ralegh found to be "a wonderful ease to great ships, both at sea and in the harbour." To him the chain pump is also attributed. Nor did he neglect the all-important question of *personnel.* Indeed, he kept the "poor sailors"

THE CHATHAM CHEST
Reproduced by permission of the Lords Commissioners of the Admiralty

always in mind, and, despite the incorrigible meanness of the Queen, contrived to raise the common seaman's pay from 6s. 8d. to 10s. a month—say, from £4 to £6 of our money. It was essential, he maintained, that the fleet should be served by respectable, God-fearing men who could "shift for themselves, and keep themselves clean—without vermin."

And it was Hawkins, of course, who in conjunction with Drake established the famous "Chest at Chatham," the forerunner of Greenwich Hospital. In 1590 he laid down that every man and boy in the fleet should contribute a small part of his pay to a common fund, and that the money should be stored "in a strong chest with five locks to that purpose especially provided," and used to assist those who, "by reason of hurts and maims received in the service, are driven into great poverty, extremity, and want."

When he learned that the Armada was actually about to sail, Elizabeth's Comptroller for a time relinquished his desk and, as Vice-Admiral, hoisted his flag on board the *Victory*. Long years of irksome office routine had shattered his health. "My sickness," he wrote, "doth abide with me continually." But his spirit and courage remained unimpaired; and, as he showed in the great battle of August 4, he still possessed his old skill in handling ships. On the following morning Lord Howard visited the *Victory* in state, and knighted him on his own quarter-deck. To receive knighthood on the field of battle was the highest honour to which any man then could aspire. Lord Howard bestowed it with a very sparing hand.

Drake made his first voyage to the West in company with Hawkins. Hawkins made his last in company with Drake.

In 1593 his son Richard, who had already won renown as a fighting sailor,[1] obtained a commission from the Queen to raid Spanish shipping in the Pacific, and for that purpose sailed from Plymouth in the *Dainty*. A fair measure of success attended the adventure till Valparaiso was reached. There a whole Spanish fleet beset the *Dainty* and, after gallantly fighting eight ships for three days and nights, "Almirante Ricardo" was forced to surrender. The Spaniards subsequently threw him into prison at Lima.

It was in the hope that he might be able to rescue his son that Sir John decided to take part in Drake's expedition of 1595. But the hardship of the voyage proved to be more than his strength could endure. He was a sick man when he left England. During the Atlantic crossing his condition grew steadily worse, and on November 12, when his ship was off Puerto Rico, the old seadog died.

Richard Hawkins remained a captive for nearly ten years—some time at Lima, some time in Spain. At length, in December 1602, he was ransomed for £12,000, the sum being paid partly by the Crown and partly from his father's estate. The rest of his life he devoted to re-establishing the family business, and, like "old Master William Hawkyns" before him, he became the leading burgess of Plymouth—the town's mayor and Member of Parliament. In 1603 he was knighted by King James I. He died in 1622.

[1] Richard Hawkins served with distinction under Drake in the descent on the Indies of 1585, and in 1588 he commanded the *Swallow* against the Armada.

XII. SIR FRANCIS DRAKE

Born c. 1541; *died* 1596

FRANCIS DRAKE was born at Tavistock in the later years of the reign of King Henry VIII. The exact date is uncertain. Controversy, indeed, rages round all the details of his youth. Here we offer—for what it may be worth—the testimony of Camden's *Annales* (published in 1615); perhaps it is the most generally accepted.

> This Drake—to tell no more than what I heard from himself—was born of mean parentage in Devonshire, and had Francis Russell (afterwards Earl of Bedford) for his godfather, who, according to the custom, gave him his Christian name. Whilst he was yet a child, his father, Edmund Drake, embracing the Protestant doctrine, was called in question by the law of the Six Articles made by Henry VIII against the Protestants, fled his country, and withdrew himself into Kent. . . . After the death of King Henry, he got a place among the seamen of the King's Navy; and soon after he was made vicar of the Church of Upnore [1] upon the river Medway—the road where the fleet usually anchoreth. But by reason of his poverty he put his son to the master of a bark, with which he used to coast along the shore, and sometimes to carry merchandise into Zeland and France.

The last assertion, at any rate, is well authenticated. Nor have we reason to doubt that "the youth, being painful and diligent, so pleased the old man that, being a bachelor, at his death he bequeathed his bark unto him by will and testament."

For some years young Drake continued to carry on his late master's business. But in 1567, finding the narrow seas too narrow for him, he sold his bark and, tempted by the promise of rich profits, accepted an offer of employment with investment from his kinsman,[2] John Hawkins, who having successfully conducted

[1] Upchurch (?).

[2] All chroniclers refer to Hawkins and Drake as kinsmen. The nature of the kinship is not known.

two slave-running ventures between the Guinea coast and Spanish America was about to engage in a third. His sovereign also became a sleeping partner in the firm. Queen Elizabeth actually consented to risk the *Jesus*, the largest ship in her Navy, to assist Hawkins in the execution of his design.

The expedition badly miscarried. Of the seven vessels which left Plymouth in October 1567 under Hawkins's command only the battered hulks of the *Minion* (Captain John Hampton) and the *Judith* (Captain Francis Drake) returned. In a fight at San Juan d'Ulloa the Spaniards for once had got very much the better of matters. The main facts of the story are set out elsewhere in these pages. "If all the miseries and troublesome affairs of this sorrowful voyage should be completely and perfectly written," wrote Hawkins, "there should need a painful man with his pen, and as great a time as he had that wrote the Lives and Deaths of the Martyrs."

In 1570, by way of recovering lost capital, Drake undertook a voyage to the West Indies on his own account. In 1571 he made another. These were of the nature of reconnaissances. Drake, who was nothing if not thorough, intended that his revenge should be full and complete, and, in order to ensure this, he required certain information.

The bulk of the wealth sent by the New World to Spain came from Chile and Peru. But it was not carried to Europe by way of the Strait of Magellan; Spanish captains fought shy of the storms which rage in the seas round the south of America. From Valparaiso and Lima treasure-galleons bore northward to Panama. Thence the cargoes were transferred by pack-mules to Nombre de Dios, on the Atlantic side of the isthmus of Darien, and there [1] stored until they could be shipped to Cadiz. Drake wished, by personal observation, to ascertain the exact details of the overland journey. For he had in mind the design of helping himself to a pack-train. The scheme cannot be justified or defended; it was piracy undisguised. Nevertheless, even the strict moralist must admire the resource and daring which its author displayed when he carried it out.

With two little ships, the *Swan* and the *Pasha*, and seventy-three men, all picked volunteers, he set out from Plymouth on

[1] In the seventeenth century the Spaniards moved the Atlantic terminus from Nombre de Dios to Porto Bello.

May 24, 1572; and on July 12 he arrived at his base on the isthmus of Darien—a snug, sheltered cove known only to himself—Port Pheasant he called it. One night, shortly afterward, under cover of darkness, he slipped into the harbour of Nombre de Dios. The capture of that place formed no part of his plan. He purposed merely to frighten the Spaniards, to puzzle them, to distract them from guessing at what he really meant to do, and then to return to his base. But the raid met with unexpected success. The garrison, completely surprised, were petrified by terror, and offered little resistance. Within an hour the lads of Devon had "the treasure house of the world" at their mercy.

Drake was just beginning to think that his revenge was going to prove altogether too easy when, as chance would have it, he was struck down with a wound in the leg. A thing nigh incredible happened then. His followers insisted on abandoning their prize and on carrying their loudly protesting leader to his ships and to safety. Those rough sixteenth-century seamen actually valued their chief more highly than riches, and they took him, helpless but still loudly protesting, back to Port Pheasant.

For several weeks he lay, nursing his hurt. He then returned to the attack, and, aided by a party of Cimaroons (India tribesmen who were sworn foes of Spain), laid a pretty little ambush midway between Panama and Nombre de Dios. The expected treasure-train did not walk into the trap. Having approached to within a few miles of the spot, its commander received a warning that danger lay ahead, and turned about, deeming discretion the better part of valour. The Englishmen gave pursuit, but the mules had clattered back to Panama before they could be overtaken.

Foiled, but not despairing, Drake again faded away to his base, where he stayed till he thought his enemies might have forgotten about him. Then he laid another ambush—this time under the very walls of Nombre de Dios. He reckoned that there, with their journey's end in sight, the guards would relax their vigilance. So it turned out. On this occasion the convoy fell an easy prey into his hands; and on August 4, 1573, he reappeared at Plymouth with a shipload of gold. His revenge indeed had been full and complete.

Being now a wealthy man, he at once aspired to advance his social interests. With this object in view he took a hand in Irish affairs. "Furnishing," wrote Stow, "at his own proper expense, three frigates with men and munition, he served voluntary in Ireland under Walter, Earl of Essex." In that troublous country he did "excellent service, both by sea and land"; and in 1577, thanks to the good offices of Sir Christopher Hatton, the Vice-Chamberlain, he was accorded the reward he desired—a "most flattering" reception at Court and the assurance that henceforth he might sail against the Spaniards, if not with the Queen's com-

SIR FRANCIS DRAKE
From the painting in the National Portrait Gallery

mission, at least as a chartered pirate. Straightway he set about to prosecute a project which he had long had in mind.

On February 11, 1573, seated among the upper branches of a "goodlie and great high tree," Drake gazed westward across the narrow isthmus of Darien upon the waters of the Pacific. Then and there, we are told, he solemnly vowed that he would never rest till he had sailed in an English ship into that sea. In the summer of 1577 he planned to carry his vow into effect.

For the purpose he fitted out a fleet of five vessels—his own ship, the *Pelican*, 120 tons; the *Elizabeth*, 80 tons (Captain John Winter); the *Swan*, 50 tons (Captain John Chester); the *Mary-*

gold, 30 tons (Captain John Thomas); and a 15-ton pinnace, the *Christopher* (Captain Thomas Moone). Lest the Spaniards should be forewarned, he made his preparations with the utmost secrecy, and on December 3 he sailed from Plymouth, "giving out his intended voyage for Alexandria."

Mogador, on the Barbary coast, reached on December 27, was the first port of call. Having there replenished supplies, the fleet coasted slowly southward to Cape Verde. Thence, favoured by the prevailing trade-winds, it struck across the Atlantic to Brazil—fifty-four days without sight of land. The ships then needed careening. Like Magellan before him, however, Drake had to proceed to Port St Julian, in Patagonia, ere he could find a suitable harbour. By that time two of his vessels had become so leaky that they had to be abandoned.

On entering Port St Julian he received another and a grim reminder of the troubles which had beset the man in whose course he was following. There, still standing, he saw "the gibbet . . . where Magellan did execution on his rebellious company." In that gloomy place, moreover, despite the dictum that history repeats itself only in the leading articles of newspapers, he too was forced to do execution—and on one whom he had long regarded as a friend, Captain Thomas Doughty.

Drake became acquainted with Doughty in Ireland. A witty and plausible rogue with a taste for choice wines and extravagant dress, the man attracted him strongly. Drake loved flattery and display, and this new friend he thought might help him to scale the social ladder he was then striving to climb. So to a paid agent of King Philip of Spain he gave not only his confidence, but an invitation to sail with him in the *Pelican* in 1577.

Doughty, it may be supposed, made himself responsible for the sumptuous manner in which the little vessel was fitted out—the fine oak furniture [1] that adorned the admiral's quarters, the silver table-utensils, and the fiddlers who made music while the officers dined. He must have been a clever fellow indeed. Drake was not often or easily fooled.

Several of the officers had suspicions of Doughty even before the expedition left Plymouth. Drake refused to listen to the reports which they made. He believed them to be inspired simply by jealousy, and for a long time, though again and again it was

[1] Some of it is preserved at Berkeley Castle.

brought to his notice that Doughty had been detected preaching sedition among the crews, his trust in his friend stood unshaken. At length, on arrival at Port St Julian, the weight of cumulative evidence forced him to probe deeper into the matter.

"In this Port," wrote Captain Winter of the *Elizabeth*,

> our General began to inquire diligently of the actions of Mr Thomas Doughty, and found them not to be such as he looked for, but tending rather to contention or mutiny, or some other disorder, whereby (without redress) the success of the voyage might greatly have been hazarded. Whereupon the company was called together and made acquainted with the particulars of the cause, which were found partly by Master Doughty's own confession, and partly by the evidence of the fact, to be true: which when our General saw, although his private affection to Mr Doughty (as he then in the presence of us all sacredly protested) was great, yet the care he had of the state of the voyage, of the expectation of her Majesty, and of the honour of his country did more touch him (as indeed it ought) than the private respect of one man.
>
> So that the cause being thoroughly heard, and all things done in good order as near as might be to the course of our laws in England, it was concluded that Mr Doughty should receive punishment according to the quality of the offence: and he seeing no remedy but patience for himself, desired before his death to receive the Communion, which he did at the hands of Mr Fletcher our Minister, and our General himself accompanied him in that holy action: which being done, and the place of execution made ready, he having embraced our General and taken his leave of all the company, with prayer for the Queen's majesty and our realm, in quiet sort laid his head to the block, where he ended his life.

With his fleet reduced to three ships, the *Pelican*, the *Elizabeth*, and the *Marygold*, Drake left Port St Julian on August 17, 1578. Three days later he came to the entrance to Magellan's Strait. There he

> caused his fleet, in homage to our sovereign Lady the Queen's Majesty, to strike their topsails upon the bunt . . . and withal, in remembrance of his honourable friend and favourer, Sir Christopher Hatton, he changed the name of the ship, which himself went in, from the *Pelican* to be called the *Golden Hind*.[1] Which ceremonies being ended . . . they entered the narrow strait with much wind, frequent turnings, and many dangers.

[1] This was the Hatton crest.

The ships passed without mishap through the perilous channel, and on September 6 sailed into the ocean beyond. There history did not repeat itself. In that ocean which Magellan, by reason of its calmness, had named the Pacific, the English navigators encountered a terrific storm. The little *Marygold*, overwhelmed by the waves, sank with all hands. The *Golden Hind* and the *Elizabeth*, meanwhile, were separated and carried far from their appointed course.

When the fury of the tempest somewhat abated, Captain Winter, believing that his leader's ship had shared the fate of the *Marygold*, set sail for home.[1] The *Golden Hind* was thus left alone. Undaunted, Drake stuck to his purpose. Somewhere to the south of Cape Horn (he was the first European to sight that point) he contrived to bring his ship about, and subsequently, taking full advantage of a following breeze, made rapid progress up the coast of Chile and Peru.

Space does not allow us to relate the amazing adventures he met with there—his fruitful raid on Valparaiso; his still more fruitful raid on Lima, "most secure, having never been assaulted," where he rifled seventeen Spanish merchantmen; or even his pursuit of the *Cacafuego*. From this famous treasure-galleon, "the great glory of the South Sea," overhauled on April 16, 1579, *en route* for Panama, he transferred to the hold of his own already overladen vessel "13 chests full of Royals of plate, 80 lbs. weight of gold, and 26 tons of silver," precious metal to the value of £150,000, together with a large consignment of diamonds, rubies, and other gems.

Thinking himself "sufficiently satisfied and revenged" and that "her Majesty would rest contented with this service," he began then to think of home. Having regard to the danger of Spanish reprisals, his first idea was to circumnavigate the American continent, in the manner afterward attempted by Captain Cook. But on June 5, when "in 43° towards the Arctic Pole," he found his men unwilling to venture into high latitudes. He changed his plan, therefore, and decided to take a "Spanish course" across the Pacific, and so, by returning to England round the Cape of Good Hope, to circumnavigate the world. Accordingly, he dropped down into 38°, "in which height it pleased God to send us into a fair and good bay." There, in perhaps the very bay

[1] The *Elizabeth* arrived at Plymouth on June 2, 1579.

which the Spaniards at a later time named Port San Francisco, he gave his men a rest. And there he made the first—albeit a barren—declaration of British sovereignty overseas.

The Californians, we are told, supposed the Englishmen to be gods, "and would not be persuaded to the contrary"; while their king insisted on resigning his kingdom into Drake's hands. "Which thing he (Drake) thought not meet to reject." So he

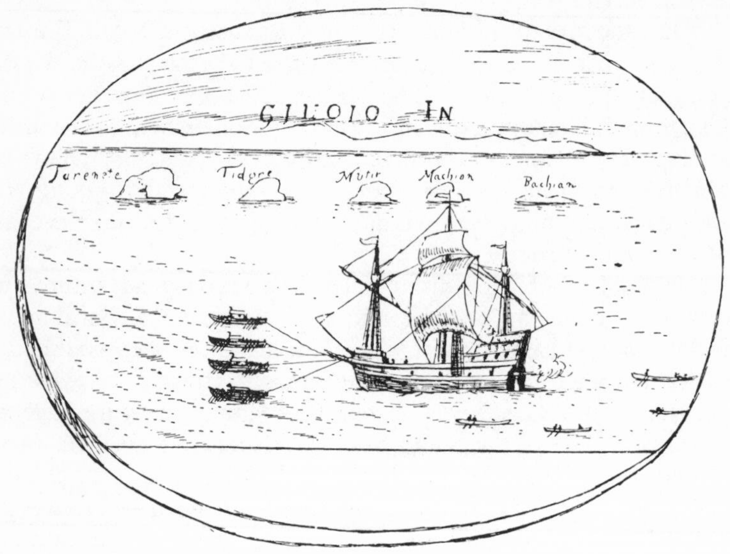

THE "GOLDEN HIND" AT THE MOLUCCAS

received it "to the use of her Majesty," and "called this country Nova Albion—and that for two reasons: the one in respect of the white banks and cliffs (*sic*) which lie towards the sea, and the other because it might have some affinity with our country in name, which sometime was so called."

The *Golden Hind* left the American coast on July 23. Her company did not sight land again till October 13, "which day we fell with certain islands" in 8° North.[1] A month later they reached Ternate. There Drake made the second declaration of British sovereignty overseas, convinced that in alliance with the natives—"enemies of the Portugals, sovereigns over seventy islands, and chief of all the Moluccas"—his countrymen might in the future achieve great things in the East.

[1] Pelew Islands (?).

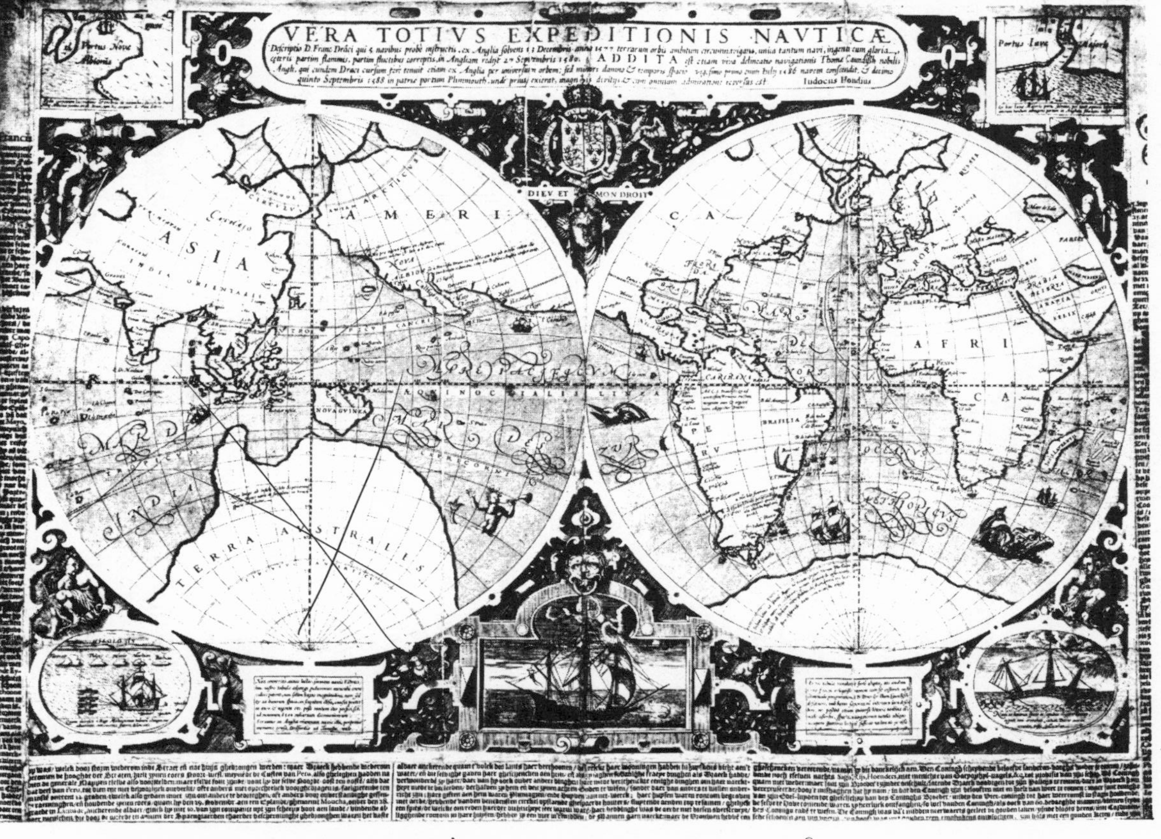

MAP OF DRAKE'S VOYAGE ROUND THE WORLD, 1577–80

Drawn by Judocus Hondius, 1595

On January 9, 1580, between Ternate and Java, the *Golden Hind* ran on a rock, and for eight terrible hours it seemed that she must be made a total wreck. Then, "as it were, in a moment, by the special grace of God," the wind changed, and the little vessel was refloated without having suffered hurt.

Drake did not tarry long at Java. Learning that there were other "such great ships as ours" in the vicinity, he deemed it advisable, having regard to his precious cargo, to push on with all possible speed. He would not allow himself even to explore the Cape of Good Hope—"a most stately thing," he declared; "the fairest we saw in the whole circumference of the earth"; and on November 3 he brought the *Golden Hind* safely into Plymouth Sound, "the place of our first setting forth, after we had spent two years, ten months, and some odd days beside, in seeing the wonders of the Lord in the deep."

At Plymouth the returned heroes received an exuberant welcome. Their leader, however, cut their merrymaking short. A few days later he made them weigh anchor again, and set sail for Deptford. Tidings of his doings on the Peruvian coast had already reached England, and he was given to understand that the Queen, to pacify the wrath of Philip of Spain, had promised he should hang if ever he came back. The sparkle of gold and diamonds, he thought, might modify that decision.

Yet for five months he was kept in suspense, while Elizabeth wavered between prudence and inclination. But the issue was never really in doubt. Wrote Stow:

> In the year next following, to wit, 1581, on the 4th of April, her Majesty dining at Deptford, after dinner entered the ship which Captain Drake had so happily guided round about the world, and being there . . . did make Captain Drake knight, in the same ship, for reward of his service.

The years from 1580 to 1585 Drake spent in England waiting for the occasion that should send him out to torment the Spaniards again. He knew it must come sooner or later, despite Queen Elizabeth's cautious endeavours to avert open war. King Philip had blazoned on his arms the motto *Non sufficit orbis*, and in the world, thus declared to be too small for Spain, England was loudly demanding a place. Peace between the two countries could not be maintained for long. So Sir Francis was content to wait, and to allow Mary Drake (*née* Newman), the wife whom he married in 1569, to enjoy for a time his boisterous company.

But he was not idle meanwhile. In 1581 he took office as mayor of Plymouth. In 1583 he entered Parliament as member for

ELIZABETH VISITS THE "GOLDEN HIND"
From a drawing by Stephen Reid

Bossiney [1] in Cornwall, and in that same year served on the royal commission which was appointed, as a precautionary measure, to inquire into the state of the Navy.

[1] Drake represented Plymouth in the Parliament of 1592–93, and in 1590 he rendered the town a very valuable service by achieving the oft attempted task of bringing in for its use a stream of fresh water from the river Meavy, near Sheepstor, on Dartmoor, where the Burrator reservoir is to-day.

In 1584 Mary Drake died. Her widower soon went wooing again, and early in the following year he married Elizabeth, the

SIR FRANCIS DRAKE
At the age of forty-three
From an old drawing

daughter and heiress of Sir George Sydenham of Combe Sydenham, in Devon. Shortly afterward arose the occasion for which he was looking.

In the summer of 1585 the crops of northern Spain failed, and thousands of people found themselves face to face with famine. To relieve their distress English merchants undertook to send corn to Corunna. When it arrived the Spanish authorities refused to make payment, and seized not only the corn but the ships and the sailors as well. This high-handed action finally aroused Queen Elizabeth. Throwing prudence to the winds, the Queen authorized Drake to go once more to the Spanish Main, this time with twenty-five sail and 2500 men, to teach King Philip manners.

Drake lost no time. Indeed, lest the order should be countermanded, he set out with a half-victualled fleet, determining in his own inimitable manner to complete his arrangements at the expense of the enemy. He left Plymouth on September 14. A few days later he put in at Vigo, and there, with his guns trained on the town, required the Spaniards to provide him with food and munitions. Having thus let King Philip know that he was "mightily at sea again," he bore across the Atlantic and, not content with doing an immense amount of damage to Spanish shipping and trade, actually captured St Domingo and Carthagena.

On his way home, inquisitiveness led him to visit the colony which Sir Walter Ralegh had lately planted in Virginia. So it came about that on July 28, 1586, he returned to Plymouth, bringing with him Governor Lane (*vide* p. 109) and the rest of Ralegh's sorely tried settlers.

This descent on the Indies was not a dazzling financial success like that of 1572, but it was a great and memorable naval achievement. It forced the Spanish Crown to throw down the gauntlet before England's growing sea-power. The "sea-dogs of Devon" eagerly accepted the challenge.

Drake's subsequent exploits are writ large in history. Yet not one of them—not his "singeing of the King of Spain's beard" in 1587, or the daring attempt which he made in 1589 to set Don Antonio on the Portuguese throne in place of King Philip, not even the defeat of "the invincible Armada"—eclipsed the voyage of 1577–80. "The master thief of the unknown world," when he

> . . . circled ocean's plain profound
> And girdled earth in one continuous round,

proved himself, as Stow justly observed, "more skilful in all points of navigation than any that ever was before his time, in his time, or since his death." Moreover, he effectively asserted his country's right to world-wide expansion and empire of the seas. Geographically, too, the voyage had important results. Hitherto Magellan's Strait had been regarded as a waterway cut through a continent which extended southward to the Pole. Drake proved that Tierra del Fuego was only an island, and that open sea lay to the south. For a quarter of a century the British Admiralty carefully guarded this secret.

For many years the *Golden Hind* lay at Deptford, an object—like Nelson's *Victory* of later times—for the wondering admiration of sightseers. At length, about 1670, her timbers having rotted beyond repair, she was broken up. But enough sound wood was salvaged to make the chair presented by Charles II to the University of Oxford, which is now in the Bodleian Library. Wrote Abraham Cowley:

> Drake and his ship could not have wished from fate
> A more blest station or more blest estate;
> For lo! a seat of endless rest is given
> To her in Oxford, and to him in Heaven.

The astrolabe which Drake used on the voyage is preserved in the museum at the Royal Navál College, Greenwich. The famous drum and other relics are at Buckland Abbey. Formerly a Cistercian monastery, standing on the banks of the Tavy midway between Plymouth and Tavistock, the house still belongs to his heirs. Sir Francis acquired it from Sir Richard Grenville, and on his death it passed, with all his other property, to the descendants of his youngest brother, Thomas. The latter, who accompanied Sir Francis on his voyage round the world, and was "with him in most and chiefest of his employments," was the only one of the twelve sons of Edmund Drake who left an heir to carry on the name. Sir Francis and the others all died without issue.

Drake made his final voyage to the West in 1595, and he made it, as he made the first, in company with Hawkins. Sir John aspired to rescue his son, Richard, who since 1593 had been a prisoner in the hands of the Spaniards at Lima. Sir Francis wished to round off his career by capturing Panama. Neither attained his object. Hawkins, an old man in his sixty-third year, could not stand the strain of an active life at sea. He died on November 12. Two months afterward his companion died also.

BURIAL OF SIR FRANCIS DRAKE

From the painting by W. R. Davison

By permission of the Curator of the Art Gallery and Cottonian Collection, Plymouth

The attack on Panama ended in a dismal failure, experience having at last taught the Spaniards to be prepared. Broken by disappointment and bitter self-reproaches, Drake fell a victim to fever; and off Porto Bello, on January 28, 1596, his sorrowing followers committed his body to the deep.

> The waves became his winding-sheet ; the waters were his tomb ;
> But for his fame, the ocean sea was not sufficient room.

XIII. JACQUES CARTIER

Born 1494; *died c.* 1557

THE discovery—or, if Viking endeavour be taken into account, the re-discovery—of the American continent is generally ascribed to John and Sebastian Cabot. Sailing under the English flag, the Cabots touched the Labrador coast in June 1497, and so reached the mainland of the New World seventeen months in advance of Columbus. But they were not really the first modern Europeans to achieve this feat. We have reason to think that Portuguese sailors did it in the days of Prince Henry the Navigator. French sailors also forestalled the Cabots.

In 1488 a certain Cousin, of Dieppe, driven from his course while cruising off the African coast, was swept right across the Atlantic, his ship at length finding shelter in the mouth of a very great river—presumably the Amazon. Cabral 'discovered' that river in similar circumstances in the year 1500. Among Cousin's crew was one Martin Pinzon. The latter, a Portuguese seaman, afterward entered the service of Spain and, as commander of the *Pinta*, took part in Columbus's expedition of 1492. Thus Columbus, it would seem, may have based his plans on definite knowledge.

During the later years of the fifteenth century French sailors also visited the coast of Newfoundland. John Cabot gave that island the name 'Baccalaos,' because, we are told, "in the sea thereabout he found so great multitudes of certain big fishes . . . which the inhabitants call baccalaos." This was simply the Basque word for 'codfish.'

By 1497 the 'banks' had become a fishing-ground much frequented by Basques, Bretons, and Normans. Fisherfolk, however, shunned the mainland beyond, also the waters to the north.

The mainland they imagined to be infested with dragons, unicorns, and other fabulous monsters, and to be peopled by ogres and giants; whilst to the north lay the dreaded Isles of Demons. These were supposed to be given over to fiends. Their traditional occupants, horned, tailed, and winged, may be seen depicted on several old maps. André Thevet, a French cosmographer of that time, wrote:

> True it is, and I myself have heard it, not from one, but from a great number of the sailors and pilots with whom I have made many voyages, that, when they passed this way, they heard in the air, on the tops and about the masts, a great clamour of voices, confused and inarticulate, such as you may hear from the crowd at a fair or market-place.

The Cabots laughed at such simple tales. They crossed the Atlantic with the idea of opening to English traders a north-west passage to China. French merchants also deemed the discovery of such a passage a consummation devoutly to be wished. They soon started a similar quest. Moreover, while people in England still looked on the lands of the West merely as a gateway to the East, Frenchmen began to regard America as desirable in itself, as a field of settlement where, in the Spanish manner, they might gain dominion and glory.

In 1524 Verrazano, a Florentine navigator in the pay of King Francis I, coasted from Florida to Cape Breton in search of a strait through which he could sail on to China. Disappointed in this, he annexed on behalf of his patron the territories lying between the twenty-fourth and forty-fifth parallels.

He returned to Europe, eager to prosecute schemes of conquest. King Francis approved the idea, and though Papal decree had divided America between Spain and Portugal, he favoured it on religious, as well as on political, grounds. By bringing heathen tribes of the New World into her fold, "the Most Christian King" aspired to requite Mother Church for the losses which, through the infection of Protestant heresy, she had lately suffered in the Old.

But the times were unpropitious for pious projects of this kind. In 1524 the French King was committed to a struggle for dominion in Italy. Nine years elapsed ere, his European ambitions finally foiled, he could be persuaded to give serious thought to the founding of an American empire. He then fitted out two ships which, under the command of Jacques Cartier, were to prospect the regions to the west of Newfoundland and, perchance, find a new route to Asia.

Born at St Malo in December 1494, Jacques Cartier was bred in a nursery of mariners, and, as a fisherman, no doubt he had often crossed the Atlantic before, in his fortieth year, he suddenly stepped into the limelight of history. Leaving his native town on April 20, 1534, he made straight for Bonavista Bay in Newfoundland. Thence he steered toward the Labrador coast, and, during the first week in June, by turning south into the Strait of Belle Isle, passed over the verge of the then explored world.

At length he brought his vessel to anchor off the Gaspé peninsula. There he disembarked, the first European to tread on the soil of Canada (an Indian word meaning land) and to behold the waters of that country's great river. From the natives he learned that the river was navigable for many leagues to the west, that it flowed through populous kingdoms, and that two wealthy cities—Stradaconé and Hochelaga—stood on its banks. Believing the long-sought North-West Passage at last to be found, he set out to explore it.

He did not advance far. Lacking the necessary supplies, he dared not risk a winter in ice-bound parts, and autumn storms already were gathering. Accordingly, he turned his prow to the east, and, well satisfied with his reconnaissance, bore back to France. He arrived at St Malo toward the end of September.

King Francis also was well satisfied with the results of the voyage. Straightway he undertook to fit out a larger and better equipped expedition. This comprised three ships, of 120, 70, and 40 tons burden respectively; and on May 19, 1535, Cartier once more spread his sails for the West.

Again he made for the Strait of Belle Isle. But this time, instead of steering southward across the gulf beyond it, he clung to the Labrador coast till he came to a bay opposite Anticosti Island. He gave the bay the name of St Lawrence, which later explorers extended to the whole gulf and to the river above. In attempting to ascend that river, knowing nothing of its intricate navigation, Cartier engaged in a hazardous venture. But his skill proved equal to the task. Eventually, sailing past the gorge of the Saguenay and the Island of Orleans (called by him the Island of Bacchus, by reason of the vines that grew luxuriantly on it), he brought his ships safely to Stradaconé. This settlement stood on the site now occupied by Quebec.

There, held by the natives to be celestial beings, the Breton navigator and his followers passed several weeks; and as the guests of Donnaconna, the chief, they were allowed freely to explore the neighbouring country. Notwithstanding the protests of his host—who was loath that a rival chief should have the privilege of entertaining so illustrious a visitor—Cartier then pushed boldly upstream. He made this part of his journey with his smallest ship only, a 40-ton galleon. The diminishing depth of the river compelled him to leave the others behind.

He reached Hochelaga on October 2 and found it, judged by Indian standards, a town of considerable size, built at the foot of a hill which he named Mont Royal. Corrupted to Montreal, the name has since adhered to the place itself. Hochelaga, Montreal; Stradaconé, Quebec: in the red man's Canada the main centres of population lay just where they lie in the white man's.

Cartier climbed to the top of Mont Royal. There met his gaze a prospect of mantling forest, stretching illimitably in every direction. Not yet, however, did he despair of his quest. Through the leafy verdure to the west ran on a broad riband of blue. Along Canada's river he still hoped to gain the China seas. French explorers continued for many long years to cling to that hope; their idea—as explained in Lescarbot's *Histoire de la Nouvelle France*—being that the St Lawrence, "taking her beginning from one of the lakes which meet at the stream of her course . . . hath two courses, the one from the east towards France, the other from the west towards the south sea."

Cartier did not attempt to verify this theory in 1535. When he reached Hochelaga autumn was well advanced. In the circumstances he prudently decided to abstain from further adventures. Accordingly, he retraced his course, and arrived at Stradaconé just before ice barred the way. Meanwhile, the crews of his two large ships, having fallen foul with the natives, had established themselves in a roughly constructed fort on the banks of the St Charles. Cartier at once set about to strengthen the fort; and there, menaced by Indians, he and his companions were soon besieged by the rigours of winter.

Ere long a more terrible enemy beset them. Early in December scurvy broke out in the fort. The disease spread with alarming rapidity and threatened to exterminate the entire company. But Cartier noticed that, whereas his men when stricken down in most cases died, the natives who were also afflicted recovered more often than not. So he contrived to seize one who had lately been ill, and from him elicited the Indian remedy. This, a decoction

JACQUES CARTIER'S ASCENT OF THE ST LAWRENCE, 1535

From the painting by Gudin in the Versailles Gallery

of the bark and leaves of the spruce, proved highly efficacious. In six days, we are told, the Frenchmen drank a tree as large as an oak. Thus assailed, the malady relaxed the hold it had fastened upon them. But it left them sadly reduced in number. Their leader, therefore, giving up his intention of investigating the waterways above Hochelaga, made for home as soon as spring freed his ships. On July 16, 1536, he again cast anchor under the walls of St Malo.

Donnaconna accompanied him to Europe. On the eve of the French fleet's departure the old chief had been lured on board to attend a farewell banquet, and had been treacherously detained. Lest an attempt should be made to release him, Cartier cunningly forced him to send word to his people that he was going to France of his own free will in order that he might confer with the King. He would return, said the message, in ten or twelve moons.

Donnaconna never went back to his native land. Five years elapsed, moreover, before Cartier recrossed the Atlantic. The tales told by his followers—tales of a harsh climate, a savage people, and a dreadful disease—did not encourage colonial endeavour in France; and, when the supposed diamonds which they had brought home were shown to be merely crystals of quartz, and the supposed gold to be a base, worthless mineral, King Francis for a time also withdrew his support.

At length, in 1540, Cartier's schemes found a new champion in the person of the Seigneur of Roberval, John de la Roche. The latter, a Picardy nobleman, persuaded the King to confer on him the viceroyalty "in Canada, Hochelaga, Saguenay, Belle Isle, Carpunt, Labrador, the Great Bay, and Baccalaos." Having also procured a substantial monetary grant, he at once set about to vindicate his high-sounding titles, and to develop the lands placed under his rule. Cartier undertook to act as his captain-general.

So it came about that on May 23, 1541, the Breton navigator, with a fleet of five ships, again set out from St Malo. His instructions bade him proceed to a spot, near Stradaconé, which he had already marked as a suitable site for a settlement. There, it was arranged, he should build a fort, clear ground, and generally prepare for the reception of a large body of emigrants. These people, criminals for the most part, were to follow in the charge of the Viceroy himself.

"Whereas," ran the king's commission to Roberval,

> we have undertaken this voyage for the honour of God our Creator, desiring with all our heart to do what shall be agreeable to Him, it is our will to perform a compassionate and meritorious work towards criminals and malefactors, to the end that they may acknowledge the Creator, return thanks to Him, and mend their lives. Therefore we have resolved to cause to be delivered to our aforesaid lieutenant such and so many of the aforesaid criminals and malefactors detained in our prisons as may seem to him useful and necessary to be carried to the aforesaid countries.

Some three hundred men and women were recruited in this way.

Cartier arrived at Stradaconé in August 1541. When the French fleet hove into sight, hundreds of natives put out in canoes to greet it—or, rather, to greet Donnaconna. But Donnaconna was not on board. Cartier sought to make out that the old chief had elected to remain in France, where he stood in high favour with the King. His words failed to carry conviction. So, fearing the hostility of the red men, he decided to push on upstream, in order that he might be under the protection of Hochalai, a neighbouring chief, who had been a very good friend to him on his previous voyage, and whom he knew to be an enemy of Donnaconna's tribe. From Hochalai he obtained permission to build a fortified post, which he named Charlesbourg Royal. Then, while his followers were clearing the ground round about, he himself, with a company of picked volunteers, attempted his long-deferred dash *à la Chine*.

He did not get very far. A few miles beyond Hochelaga the strength of the current below the Lachine (*sic*) rapids rendered navigation impossible. Leaving his ship, he took to the bank of the river, but, though he explored the rapids on foot for some little way, he soon wearied of forcing a passage through dense, virgin forest, and so retraced his steps. He reached Charlesbourg Royal just before winter set in.

Roberval had not yet appeared. Nor did the Viceroy appear in the spring, and, though spring changed to summer, still no word from him came. Yielding, therefore, to the demands of his sailors, who shrank from facing a second Canadian winter, Cartier agreed to abandon the settlement.

On his way home he put in at the harbour of St John's, in Newfoundland. There he was astonished to find Roberval's fleet, which, owing to the shortcomings of contractors, had been prevented from sailing from France on the appointed date. The Viceroy was even more greatly surprised at his captain-general's arrival; and an angry interview followed. Cartier, however, bitterly resenting his chief's reproaches, refused to turn back. That night, under cover of darkness, he slipped away from St

JACQUES CARTIER
From the original painting of 1829 in the Hôtel de Ville, St Malo

John's, and continued his voyage to Europe. Roberval, none the less, doggedly stuck to the enterprise he had taken in hand, and, pursuing his course, at length came to the deserted fort at Charlesbourg Royal, where he duly planted his criminals.

Cartier, repenting his impetuous action, visited the colony in the following year, bringing—by way of atonement—much-needed supplies. But he departed again almost at once; and with him he took away Roberval, whom the King had summoned to France. The luckless settlers were thus thrown on their own resources.

Perhaps they would have fared better had they never been set free from gaol. The majority soon died of cold and disease. The remainder were slain by the Indians.

During the second half of the sixteenth century the people of France, convulsed by religious and civil wars, had had little opportunity of giving attention to lands overseas. Not until 1604 was another serious attempt made to colonize the St Lawrence valley. Then Pierre du Gast, the Seigneur of Monts, at last planted a permanent settlement at Port Royal (Annapolis) in Arcadia (Nova Scotia). Four years later, Samuel Champlain established the French at Quebec.

History acclaims Champlain as "the father of Canada." But does not this title rightly belong to Jacques Cartier? As Ralegh founded the first British American empire, the lands lost in 1783, so surely Cartier founded the second, those lands which for two hundred years prior to their conquest by Wolfe were the most highly treasured of France's possessions overseas.

Of Cartier's later years little is known. Created a seigneur by King Francis on his return from the West in 1542, he seems to have passed the rest of his days quietly on his estates at Limoilon, just outside St Malo. He was still alive in 1554. The date of his death is uncertain. Whether the portrait (painted in 1829) which hangs in the town hall at St Malo can be accepted as a likeness we have no means of telling.

XIV. HENRY HUDSON

Died 1611

ON May 1, 1607, Henry Hudson set out from London on the first of the four voyages which made him famous. Of his previous exploits little is known. This, perhaps, is remarkable, for he was not a man of obscure or humble antecedents. His grandfather, the Henry Hudson mentioned by Hakluyt, was one of the founders of the Muscovy Company. An alderman of the City of London, he died, according to Stow, in December 1555, "of the late hot burning fevers whereof died many old persons," leaving numerous offspring, who, as contemporary records testify, were closely associated with various bodies engaged in the overseas expansion of Tudor England—with the Muscovy Company, in particular.

Hudson the navigator, no doubt, received his early training in the service of the corporation which his relations had helped to establish. In 1607, it may be assumed, he was at length raised to the rank of captain.

In that year, on "April the nineteenth," wrote Samuel Purchas in his *Hakluytus Posthumus* (published in 1625),

> at St Ethelburge, in Bishops Gate Street, did communicate with the rest of the parishioners these persons, seamen, purposing to go to sea four days after,[1] for to discover a passage by the North Pole to Japan and China. First, Henry Hudson, master. Secondly, William Colines, his mate. Thirdly, James Young. Fourthly, John Colman. Fifthly, John Cooke. Sixthly, James Beubery. Seventhly, James Skrutton. Eighthly, John Pleyce. Ninthly, Thomas Barter. Tenthly, Richard Day. Eleventhly, James Knight. Twelfthly, John Hudson, a boy.

The Muscovy Company had been incorporated with a view to opening up trade between England and Russia. But the discovery of a north-east passage from Europe to the East was also one of the main objects of its promoters. To find such a passage the directors sent out several expeditions. These ventures, while

[1] For some reason their departure was postponed to May 1.

consuming a deal of money, produced very few tangible results. Hudson, therefore, when he put forward another scheme by which the desired object might be attained, was given an attentive hearing. He proposed to sail right across the Pole—to seek, in short, a northern passage.

The idea was not new. As far back as 1527, Robert Thorne, a Bristol merchant whose father had sailed with the Cabots, tried to induce King Henry VIII to put it in hand. The following is an extract from a treatise he wrote on the subject:

> After they be past the Pole, they (the mariners) are to go straight towards the Pole Antarctic; and then to decline towards the seas and lands situate between the Tropics and under the Equinoctial, where without doubt they shall find the richest lands and islands of the world—with gold, balms, spices, precious stones, and other things that we here most esteem, which come out of strange lands—and may return the same way.

Thorne reckoned the distance to the Indies by the Portuguese route round the Cape of Good Hope and by the Spanish route through Magellan's Strait at 4000 leagues. "Our way by the Pole to the Spiceries" he estimated at 2000 leagues, and he scoffed at the fear that the intense cold of the arctic regions might render it impracticable. That fear, he boldly affirmed, would prove as illusory as the old-time fears of tropical heat; just as "on this side of the Tropic there is found greater heat than under the Line itself," so ships as they neared the Pole would strike warmer, not colder, air. "No land is uninhabitable, and no sea is unnavigable. *Nihil fit vacuum in Rerum Natura*."

These strange beliefs were widely shared at the time. Wrote an eminent Dutch cosmographer, Peter Plancius:

> Near the Pole the sun shines for five months continually; and although his rays are weak, yet on account of the long time they continue, they have sufficient strength to warm the ground, to render it temperate, to accommodate it for the habitation of man, and to produce grass for the nourishment of animals.

Samuel Purchas advanced similar theories.[1] Hudson, however, in undertaking his voyage of 1607, attempted for the first time to put them to the test of experience.

[1] Dr Stefansson has in various of his books called attention to the fertility of large tracts within the Polar Circle during the short Arctic summer.

Sailing from Greenwich in the *Hopewell*, a ship of 80 tons burden, he bore up the North Sea, and was off the Shetland Islands on May 26. Three weeks later, having passed to the north of Iceland, he sighted the east coast of Greenland—in the vicinity of King Oscar's Fiord. "We saw," to quote the words of John Pleyce, one of the crew,

> some land on head of us, and some ice; and it being a thick fog we steered away northerly. . . . Our sails and shrouds did freeze. . . . All the afternoon and all the evening it rained. . . . This was a very high land, most part covered with snow.

From King Oscar's Fiord the *Hopewell* coasted northward. Hudson intended to continue on this course until his ship touched the Pole. But, on June 27, the great ice barrier headed him off, and he was constrained to explore its fringe "to the north-west of Newland" (Spitzbergen). Yet even there—though he finally reached the latitude of 80° 23′ N.[1]—he failed to break through to the warmer waters which, he believed, lay round the Pole. To return to England, therefore, was the only thing to be done. He arrived at Tilbury on August 16.

In the following year, as master of the *Hopewell*, he sailed again to the north. This voyage, designed to open a passage to the Pole between Spitzbergen and Nova Zembla, was as unsuccessful as the last. Nevertheless, it marked a further stage toward the unravelling of the secrets of the Arctic. It also resulted in the establishment of the Spitzbergen whale fishery. Hudson was the first man to recognise the economic possibilities of an industry which for many years provided the Muscovy Company with a rich source of income. To the cleansing properties of soap prepared from the blubber of Spitzbergen whales the laces and ruffs of Stuart England owed much of their whiteness and charm.

In the autumn of 1608, soon after his return to England, Hudson received from his friend, Captain John Smith, one of the pioneers of the English settlement in Virginia, a map—based on Michael Lok's planisphere (1582)—showing the American continent reduced to a mere strip at about 40° lat. Thinking that through this isthmus might lie a way to the China Sea, he urged his employers to send him out to find it. The Muscovy Company rejected the

[1] A "farthest north" record that remained unbroken till 1773. In that year Captain Phipps touched 80° 48′ N.

EXPLORING THE FRINGE OF THE ARCTIC

proposal. The directors had decided to concentrate their energies on the Russian trade and the Spitzbergen fishery, and to eschew the cost of voyages of discovery. Hudson, therefore, transferred his services to a rival corporation—the Netherlands East India Company.

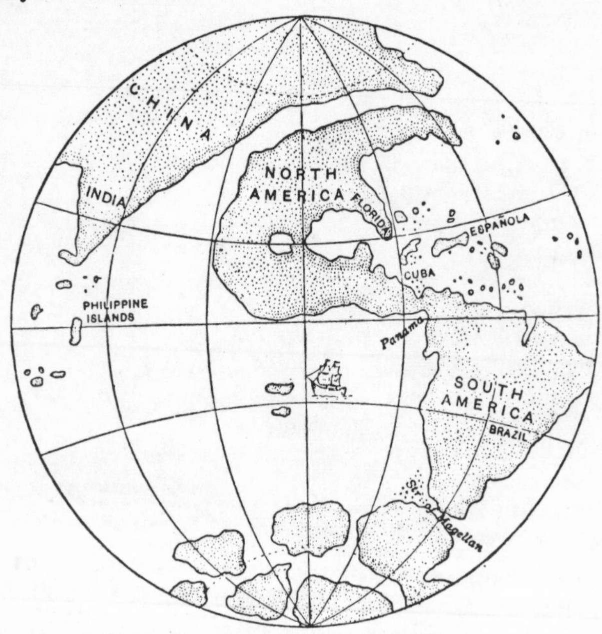

AN OLD MAP OF THE NEW WORLD
Showing the supposed passage into the Indian Seas

A seventeenth-century manuscript history of that company, which was brought to light some years ago, contains a copy of the contract between him and his new masters. Below is a translation of the document:

On this eighth of January, in the year of our Lord one thousand six hundred and nine, the Directors of the East India Company of the Chamber of Amsterdam . . . of the one part, and Master Henry Hudson, Englishman . . . of the other part, have agreed in manner following, to wit:

That the said Directors shall in the first place equip a small vessel or yacht of about thirty lasts burden,[1] well provided with

[1] That is, about 60 tons.

men, provisions, and other necessaries, with which the above-named Hudson shall, about the first of April, sail in order to search for a passage by the north around the north side of Nova Zembla, and shall continue along that parallel until he shall be able to sail southward to the latitude of sixty degrees. He shall obtain as much knowledge of the lands as can be done without any considerable loss of time, and, if it be possible, shall return immediately to make a faithful report and relation of his voyage to the Directors, and to deliver over his journals, log-book, and charts, together with an account of everything whatsoever shall happen to him during the voyage without keeping anything back.

For which said voyage the Directors shall pay the said Hudson . . . the sum of eight hundred guilders.[1] And in case—which God prevent—he shall not come back within a year, the Directors shall further pay to his wife two hundred guilders in cash, and thereupon they shall not be farther liable to him or to his heirs, unless he shall either afterwards or within the year arrive and have found the passage good and suitable for the Company to use: in which case the Directors shall reward the before-named Hudson for his dangers, trouble, and knowledge, in their discretion.

Hudson went to Holland hoping that the Dutch company would take up the scheme which had been turned down in London. In this hope, as the terms of the contract show, he was disappointed. He found the Dutch company, like its English rival, bent on the discovery of a north or north-east, rather than a western, passage. Yet, though his sailing orders explicitly laid down that he was "to think of discovering no other route or passages except the route round the north and north-east above Nova Zembla," he left Texel, it would seem, in the *Half Moon* (60 tons), on April 3, 1609, with the set purpose of crossing the Atlantic.

The log of the voyage, printed in Van Meteren's *Historie der Nierderlanden* (1614), tells us that in Barents Sea his mixed crew of Englishmen and Dutchmen, "after much trouble, with fogs sometimes, and more dangerous ice," became mutinous, and that in agreeing to sail westward he acted under compulsion. The story is not entirely convincing. The ship's company, seeing that they had been recruited mainly from Dutch East India merchantmen, may well have found the Arctic little to their liking. It is suggested, however, that Hudson himself engineered the 'mutiny.' Then, since an immediate return to Holland would have exposed

[1] About £70.

all to the risk of punishment, it was an easy matter for him to persuade his men to sail with him into warm western seas on a voyage of discovery that offered boundless prospects of gain.

In August, after many adventures, he brought the *Half Moon* to the coast of Virginia "under 37° 45′," the point at which Captain Smith had left off his survey. Thence he coasted northward, passing unnoticed the overfall of the Delaware, till in 40° 45′ he "found a good entrance between two headlands . . . with good anchoring grounds on both sides," and so, on September 12, entered the great river which bears his name, and which he fondly believed to be a strait connecting the Atlantic and the Pacific.

He sailed up the river one hundred and fifty miles, carefully surveying as he went, before he was finally disillusioned. A French expedition under Samuel de Champlain, meanwhile, was seeking a passage from the St Lawrence southward into the China Sea through Lake Champlain and Lake St Sacrament. On October 4 Champlain and Hudson, by opposite routes, actually arrived within sixty miles of each other.

On that same day the *Half Moon* weighed for Texel. A month later she put in at Dartmouth. There, though the ship was allowed to proceed, her captain was detained by order of the Government on the ground that he had "undertaken a voyage to the detriment of his own country." But no further action was taken against him. It may be that his old employers, impressed by the daring and resource he had shown, interceded on his behalf. Shortly afterward, at any rate, two of the leading members of the Muscovy Company, Sir Dudley Diggs and Sir Thomas Smith, urged him to attempt a north-west passage, undertaking to provide a ship for the purpose. Hudson eagerly accepted the offer.

So it came about that, on April 17, 1610, in "the bark *Discoverie*," he started from London "to try if, through any of these inlets which Davis saw, but durst not enter, any passage might be found to the other ocean called the South Sea." This voyage, which cost him his life, resulted in the first exploration of the strait and it being named after him.

By the middle of September, having traversed Hudson Bay, he had penetrated to the extreme south-eastern corner of James's Bay. There he decided to take up winter quarters, and his ship was soon frozen in. Not until June 1611 could he again weigh anchor. He then coasted northward until, on Midsummer Day, when about half-way back to the strait, he and his little son, John, who had accompanied him on all his travels, together with two loyal followers, were turned adrift in a shallop to perish miserably, "without food, drink, fire, clothing, or any necessaries."

The story of the mutiny has been often told. Yet the circumstances are still in dispute. Hudson, by all accounts, was not an exacting or harsh-tempered commander, and his crew were picked men. Their action can be satisfactorily explained only if it be attributed to the nerve-shattering effects of a winter spent in Arctic regions—effects which many an explorer has noted. Wrote Colonel Brainard of the Greely Expedition of 1881–84:

> Take any set of men, however carefully selected, and let them be thrown together as intimately as are the members of an exploring expedition—hearing the same voices, seeing the same faces, day after day—and they will soon become weary of one another's society, and impatient of one another's faults.

On the voyage home, several of the mutineers suffered at the hands of their fellows as Hudson had suffered. The *Discoverie*, however, eventually arrived at London. What subsequently happened to the survivors is a question which has long intrigued historians.

In a publication of 1613 it is stated:

> They have been thrown into prison for their crime, and will be kept in prison until their captain shall be safely brought home. For that purpose some ships have been sent out last year by the late Prince of Wales [1] and by the Directors of the Muscovia Company, about the return of which nothing as yet has been heard.

It is now possible to carry the story forward another stage. In 1618 the ringleaders at last were put on trial. A document relating to the proceedings has recently been brought to light in the Public Record Office at London. From it we learn that the jury returned a verdict of "not guilty" on every count.

Hudson failed to achieve the immediate objects he had in view. Yet the consequences of his efforts are writ large in history. His first and second voyages led, as we have seen, to the setting up of the English whale fishery at Spitzbergen. His third voyage led to the establishment of the Dutch settlements in North America: the city of New Amsterdam—renamed New York when, in 1667,

[1] Prince Henry, Charles I's elder brother, who died in 1612.

the British took possession of it—was founded [1] as a direct result of his report to his Dutch employers. His fourth voyage brought into being the Hudson's Bay Company which, started by Prince Rupert, received its royal charter from Charles II in 1670.

No authentic portrait of Hudson has come down to us; the

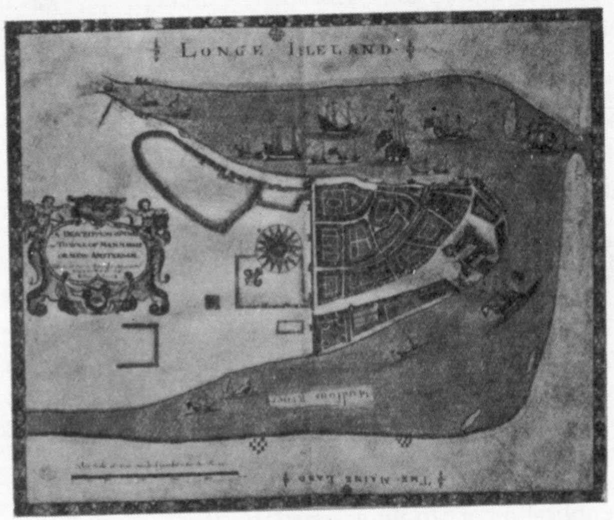

THE EARLIEST MAP OF NEW YORK
From a print in the British Museum

Hon. John Collier's well-known painting serves well to illustrate the tragic story of his death, the story immortalized in verse by Dr van Dyke:

> One sail in sight upon the lonely sea,
> And only one! For never ship but mine
> Has dared these waters. We were first,
> My men, to battle in between the bergs
> And floes to these wide waves. This gulf is mine;
> I name it! and that flying sail is mine!
> And there, hull down below that flying sail,
> The ship that staggers home is mine, mine, mine!
> My ship *Discoverie*!

Hudson had two sons, Oliver and Richard, in addition to his faithful companion, John. Of Oliver, nothing is known. Richard, after a successful career in the East, became the East India Company's chief representative in the Bay of Bengal. Mrs

[1] The Netherlands West India Company was incorporated in 1621.

Hudson also entered the service of the East India Company. On the ground that it behoved them to help the dependants of one "who had lost his life in the service of the Commonwealth," the

THE LAST VOYAGE OF HENRY HUDSON
By the Hon. John Collier
Photo W. A. Mansell & Co.

directors yielded to her importunity, and actually allowed her to go out to India with special trading privileges. The enterprising widow made such good use of the opportunity that she quickly amassed a considerable fortune. She died in 1624 and was buried at St Botolph, Aldgate, leaving her wealth to be divided between her sons.

XV. ABEL JANSSEN TASMAN

Born 1603; *died* 1659

AUSTRALIA was the last of the continents to be exploited by the ubiquitous white man. Not till 1789 did Europeans begin to make it a field of settlement. Its existence had then been known for two hundred and fifty years at least. Portuguese navigators touched its coasts early in the sixteenth century. But the Portuguese, who went to the south and east in quest of spices and gold, did not pursue their investigations far. They found that Australia was not a spice-producing land, and it seemed to be lacking in mineral wealth. Nevertheless, they were careful to say very little about it.

In 1494 Pope Alexander VI, hoping to promote peace in Christendom, had divided the seas, countries, and trades beyond Europe between Spain and Portugal, the only powers which at that time aspired to colonial empires. The partition allowed Spain practically the whole of the American continent; only Brazil was reserved to Portugal. Portugal acquired Africa and India, also the greater part of the Malay Archipelago. Australia had yet to be discovered. When discovered, it was found to lie largely in the Spanish zone. Hence the silence of the Portuguese: the merchants of Lisbon, though they themselves had no use for the country, did not wish to see Spaniards established on the fringe of their spice preserves.

In the seventeenth century the Dutch hounded the Portuguese from Malaya. The new-comers were a commercial people, too. Save while Anthony Van Diemen had charge of their overseas interests, they likewise gave but a cursory glance at Australia, or New Holland as it was then called.

Van Diemen was cast in a bigger mould than most of his compatriots. He aspired to be a second Prince Henry the Navigator, and in 1636, on taking up office at Batavia as Governor-General of the Netherlands East India Company's territories, he set about to extend Dutch influence all over the South Pacific.

As a result of the discoveries, he wrote of "the highly renowned naval heroes, Christopher Columbus and Americus Vesputius," and of "Vasco da Gama, and other Portuguese captains . . . with what invaluable treasures, profitable trade-connexion, useful trades, excellent territories, vast powers and dominions, have the Kings of Spain and Portugal . . . enriched their kingdoms and crowns?" And yet "no Christian Kings, Princes, or Common-

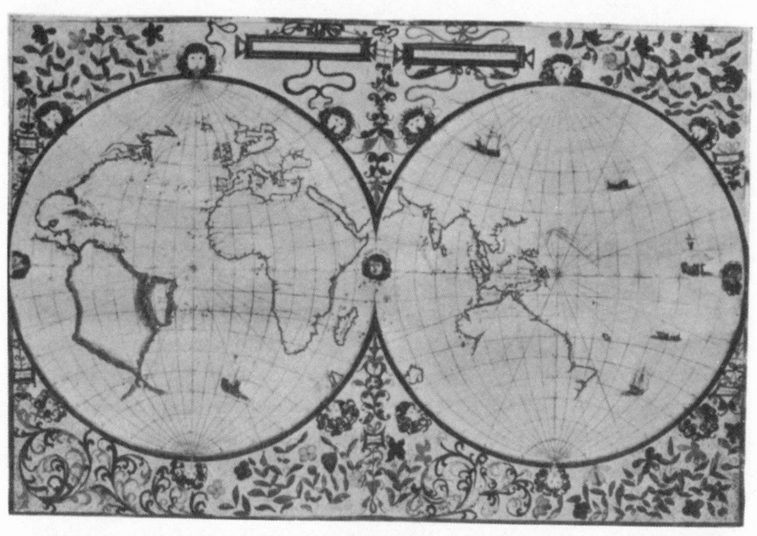

THE WORLD, DRAWN IN 1542, BY JOHN ROTZ, HYDROGRAPHER TO HENRY VIII
It has been contended that this map shows Australia.
British Museum

wealth have seriously endeavoured to make timely discovery of the remaining unknown part of the terrestrial globe, situated in the South." Why? Are there not "good reasons to suppose that it contains many excellent and fertile regions, like the provinces of Chile and Peru which stand in the same Southern Latitude?" Indeed, "it may be confidently expected that the expense and trouble that must be bestowed in the eventual discovery of so large a portion of the world will be rewarded with certain fruits of material profit and immortal fame."

The directors at Amsterdam, impressed by the argument, authorized the Governor-General to send out expeditions. If only he could solve the riddle of the Great South Land, which had long intrigued geographers; if only he could locate Marco

Polo's "Land of Beach," which was supposed to form part of it, and to abound in elephants, spices, and gold; if only he could find a safe and easy route to Chile, and so make it possible for Dutch traders to tap the sources of the Spaniards' wealth . . . the brilliance of the prospect dazzled them.

But Van Diemen's scheme, while entailing heavy charges, did not yield immediate profits. The directors soon wearied of it.

THE DUTCH EAST INDIES HOUSE, AMSTERDAM, IN THE SEVENTEENTH CENTURY

In 1644 they decided to revert to their old conservative policy. "We cannot," they wrote to the Governor-General and his council,

> anticipate any great results from the continuation of such discoveries. . . . Gold and silver are not extracted from the earth without excessive outlay, as some would seem to imagine. These plans of your Worships somewhat aim beyond our mark. The gold and silver mines that will best serve the Company's turn have already been found: which we deem to be our trade with the whole of India, and especially in Formosa and Japan, if only God be graciously pleased to continue the same to us.

In the following year Van Diemen died.

The wisdom of the directors' decision is hard to gainsay. Had exploring activities been continued, some Dutchman must soon have stumbled on Australia's secret—that fertile south-east corner which Captain Cook discovered in 1770, and which is the main centre of the wealth and population of the modern Commonwealth. But how would such a find have profited his countrymen?

The Dutch in the seventeenth century were not a numerous people. Already they knew of as many lands as they were able to trade with. An important new discovery could only have resulted in the immediate opening of the door of the spice world to rival nations; and that was the very contingency which it was their prime concern to prevent.

Abel Janssen Tasman, a Dutchman, born at Luytjegast, a village in the province of Groningen, in the year 1603, was the most notable of the navigators whom Van Diemen employed on his projects. History has little to say of his youth, but this is hardly surprising. In a record of his marriage, dated December 1631, he is described as a "common sailor" dwelling in a mean quarter of Amsterdam. In 1632, having entered the service of the Netherlands East India Company, he went out to Batavia. There he was given command of a small trading vessel and, by reason of his daring and his high technical skill, soon made himself conspicuous among the many able captains whom occasions, lawful or otherwise, had attracted to the seas around Java.

He set out on his first official voyage of discovery in June 1639. This was a venture directed to the North Pacific, its object being the rediscovery of a certain "large and high-rising island" to which, according to tradition, some Spanish ships had once been driven by a storm. The island was supposed to lie to the east of Japan, and on the shore—so ran the story—"gold and silver were almost to be picked up at discretion." The Spaniards had made many vain attempts to find it again. Therefore, argued Van Diemen, "the Lord God, considering the wickedness of the Spanish projects," must have reserved it for His Dutchmen. Its discovery, he wrote, surely would "bring the Company into the real enjoyment of the profits of the East Indian trade."

Two ships were fitted out for the purpose, and placed under the command of Tasman and a certain Matthew Quast. To them the Governor-General issued comprehensive instructions. They were not to content themselves merely with locating the island. Afterward they were to explore the coast of Korea, a country which might prove useful to the Company if, "contrary to our hopes, the trade with Japan should prove less profitable in the future." Then, if circumstances allowed, they were to proceed to the Ladrones, and, by careful observation, ascertain the exact route taken by Spanish trading ships between Manila and America, "so that the Company's ships might be enabled to cruise with more hope of success in search of that rich booty."

The expedition did not realize the aim of its author. Its only tangible result was the discovery of the Bonin Islands. Thence Tasman and Quast sailed northward to a point in latitude 38° 40′ N., some six hundred miles east of Japan, and for many days scoured the surrounding ocean. But they failed to sight land. Finally, disease compelled them to abandon the enterprise, and on November 21, after touching at Japan, they anchored off Tainan, in Formosa, "in a very bad plight"; more than half of their men had died of scurvy.

Despite this, Van Diemen did not despair. If his captains had not found the golden island they had "observed"—so they reported—"numerous unmistakable signs of the same." In 1641 he again sent ships in search of it.

Of this voyage, also unsuccessful, few details have been preserved. Tasman, however, did not take part in it. In 1641 he was employed elsewhere—trading in Cambodia, and punishing "certain Chinamen" who, according to the Company's records, had dared to "put great affronts upon us." He returned to Batavia in May 1642. A few weeks later Van Diemen offered him the command of a fleet which was then being equipped "for the discovery and exploration of the supposed rich Southern and Eastern lands." To this discovery, we are told, he was "strongly inclined."

With two ships—the *Heemskirk* and *Zeehaan*, victualled for eighteen months and well furnished with merchandise—he left Batavia on August 14, and, running before the south-east trade wind, made for Mauritius. Thence his instructions bade him bear south to latitude 54°, or until he came to land. He was then to turn east and sail across the Pacific to the longitude of the east coast of New Guinea, carefully surveying any territories he might chance to discover. From that point he was to head in a northerly direction, and finally find his way back to Batavia by what should seem the most practicable route, always remembering that a great object of the voyage was the opening up of a new passage to

A DUTCH MERCHANTMAN OF THE MIDDLE OF THE SEVENTEENTH CENTURY

From a model in the Nederlandsch Historisch Scheepvaart Museum, Amsterdam

America so that the Dutch might be in a position "to do great things with the Chilese, and to snatch rich booty from the Castilian."

Preserved among the archives in the Colonial Office at The Hague is an intensely interesting document, his "daily register," illustrated by numerous drawings—the *Journal or Description drawn up by me, Abel Janssen Tasman, of a voyage made from Batavia in East India, for the discovery of the unknown South Land, in the year of our Lord*, 1642. Some years ago, thanks to the enterprise of Professor Heeres, the leading authority on the history of the Netherlands East India Company, a facsimile was published.

On September 5, after a remarkably quick passage of twenty-two days, the *Heemskirk* and her consort arrived at Mauritius. There they were detained for a month. The *Zeehaan* was found to be in such a "hopelessly unsatisfactory" condition that "a great part had to be repaired and renewed." The two ships eventually got away on October 8, and, aided by favouring winds, reached latitude 44° S. by the end of the month.

Farther south than that Tasman dared not proceed. Owing to "dense fog and darkness" it was "hardly possible to survey known shores, let alone to discover unknown lands." Moreover, "the sea ran very high, and our men began to suffer badly from severe cold." Accordingly he bore to the east and sailed along the forty-third parallel until at length, on November 24, "in the afternoon about 4 o'clock," he sighted the mountains on the west coast of the island which in 1853 was fittingly renamed Tasmania.

Tasman called the country Van Diemen's Land, "in honour" —to quote the words of his *Journal*—"of the Hon. Governor-General, our illustrious master, who sent us to make the discovery." The widely accepted story that he gave it the name of his lady-love, the Governor-General's daughter, must be dismissed as fictitious. Professor Heeres assures us that Van Diemen was childless.

For some days stormy weather prevented the Dutch ships approaching the shore. On December 3, however, a landing was effected in the inlet now known as Blackman's Bay. There, "near four tall trees, easily recognizable," Tasman set up "a pole with the Company's mark carved into it . . . that those who come after us may be aware that we have been here, and have taken possession of the said land as our lawful property." Little did he think that a century and a half would elapse ere Europeans again sought out the spot.

The Dutchmen met with no opposition when landing. They heard human voices, and the sound of trumpets and gongs; but the natives remained carefully concealed, though "we suspected," wrote Tasman, "that some of them were at no great distance watching our proceedings." The adventurers, perhaps, since they pictured the natives as giants, were not sorry to avoid an encounter. Trees which they noticed "bore notches made with flint implements, the bark having been removed for the purpose. These notches, which formed a kind of steps to enable persons to get up the trees . . . were fully five feet apart." Therefore, it seemed, "the natives must be of very tall stature."

Next morning Tasman set sail again, and made his way to the north in search of a better watering place. But toward evening—since he "could no longer steer near the coast, the wind being almost ahead"—he decided to stand out to sea, and to resume his easterly course. This he continued to follow till December 13, when, "about noon," he sighted the Southern Alps of South Island, New Zealand—"a large high-lying land being south-east of us about sixty miles distance."

It "seems," he wrote, "to be a very fine country, and we trust it is the mainland of the coast of the unknown South Land." Therefore, he named it Staten Land, hoping it would prove to be a part of that Staten Land which a fellow-countryman, Le Maire, had discovered in 1616 to the south of Tierra del Fuego. It acquired its modern name, New Zealand (*Nova Zeelandia*), in 1647, after Le Maire's southern continent had been shown to be but an island.

Coasting northward, Tasman rounded the promontory now known as Cape Farewell on December 16, and two days later entered the bay which still bears his name. While his ships were being anchored, prows came out from the shore, filled with men who "began to call to us in a rough, hollow voice" and to blow on instruments which made a sound "like that of a Moorish trumpet." His *Journal* is illustrated with a sketch of these natives. The accompanying description—the first European description of the Maori—runs as follows:

As far as we could observe, these people were of ordinary height. They had rough voices and strong bones. The colour of their skin was between brown and yellow. They wore tufts of black hair right upon the tops of their heads, tied fast in the manner of the Japanese at the back of their heads, but somewhat longer and thicker, and surmounted by a large, thick, white feather. Their boats consisted of two long, narrow prows side by side, over which a number of planks or other seats were placed. Their paddles are upwards of a fathom in length, narrow and pointed at the end.

VIEW OF MURDERER'S BAY

From *Voyages and Discoveries in the South Pacific Ocean*, Dalrymple, 1770

With these vessels they could make considerable speed. For clothing, it seemed to us, some of them wore mats, others cotton stuffs. Almost all of them were naked from the shoulders to the waist.

Thinking that the natives wished to be friendly, the Dutchmen tried to entice them to their ships by displaying merchandise over the sides. The natives refused to be drawn. The captain of the *Zeehaan*, therefore, having launched his cockboat, pulled out toward them. The crew of one of the prows immediately began to paddle furiously, and rammed the cockboat. What followed can best be told in Tasman's words:

The foremost man in this prow of villains with a long, blunt pike thrust the quartermaster, Cornelis Joppen, in the neck several times, with so much force that the poor man fell overboard. Upon this the other natives, with short, thick clubs . . . and with their paddles, fell upon the men in the cockboat, and overcame them by main force. . . . After this outrageous and detestable crime the

MAORI

murderers sent the cockboat adrift, having taken one of the dead bodies into their prow, and thrown another into the sea.

Meanwhile, though the crews of the *Heemskirk* and *Zeehaan* "diligently fired with muskets and guns," the natives suffered little hurt. In the end, all got away.

Seeing that he "could not hope to enter into any friendly relations with these people, nor to be able to get water or refreshments" from them, Tasman decided to seek another landing-place. Accordingly, he weighed anchor and, crossing Cook Strait (which he thought to be a bay), coasted slowly northward till, on January 4, he found himself in a channel between a bold promontory on the mainland and an island. The latter he called Three Kings (*Drie Coningen*) Island, "because we came to anchor there on Twelfth Night even." To the cape he gave the name of Maria Van Diemen, stating, be it noted, that this was "the name of the Governor-General's wife."

On the following day an attempt was made to procure water and food from the island. The sailors sent for the purpose, however,

MAORI GREENSTONE AXES
Photo Dominion Museum, Wellington, N.Z.

could not be persuaded to leave their boat; in the distance they observed a body of natives whom they believed to be akin to the giants of Van Diemen's Land, men of very tall stature who "in walking took enormous steps or strides." So again Tasman weighed anchor; and finally—since, on rounding the cape, he found the sea "running very high from the east"—he bore on to the north without even setting foot on the land of the Maori.

After a fortnight's sailing the Dutchman came to the Tonga Islands. Captain Cook, when he visited these islands in 1773, named them the Friendly Islands. Tasman likewise found them friendly. The largest he called Amsterdam, "because of the abundance of refreshments we got there"; another he called Rotterdam, for "here we got our casks filled with water." The

Fiji group, his next important discovery, he reached on February 5. Thence he made his way cautiously to the known north coast of New Guinea, and on June 14, having braved and survived countless perils of tempest, rock, and shoal, arrived at his starting-point. So his *Journal* concludes: "Item, the 15th do. In the

THREE KINGS ISLAND
From *Voyages and Discoveries in the South Pacific Ocean*, Dalrymple, 1770
From the Macpherson Collection

morning, at daybreak, I went to Batavia in the pinnace. God be praised and thanked for this happy voyage. Amen."

With the results of the expedition, its leader felt that he had good reason to be satisfied, Van Diemen thought otherwise. Why, he wanted to know, had not Tasman explored Staten Land more thoroughly? Why had he not proved its connexion with the land discovered by Le Maire, and sailed on to Chile? Why had he not done this and done that? Tasman stoutly defended his actions. If he had erred, he maintained, he had erred on the side of boldness rather than caution. He and his few followers, he said, would have been courting disaster in attempting to take possession of a country peopled by warlike savages; and they would have been equally foolish, having regard to the condition of their ships and their lack of supplies, had they prolonged their course to the east.

In the end the Governor-General was convinced by these arguments, and undertook to equip a more powerful expedition. He arranged that this should sail, under Tasman's command, in the following October. Circumstances, however, compelled him to postpone its departure; owing to a renewal of hostilities with "the overbold Portuguese" he required the ships for service elsewhere.

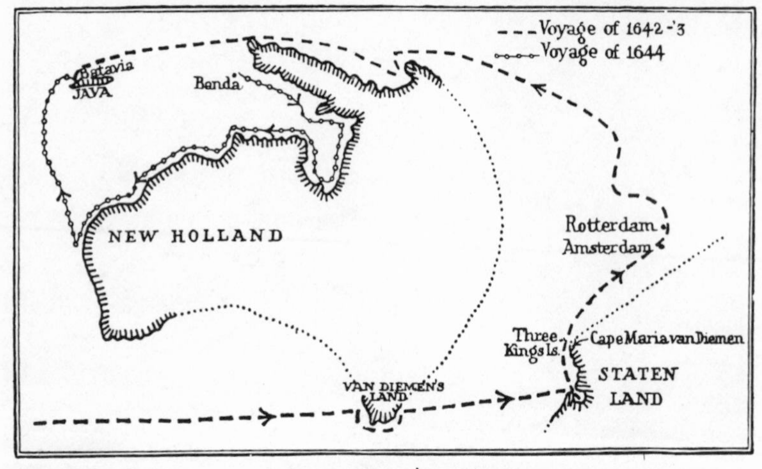

CHART OF TASMAN'S VOYAGES

Meanwhile, eager, "by God's aid, to obtain rich booty" he decided to send their appointed commander, in charge of three yachts, to seek some shorter route to the south.

So it came about that, in February 1644, Tasman sailed from Banda into the Gulf of Carpentaria.[1] Since no navigator had yet touched its southern shore, he hoped he might find the gulf to be the entrance to a strait. Should his theory prove wrong, he purposed to sail westward and "fully discover" the then little known north coast of Australia. This plan he carried out to the letter. Geographically, therefore, his voyage of 1644, though less spectacular, was of more value than that of 1642–43. But it was the last voyage of discovery he made. When he returned to Batavia the directors at Amsterdam had already issued their fiat vetoing Van

[1] Named after Peter Carpenter, sometime Governor of the Netherlands East India Company.

Diemen's schemes. Thus Tasman the explorer again became Tasman the trader.

In this latter capacity he met with considerable success. At any rate, by 1659, the year of his death, he had amassed a very large

ABEL JANSSEN TASMAN, *c.* 1603–59
From the portrait by Van der Helst
By permission of *The Pall Mall Magazine*

fortune. The means by which he acquired it will not bear scrutiny. In the seventeenth century the Dutch in the East were not—to state the case mildly—a scrupulous people. Tasman offended even against their lax code, and in 1649, on the ground that he had been acting "against all forms of law," his employers suspended him "from the exercise of his functions and office."

Two years later, "at his urgent request," he was restored to his rank and pay (a hundred guilders a month)—"seeing," wrote the directors, "that in divers parts of the world he has rendered the Company good service, and may continue to do so." This pardon, it would seem, counted for little. From the society of his countrymen he continued to be an outcast, despite all his riches, and in a document dated 1653 he is still referred to as the "ex-commander" sailing a "private vessel." Yet, whatever may have been his faults as a man, he was a very great sailor.

He died at Batavia in October 1659. A substantial part of his wealth he bequeathed to the poor of his native village in Holland; the rest he divided between his wife and his grandchildren.

XVI. ROBERT BLAKE

Born 1598; *died* 1657

ENGLAND'S struggle with Spain in the sixteenth century resulted, *inter alia*, in the establishment of the Royal Navy as a profession. Since an efficient striking force had to be kept constantly in being, officers were encouraged to enter the service as youngsters, and to remain in it all their active years. Non-professional officers of the old type became rarer and rarer. By the close of Elizabeth's reign they had mostly disappeared.

James I, a penurious pacifist, shamefully neglected his fleet. Yet, even under him, the Navy retained its professional status; and men like Sir William Monson—who, as boy and man, served afloat almost continuously from 1583 to 1635—complacently regarded the possibility of sea forces again being led by landlubbers as a contingency fantastically improbable.

"Suppose," wrote Monson,

> the best and ablest-bred seaman should buckle on armour, and mount a courageous great horse, and so lead a troop of horse, he would no doubt be accounted very indiscreet, and men would judge that he could perform but very weak service; neither could his soldiers hope of good security, being under an ignorant captain that knows not scarce how to rein his horse, much less to take advantage for execution or retreat. And yet it is apparent to be far more easy to attain experience for land service than on the sea.

Or, again:

> The best ships of war in the known world have been commanded by captains bred seamen; and merchants put their whole confidence in the fidelity and ability of seamen to carry their ships through the hazard of pirates and men of war, and the dangers of rocks and sands, be they never of so much value; which they would never do under the charge of a gentleman, or an inexperienced soldier, for his valour only.

Monson's *Naval Tracts* were published posthumously in 1643. The Civil War had then begun. That war strangely disproved some of the author's theories. Other wars—among them, the Great War of our own day—have falsified equally sane, well-reasoned arguments.

Deane, Popham, and Penn—to name three of the famous sea captains of the seventeenth century—were, by training, essentially landsmen. So, too, were George Monk (Duke of Albemarle) and the gallant Prince Rupert. Yet, as Monson truly observed,

> the sea language is not soon learnt, much less understood, being only proper to him that has served his apprenticeship. Besides that, a boisterous sea and stormy weather will make a man not bred to it so sick that it bereaves him of legs, stomach, and courage, so much as to fight with his meat. And in such weather, when he hears the cry 'starboard' or 'port,'[1] or to 'bide aloof,' or 'haul home a clue-line,' he thinks he hears a barbarous speech which he conceives not the meaning of.

On one occasion—so runs the story—Monk, carried away by the excitement of action, astonished his sailors by giving the order: "Wheel to the left." On another occasion he was asked, "Starboard, sir, or larboard?" "Ay," he replied, "board her by all means; board her by all means!" Like Rupert, however, likewise an "admiral in spurs," he was an amphibian genius; which was his proper element, the sea or the land, it is hard to determine.

A first-rate leader of cavalry, Prince Rupert had the makings of a really great general. Indeed, he might now be regarded as such had he not been pitted by fate against Cromwell, a farmer who, in violation of the rules which govern these matters, proved himself one of the master soldiers of history. He also had the makings of a really great admiral. But he was even unluckier at sea than on land. At sea he had to contend with Blake; and Blake, though he was fifty years old when he first set foot in a warship, stands very high in the list of the world's fighting sailors.

The eldest son of a west country merchant, Robert Blake was born at Knoll Hill, near Bridgwater in Somerset, in August 1598. He received his early education at the local grammar school, and at the age of sixteen went to Oxford. There, as an undergraduate at Wadham, a college which the widow of Nicholas Wadham, an old friend of his father, lately had founded, he won

[1] The use of 'port,' instead of 'larboard,' is not so modern a habit, it will be seen, as is generally supposed. The term to 'bide aloof' suggests an origin of the later 'luff.'

golden opinions. But his industry and learning failed to gain him a Fellowship. The Warden, it is said, took exception to his "low and squat" figure. Perhaps, also, the worthy Warden took exception to his views, freely expressed, on religious and political questions.

In 1623, despairing of academical preferment, Blake returned to Bridgwater, and for sixteen years acted as manager of his father's business. In this capacity he quickly made himself a man of mark among his neighbours. The burgesses of Bridgwater listened more sympathetically than had the dons of Oxford to what he had to say on Ship Money, the legality of the Court of High Commission, and other controversies of the time. So it came about that in April 1640 he was elected to represent his native borough in the Parliament which, after eleven years of arbitrary rule, financial necessity forced Charles I to summon.

This Parliament, the so-called Short Parliament, lasted barely three weeks. To its successor, the Long Parliament, which met in the following November, Blake did not seek election. Yet his brief venture into the arena of active politics had a determining influence on his career. It brought him into contact with the leaders of the party opposed to the King; and in 1642, on the outbreak of the Civil War which had long threatened England, he at once declared himself a Parliament man. Moreover, as Dr Johnson has pointed out, deeming a mere espousal of the cause of right to be by no means all the duty of an honest citizen, he proceeded to raise a troop of horse, and rendered such efficient service that in 1643, at the time of Prince Rupert's victorious progress in the west of England, he was entrusted with the command of one of the forts protecting Bristol.

This he held gallantly throughout the siege. Subsequently, having been promoted to the rank of colonel, he added fresh laurels to his military reputation by his spirited defence of Lyme, in Dorset, and by his exploits at Taunton. Lying on the main road between Bristol and Plymouth, Taunton was a place of high strategic importance. In 1644, at the head of a handful of men, Blake took the town by storm; and for more than two years—till Fairfax at length brought relief—he successfully defied the repeated efforts which the Royalists made to recover it. "His defence at Taunton," Dr Fitchett has written, "was perhaps the most brilliant single episode, on the Parliamentary side, in the great Civil War." A bust in the church commemorates the achievement.

In 1647 Charles I fell a prisoner into the hands of his enemies. Believing the war to be finished, Blake resigned his command, and, as member for Taunton, re-entered Parliament. But the Stuart cause was not yet dead. The execution of the King, moreover, served to strengthen rather than weaken it. In January 1649 a large part of the fleet, loath to submit to a dictatorship, went over to Charles II. Parliament thus lost the supremacy at sea which it had hitherto enjoyed, and Prince Rupert, in command of the Royalist ships, was able seriously to menace the trade of the young English republic.

Resolute leadership had given Parliament victory on land. By resolute leadership Cromwell purposed to gain it at sea; and, being a rare judge of character, he selected Colonel Blake to act as the leader.

In his youth, no doubt, Blake made voyages in his father's ships. Probably, therefore, he knew more of matters nautical than most of the parliamentary chiefs. But there is no evidence to support the theory, sometimes advanced, that in 1649 he was already an experienced navigator. Few men were more surprised than was he when Cromwell invited him to take charge of the naval forces of England. His surprise was the greater because he had strongly opposed the policy of the regicide Government in bringing the late King to trial.

But, though he did not see eye to eye with the Government in all things, he remained a stout champion of popular rights. As such, despite the execution of Charles, he still adhered to the Parliamentary side; and the astute Protector knew well that he would never be a party to designs for restoring the Stuarts. Cromwell also knew that he could rely on him to instil in the fleet that same sense of duty and discipline which had made the Ironsides invincible. The rest, he felt, he could safely leave to the seamanship and fighting qualities of English sailors. Nor was this surmise at fault. Blake, as Julian Corbett has written, "transformed the Navy to its modern scope and established England as the great naval power of the world."

Having accepted Cromwell's commission, Blake, as "General at Sea," hoisted his flag on the *James* in February 1649, and, marvelling at the trick which fortune had played on him, set sail to match his strength against Rupert's. The Prince had established his base at Kinsale, in Ireland. Thither Blake made his way; and for six months he held the harbour closely blockaded, thus effectively checking the activities of the Royalist marauder. Having regard to the state of his ships, the Prince dared not risk a set battle.

In September, bad weather drove Blake from the coast. Rupert then contrived to escape and, with his vigilant foe hot in pursuit, scurried southward to Lisbon. Blake demanded of the Portuguese authorities that "the pirate" should be expelled from his place of refuge. The Portuguese authorities, anxious to keep on good terms with both parties, tried to prevaricate. Blake was not a man to be trifled with. Since protests produced no effect, he fell on a home-coming Brazilian treasure fleet, capturing seventeen richly laden vessels. This had the desired result. Rupert was ordered to put out to sea.

Again the Prince eluded his adversary. This time he slipped through the Strait of Gibraltar, and found shelter at Cartagena. Eventually, in January 1651, Blake brought him to battle off Malaga. Rarely has the issue of a fight been more decisive. Only Rupert's [1] and one other of the Royalist ships avoided destruction.

The battle of Malaga, a noteworthy event in itself, is particularly noteworthy as marking the extension of British naval power to the Mediterranean, a sea which hitherto had been deemed beyond the range of our admiralty. Quick to appreciate the significance of Blake's victory, Cromwell determined to make England's influence permanently felt in it, and so at once to protect trading interests and to lend to diplomacy the support of force. Even in 1651, it is said, he conceived the design of taking and holding Gibraltar. First, however, he had to regain for his country the command of the Narrow Seas.

Elizabeth had left England the leading maritime power in Europe. During the reigns of James I and Charles I, Holland

[1] Prince Rupert remained at sea till 1653, doing such damage as he could to English shipping in the Atlantic. At the invitation of Louis XIV he then settled in France and gave himself up to scientific pursuits. After the Restoration he returned to England, and at sea, during the Dutch War of 1665–67, rendered valuable service. He died at Windsor in 1683. A man of many parts, he discovered the process of mezzotint engraving, and is credited with having invented a torpedo. He was also the founder and first governor of the Hudson Bay Company.

usurped the leadership, and when Cromwell took up the reins of government the Dutch had acquired a monopoly of the seaborne trade of the continent. With a view to helping the English mercantile marine to recover the position it had lost, Parliament, at Cromwell's instigation, passed the Navigation Act of 1651. The Act, which laid down that goods must be imported into England either in English ships or in ships belonging to the countries which produced them, was intended as a challenge to

THE ROCK OF GIBRALTAR

the Dutch. As such the Dutch accepted it, and both by them and their rivals preparations for war were feverishly pushed forward. It but remained to find a pretext for hostilities. This was provided by an incident which occurred in May 1652.

The English had long claimed that foreigners sailing the Narrow Seas should strike their flags or lower their topsails in the presence of an English ship. Under the Tudors [1] the claim had been strictly enforced. In 1570 a Spanish fleet homeward bound from Flanders—with Anne of Austria, Philip II's third queen, on board—put in at Plymouth and dropped anchor without paying the customary salute. A small English squadron under Sir John Hawkins chanced to be lying in the Cattewater. Hawkins at once

[1] The national flag at that time was still the simple cross of St George on a white ground, the flag which now—flown at the main—is used by admirals as an ensign of rank.

H.M.S. "PRINCE ROYAL"

opened fire on the Spanish flagship. The strangers hurriedly lowered their topsails.

The officers of James I and Charles I proved less exacting. The Dutch in consequence neglected, and in the end refused, to conform with the established etiquette of the sea. Cromwell resolved to put an end to this state of affairs; ever jealous of national pretensions, he instructed his admirals to require a punctilious observance of the honour of the flag. So it came about, in May 1652, that Blake beat into Dover Roads and, in the manner of Hawkins, let off a gun to remind a Dutch commander—who was sheltering from a storm—that, when anchoring, he had not saluted the Castle. The Dutchman, the mighty Tromp, replied with a broadside. Seeing that he had fifty sail in his command against Blake's fifteen, he believed he could afford to be insolent. Blake quickly disillusioned him.

ADMIRAL TROMP
By J. Lievens

During the general engagement which followed, superior gunnery more than counterbalanced the numerical inferiority of the English fleet; and, when night fell, Tromp, worsted in action for the first time in a long fighting career, made off with all possible speed. Two of his ships had been lost. The remainder were in no condition to continue the conflict.

War between England and Holland was formally declared in July. Blake, meanwhile, knowing well the meaning of sea power, scoured the North Sea and the Channel, ruthlessly rounding up returning merchantmen. Prizes innumerable fell into his hands ere the main Dutch fleet under De Ruyter—Tromp had been temporarily superseded—at length brought him to battle among the shoals of the Goodwin Sands.

The fight began at 4 o'clock in the afternoon of September 28,

ADMIRAL DE RUYTER

and raged far into the night. Afterward each side claimed it a victory. But De Ruyter broke off the action and, though several Dutch ships were sunk, not one English vessel was totally disabled. The advantage, therefore, unquestionably lay with Blake. Cromwell, indeed, confident that the Dutch would not venture to sea during the ensuing winter, actually authorized a large reduction of naval strength.

Cromwell's judgment was at fault. On November 29, while lying in Dover Roads with thirty-seven ships, Blake learned that Tromp had entered the Strait with eighty line-of-battle ships and fifteen smaller vessels. Determined to uphold the honour of the flag, he sailed out to meet the enemy, and bravely suffered the defeat which he courted. Under cover of darkness the battered English fleet withdrew toward the Thames estuary, leaving Tromp—with, says tradition, a broom at his masthead—to sweep the Channel. Yet the battle of Dungeness may be accounted, perhaps, the most glorious of Blake's exploits. In a fight against overwhelming odds the English commander and his men acquitted themselves nobly.

MEDAL STRUCK IN COMMEMORATION OF BLAKE'S VICTORY OF FEBRUARY 1653

Cromwell—be it said to his credit—did not try to foist on his defeated admiral the blame for what had happened. He himself accepted full responsibility. To Blake, indeed, he sent a gracious letter of appreciation, at the same time promising speedily to refit the ships which had been dismantled. The promise was fulfilled. Early in 1653, therefore, Blake again put to sea, and on February 18, off Portland, with seventy-three sail in his command, he came upon Tromp, who was convoying two hundred merchantmen up Channel. The battle that followed—a battle between equally matched fleets, the entire forces of the two chief naval powers of Europe—lasted three days, and

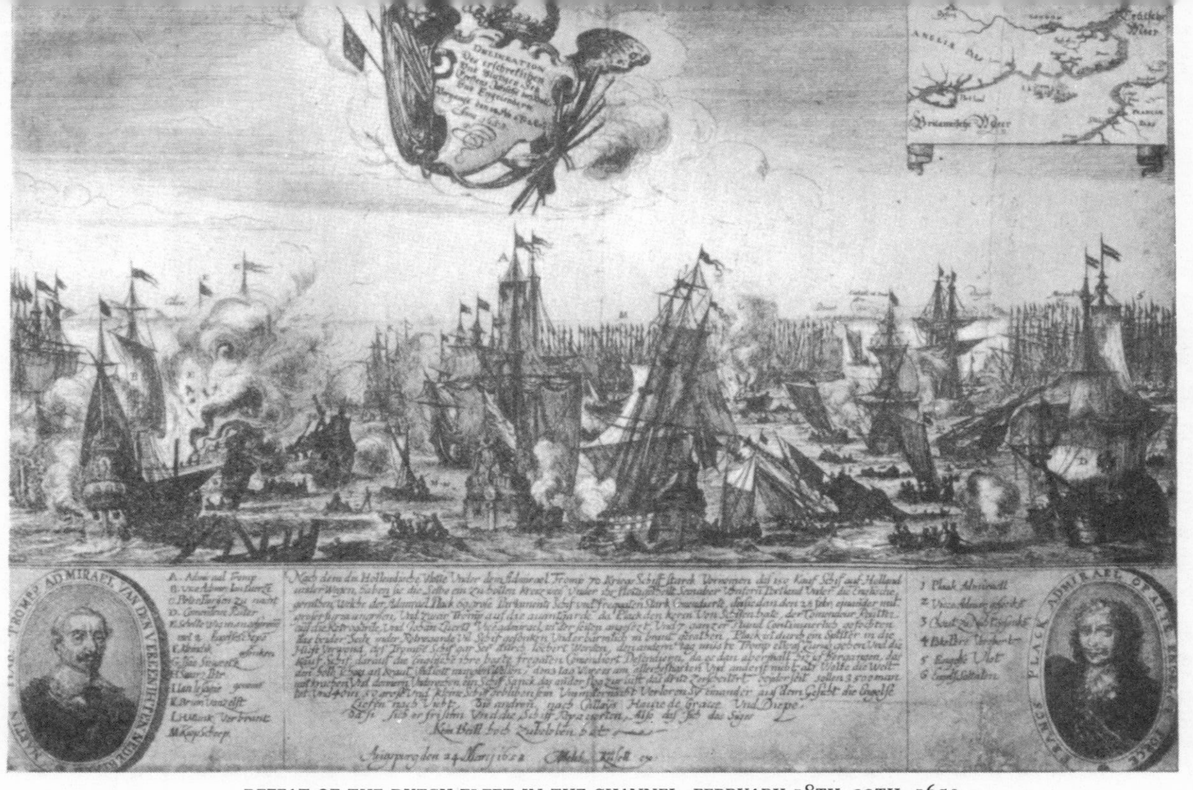

DEFEAT OF THE DUTCH FLEET IN THE CHANNEL, FEBRUARY 18TH–20TH, 1653

From an old engraving

resulted in as great a triumph as British arms have ever won at sea.

Blake, who was severely wounded on February 20, took no part in the two battles which had yet to be fought before the Dutch finally capitulated. These engagements, however, were of minor importance. The battle of Portland was the decisive event of the war. More than that, it was one of the decisive battles of history. It gave Britain the proud title of "Queen of the Ocean," which she has retained to this day.

The Dutch menace disposed of, Cromwell again turned his thoughts to the Mediterranean, where English commerce was still hampered by the high-handed actions of princes and pirates. This was intolerable to a ruler of the Protector's temperament. In November 1654, therefore, Blake, who had then recovered of his wound, was sent out with twenty-three ships to vindicate the rights of his countrymen, to "make the name of Englishmen"—as Cromwell bade him—"to be as much dreaded as ever was the name of *civis Romanus*."

Faithfully he carried out his commission. First, he exacted reparation, in the shape of a substantial sum of money, from the Duke of Tuscany for wrongs done to English merchants. He next crossed to Tunis, and demanded similar redress from the Dey. The latter, relying on the strength of his batteries, haughtily refused to negotiate. So Blake, who—to quote the words of Clarendon, a critic not biased in his favour—"first brought ships to contemn castles on the shore," sailed into his harbour and, with the loss of five men killed and forty wounded, destroyed not only all the shipping within, but the land armaments as well.

From Tunis he sailed to Algiers. Taking warning from the fate of his Tunisian brother, the Dey of Algiers offered an abject submission. Thus the English admiral was able to proceed on his way, and for several months he carried his flag, a symbol of terror and power, from one Mediterranean port to another. He then dealt with Spain.

Cromwell had demanded two things from Spain: the right to trade with Spanish America, and the exemption of Englishmen from the jurisdiction of the Inquisition. The claim was rejected. "My master," said the Spanish ambassador, "has but two eyes, and you ask him for both." In the autumn of 1654, therefore, war was declared.

Cromwell's plan of campaign was simple and bold. While an expedition, under Admiral Penn and General Venables, went out to mop up islands in the West Indies, Blake was instructed to contain the Spaniards in Europe.

ADMIRAL ROBERT BLAKE

The venture to the west, though it resulted in the capture and annexation of Jamaica, did not wholly realize its author's expectations. Blake was not to blame for this. For two long years, until April 1657, he held the main Spanish fleet at Cadiz in the grip of an iron blockade. Food, even water, ran short. Barnacles grew thick upon his hulls. Scurvy raged among his crews. "Our ships," he wrote, "are extremely foul, our stores failing, our men fallen sick through badness of drink. Our only comfort is that we have a God to lean upon, although we walk in darkness and see no light." Yet, through summer and winter, storm and tempest, he steadily maintained his tireless vigil.

At length news came to him that a plate fleet, not daring to approach the coast of Spain, had made for the Canaries and had sought safety in the strongly fortified harbour of Santa Cruz. He at once determined to dig it out, and, on April 20, he actually succeeded. Nelson, also at Santa Cruz, when attempting a similar exploit under much easier conditions failed.[1] What higher tribute could be paid to Blake's genius?

In April 1657 the Spaniards fought with devoted courage, but valour availed them not. The English intruders quickly silenced the batteries on shore. Within four hours of the forcing of the entrance to the harbour, moreover, the plate fleet was reduced to drifting wreckage, and Blake, whose masterly seamanship was aided by a providential change of wind, had brought his vessels, almost unscathed, out to sea.

"The whole action," wrote Clarendon,

> was so miraculous that all men who knew the place wondered that any sober man, with what courage soever endued, would ever have undertaken it, and they could hardly persuade themselves to believe what they had done; whilst the Spaniards comforted themselves that they were devils and not men who had destroyed them in such a manner. So much a strong resolution of bold and courageous men can bring to pass that no resistance and advantage of ground can disappoint them, and it can hardly be imagined how small loss the English sustained in this unparalleled action; no one ship being left behind, and the killed and wounded not exceeding two hundred men, when the slaughter on board the Spanish ships and on the shore was incredible.

The English Parliament, on receiving the news, voted its thanks and a large sum of money to the victorious admiral; whilst Cromwell, to signify his personal admiration, sent him a diamond ring—"as a token," he wrote in the letter which accompanied it. Thus encouraged, Blake contrived, despite his failing health, to continue his watch on Cadiz during the months of May and June. In July,

[1] It was in 1797, at Santa Cruz, the scene of his one defeat, that Nelson lost an arm.

however, he was forced to ask that he might be relieved by another commander. The request was granted, and in August he set sail for home. But, worn out in body and mind, he was not spared to set foot on his native land. He breathed his last on August 17, just as the *St George*, the good ship that bore him, was passing under Plymouth Hoe to her anchorage.

His bones now lie in the churchyard of St Margaret's, Westminster. The corpse originally was buried in the great Abbey near by. In 1660, however, it was dug up by order of Charles II. The restored Stuart can be forgiven, perhaps, the petty spite which prompted him to desecrate the tomb of the 'usurper' Cromwell. No excuse can be found for his treatment of Blake's remains. Blake, as noble and unselfish a patriot as England has ever reared, was not a politician, and he heartily disliked most of the Protector's constitutional changes, even though he did not openly question them. "It is not," he said, "the business of a seaman to mind state affairs, but to prevent foreigners from fooling us."

Blake never married. That younger Blake who served with much distinction under him, and subsequently rose to a high position in the Navy, was a nephew, the son of a brother who fell fighting in the Civil War. Robert Blake adopted the lad and made him his heir.

XVII. SIR HENRY MORGAN

Born 1635; *died* 1688

IN 1492, when Columbus discovered it, the island of Hispaniola ("Little Spain")—miscellaneously known as Haiti and St Domingo—had two million inhabitants. Within thirty years the natives had been practically exterminated. Not content with working them to death, their conquerors brutally slaughtered them, simply—as a contemporary writer puts it—"to keep their hand in use." As early as 1505, with a view to solving labour problems, the Spaniards began to import from Africa the negro slaves whose descendants now own the soil.

The remedy did not immediately cure the disease. During the sixteenth century the prosperity of the island rapidly declined, and many of the Spanish settlers, tempted by richer spoils, migrated to the Main, the American mainland. Those who remained, labouring under the burden of official neglect, were driven to look for a livelihood to the visits of foreign privateers. With the masters of such vessels, British, Dutch, and French, they carried on a lucrative trade—mostly in hides and meat. From the natives they had learned a method of preserving the flesh of the cattle which roamed in large herds on the island. Cutting it into strips, they dried it upon gratings over slow wood-fires. The gratings were called *boucans* in the Carib-Indian language. *Viande boucannée* was a fare well known to mariners of that period.

As time went on, outcasts of various nationalities—crews of wrecked ships, deserters, runaway convicts, and suchlike—found their way to the island. These folk settled on the hitherto untenanted northern and north-western coasts, and, as cattle-hunters, they likewise took to supplying the needs of passing vessels. The Spaniards strove to eject them. The new-comers merely withdrew to Tortuga, a neighbouring islet. This, while they still hunted on Hispaniola, they made their storehouse and stronghold. Such was the genesis of the buccaneers, a fellowship of rogues whose exploits figure largely in the annals of the seventeenth century.

About 1640 Tortuga became a dependency of France. But its old masters continued to live there, and, under the new *régime*, their activities received official encouragement. The French sought by this means to advance their own interests in the West. Subsequently, with the approval of the British and the Dutch, the buccaneers established bases at Jamaica and St Eustatius also.

Having already ceased to restrict their energies to cattle-hunting, they now began, as chartered pirates, openly to prey on Spanish commerce. Finally, they organized a sort of mercenary navy, which they held in readiness to fight for Spain's rivals, provided they were assured by their patrons a market for booty.

At first they sailed mostly in barques, ships of one mast rigged with triangular sails. These little vessels, being fast and easy to manœuvre, were admirably adapted for attacking galleons lumbering, heavily laden, toward Europe. As Spain's prosperity declined the number of treasure-galleons to be met with at sea steadily diminished. So the buccaneers turned their attention to the settlements on the isthmus of Central America. Between 1655 and 1671 they captured and sacked no fewer than twenty-four wealthy and populous cities. Such ventures called for larger vessels. Gradually the older barques were replaced by brigantines and corvettes.

Posing as the avengers of Spanish cruelty to the native Indians, the early buccaneers, we are told, never embarked without offering up prayers for success, "nor ever returned without thanks for the same." Each received a definite allowance of arms and food, and the plunder was divided strictly according to merit and rank, provision having first been made for the wounded. In this matter a fixed scale was prescribed:

> For the loss of a right arm 600 pieces of eight,[1] or six slaves; for the loss of a left arm 500 pieces of eight, or five slaves; for a right leg 500 pieces of eight, or five slaves; for the left leg 400 pieces of eight, or four slaves; for an eye 100 pieces of eight, or one slave; for a finger of the hand the same reward as for an eye.

For other wounds a proportionate compensation was paid.

The leader of an expedition could claim by right six shares of the plunder, and the ordinary seamen one share apiece. Individuals who distinguished themselves were usually awarded addi-

[1] A piece of eight was worth, roughly, 5s. at Jamaica in 1660.

tional grants. Right down to the time of their suppression the buccaneers generally acknowledged this code.

For an account of the conditions of life on their ships the reader should turn to Exquemelin's *Bucaniers of America*. Written in Dutch, and published in 1678, this book has been widely translated. An English edition appeared in 1741.

The author, a Fleming, went to Tortuga in 1666 as an *engagé*, or indentured servant, of the French West India Company. Subsequently, having learned the rudiments of medicine, he secured employment on a pirate vessel, and, in the capacity of barber-surgeon, took part in many buccaneering adventures. His picturesque descriptions, therefore, have the merit of being really first-hand.

The losses sustained at this time by the Spaniards through the action of pirates are beyond computation. Yet the peoples who used the buccaneers as their agents suffered more heavily. Despite an inflexibly exclusive commercial policy, Spain did not monopolize the trade with her colonies. Of all European countries, indeed, she probably derived the least benefit from it. British, Dutch, and French merchants freighted the fleets which sailed from Cadiz and Seville. The same merchants appropriated the greater part of the treasure brought back. When, therefore, a galleon was sunk, or an American city was sacked, much of the cost fell on them.

Gradually they awoke to this fact, and realized that they could absorb the riches of the New World more profitably through friendly concession than by striving to perpetuate the methods of the Tudor sea-dogs. During the closing years of the seventeenth century the Governments of Britain, France, and Holland took concerted action for the suppression of piracy in West Indian waters.

Edward Mansvelt, a Dutchman, and perhaps the greatest of the buccaneer leaders, had visions of the inevitable as far back as 1665. In the hope of averting it he urged his followers to occupy New Providence (later to become the headquarters of the American bootleggers), or some other island in the Bahama group, and there, under a strict form of government, to set up a buccaneer commonwealth, conserving their gains, and tempering piracy by settled labour.

Any chance of success which the scheme may have had vanished in 1667. In that year Mansvelt died. The mantle of leadership then fell on Henry Morgan, a reckless and rascally Welshman.

The son of a well-to-do Glamorganshire farmer, Morgan was born in 1635. According to the *Bucaniers of America*, he and Exquemelin became pirates in somewhat similar circumstances, Morgan having been kidnapped when a boy and sold as a slave to a West Indian planter. This statement, and many of the other things said about him in his Dutch colleague's book, Morgan hotly denied. In 1684, when the English translation appeared in London, he brought an action for libel against the publisher, William Crooke, and was awarded £200 damages.

Some of Exquemelin's defamatory assertions were only too true. The kidnapping story is probably false. The Morgan family had interests in the West Indies in the days of the Stuarts, and Henry, it would seem, a seafaring man, went to Jamaica about 1660 to join his uncle, Colonel Edward Morgan, sometime the Lieutenant-Governor of the island. There at once he threw in his lot with the buccaneers. This he did, no doubt, at his uncle's suggestion; buccaneering was the most lucrative career the colony had to offer.

A skilful navigator, devoid of fear or of scruple, and possessed withal of a singular charm of manner, Morgan quickly won the confidence of Mansvelt, who raised him to the rank of vice-admiral of the pirate forces. On Mansvelt's death he automatically succeeded to the leadership, and for three years ruthlessly harried the Spaniards. A daring attack on Porto Bello crowned his achievements.

Now a mean village, Porto Bello was once the chief city on the Main, the depot whither the riches of Chile and Peru were conveyed by mule transport for shipment to Europe. Morgan carried the place by storm, looted it, and returned to Port Royal [1] with plunder of enormous value.

Political considerations rendered it inadvisable at the time for Spain's rivals openly to connive at this sort of thing. The British Government, therefore, denounced the raid, and King Charles II, hoping to promote more cordial relations between Whitehall and Madrid, set about to negotiate a treaty of "universal peace and friendship" in the New World. The pact,

[1] The old town of Port Royal, the former capital of Jamaica, was submerged by an earthquake in 1692.

concluded in 1670, provided for the immediate withdrawal of commissions granted to privateers. Further, it pledged Englishmen to forbear trading with any Spanish port except under licence lawfully obtained. The Spanish Crown, for its part, agreed—a notable concession—to recognize Charles's claim to the sovereignty of Jamaica and certain other lands held in the West.

The negotiations occasioned dismay at Jamaica. Morgan remained unperturbed; he determined yet to perform some deed which would make his name resound through the world. Accordingly, before definite instructions could arrive from London, he urged the local authorities to commission him to raid Hispaniola; the Spaniards, he said, were there laying plans for an assault on Port Royal.

Early in 1671 he obtained his commission, and put to sea with a fleet of thirty-nine ships, carrying in all some two thousand men. Only then did he disclose his real intention. This was to attack Panama, and so carry the buccaneers' sword to the shores of the Pacific. Instead of sailing westward, therefore, he made straight for the Mosquito Gulf, landing his followers at the mouth of the River Chagres, a few miles from the Castle of San Lorenzo. A surprise attack yielded this place into his hands. Leaving a garrison to cover his retreat, he then proceeded up the river with fourteen hundred men in canoes.

The journey through the tropical jungle of the isthmus took ten days to accomplish, and was attended by inconceivable difficulties. The buccaneers had counted on being able to live on the country. The Spaniards, however, fled before their advance, destroying all settlements. Nowhere could the invaders find food. By the fourth day hunger had reduced them to the last extremity.

"This day"—to quote Exquemelin's narrative—

> about noon they found themselves nigh unto a post, called Torna Cavallos. Here the guide of the canoes began to cry aloud he perceived an ambuscade. His voice caused infinite joy unto all the Pirates, as persuading themselves they should find some provisions wherewith to satiate their hunger, which was very great. But, being come unto the place, they found nobody in it, the Spaniards who were there not long before being fled every one, and leaving nothing behind unless it were a small number of leather bags, all empty. . . .
>
> Being angry at this misfortune, they pulled down a few huts which the Spaniards had made, and afterwards fell to eating the

leathern bags, as being desirous to afford something to the ferment of their stomachs. . . . Thus they made a huge banquet . . . which doubtless would have been more grateful unto them if divers quarrels had not arisen concerning who should have the greatest share.

For the benefit of incredulous readers, Exquemelin added:

> Some persons, who were never out of their mothers' kitchens, may ask how these Pirates could eat, swallow, and digest those pieces of leather, so hard and dry. Unto whom I only answer: That could they once experiment what hunger, or rather famine, is, they would certainly find the manner, by their own necessity, as the Pirates did. For they first took the leather, and sliced it in pieces. Then did they beat it between two stones and rub it, often dipping it in the water of the river, to render it by these means supple and tender. Lastly they scraped off the hair, and roasted or broiled it upon the fire. And, being thus cooked, they cut it into small morsels, and eat it, helping it down with frequent gulps of water.

On the sixth day of their march the invaders met with better fortune, coming upon a barn full of maize, which the retreating Spaniards had neglected to destroy. Nevertheless, they were an exhausted, dispirited band when at length they sighted Panama. Yet, thanks to their leader's masterly generalship, they captured the city. Morgan attacked the place from a direction which had not been thought possible. The defenders, in consequence, found their guns so placed as to be utterly useless.

On the luckless inhabitants the buccaneers perpetrated abominable atrocities. Morgan would have us believe that this was no fault of his, and that, to lessen excesses, he had strictly forbidden his men to touch liquor, telling them he had received private intelligence that all the wine in the place had been poisoned. "Howbeit," wrote Exquemelin,

> it was the opinion of many he gave these prudent orders to prevent the debauchery of his people . . . fearing lest the Spaniards, seeing them in wine, should rally their forces . . . and use them as inhumanly as they had used the inhabitants.

Panama remained for three weeks in the hands of its captors. Then, having loaded on pack-mules a vast store of treasure, valued by Spanish authorities at five million crowns, the victorious buccaneers set fire to the city and began their march eastward. On February 26 they rejoined their fellows at San

Lorenzo. There the spoil was divided. That night, however, if Exquemelin's narrative can be trusted, Morgan and a few chosen friends secretly made off with the greater part of the booty. Their late companions-in-arms were left, we are told, with but £10 apiece, and had "much ado to find sufficient victuals and provisions for their voyage to Jamaica."

This story formed the main ground for the libel action of Morgan *versus* Crooke. Its truth, therefore, perhaps may be questioned—the more so seeing that the pirate leader was given a tremendous ovation on his return to Port Royal, and was formally thanked by the Council for services rendered. Such a reception would hardly have been accorded to him had he cheated his comrades, themselves mostly Jamaican men.

In any case, the Panama expedition of 1671 was a very remarkable military exploit. With miserably inadequate means, Morgan accomplished a feat which had been Drake's fondest dream, and which Admiral Vernon in 1741, with a much greater force, did not dare even to attempt.

The British Government of the day, having regard to treaty obligations, could not view it with favour. Wrote the Ambassador in Spain to Lord Arlington, one of the Secretaries of State:

> It is impossible for me to paint to your Lordship the face of Madrid upon the news of this action . . . nor to what degree the Queen [1] and ministers of State, the particular councils and all sorts of people here, have taken it to heart.

In the circumstances, something had to be done.

It was obvious that an inquiry instituted at Jamaica must prove a farce. The Government, therefore, issued orders for Morgan to proceed straightway to London, that he might there account for his doings. The pirate was duly arrested. Shortly afterward, in April 1672, he sailed from Port Royal in the *Welcome* frigate.

Sir Thomas Lynch, the Governor of Jamaica, in the hope of smoothing the path of the "brave, honest fellow," entrusted to the captain of *Welcome* a strong plea in his favour, addressed to Lord Arlington. Major James Bannister, commanding the garrison, sent a similar letter, describing the prisoner as a "well

[1] The Queen Mother, Maria Anna, a sister of the Emperor Leopold. She was then ruling in the name of the infant King Charles II, the last of the Spanish Hapsburgs, whose death (1700) plunged the world into war.

deserving person, and one of great courage and conduct, who may with his Majesty's pleasure perform good service at home and be very advantageous to the island if war should break out with Spain."

The subject of these eulogies had little need of such help. A

SIR HENRY MORGAN
From an old engraving

real live buccaneer proved something of a novelty to the frail ladies at Whitehall. Morgan, by showering upon them his riches and gallantry, soon won their hearts. So was it easy for him to gain the ear of the King. As a matter of fact, Charles and he at once evinced a real liking for each other. The Merry Monarch, therefore, instead of punishing the merry pirate, dubbed him a knight and, with an Elizabethan contempt for Spanish feelings, sent him back to act as Colonel and Deputy-Governor of Jamaica, an office which his uncle, Lady Morgan's father,[1] had formerly filled.

At Jamaica he continued to reside during the remaining years of his life, successfully running with the hare and hunting with the hounds. While it behoved him in his public capacity to initiate measures for the suppression of piracy, he was able in a private capacity, by reason of his wide experience and knowledge, greatly to facilitate the operations of his former associates. This he did much to his own and his family's advantage. His will, filed in the Public Record Office at Spanish Town, affords interesting reading.

The ex-buccaneer died on August 25, 1688, leaving Jamaica to mourn the loss of one who, despite a domineering and lawless nature, had endeared himself to all sections of the community. Friends and old foes alike paid tributes to his many fine qualities. The following is an extract from the journal of Captain Lawrence Wright, commanding H.M.S. *Assistance*, a frigate which took part in the funeral ceremonies:

> *Saturday* 25. This day about eleven hours noon Sir Henry Morgan died, and the 26th was brought over from Passage-fort to the King's house at Port Royal, from thence to the Church, and after a sermon was carried to the Pallisadoes and there buried. All the forts fired an equal number of guns; we fired two and twenty, and after we and the *Drake* had fired, all the merchant-men fired.

As a navigator, Morgan cannot be credited with any outstanding achievement, and he made no direct contribution to the exploration of the world. Yet, in that he reopened to the men of his race the way to the Great South Sea, upon which none of them had sailed since the days of Drake, he and his successors had a determining influence on England's conquest of the ocean. After 1671—though they still looked on the Caribbean as their special preserve—the buccaneers made the Pacific their chief sphere of activity. Sailing thither *via* the Horn, they ranged for twenty-five years along the Chilian and Peruvian coasts. Anson and other travellers of the eighteenth century often had occasion to find fault with their maps. Yet upon those maps is based much of our modern geographical knowledge.

[1] Sir Henry married Colonel Edward Morgan's daughter in 1671.

XVIII. WILLIAM DAMPIER

Born 1652; *died* 1715

THE age of discovery inaugurated by the Portuguese was rounded off by "the sea-dogs of Devon." Between it and the next—the age of discovery inaugurated by Cook and Anson, and crowned by the achievements of Amundsen, Peary, Scott, and Shackleton—lies a perceptible hiatus. The period from 1630 to 1730 produced buccaneers, privateers, sea-adventurers of all kinds, famous and infamous, but it did not produce many sailors who, tempering greed with observation, added much that was of value to the store of human knowledge.

Yet it produced a few; and at any rate to one of them, to William Dampier, must be accorded a high place in the illustrious order of great navigators. Captain Lemuel Gulliver, it will be remembered, hailed Captain William Dampier as cousin. The tribute which Swift thus made his incomparable discoverer in the region of the fantastic pay to a contemporary discoverer in the region of the actual was richly deserved.

William Dampier was born in 1652 at East Coker, in Somerset. He passed his boyhood on his father's farm. But in 1669, on the death of his parents, his guardian—"complying," we are told, "with the inclination I had very early of seeing the world"—entrusted him to the charge of the master of a ship bound for the West. Early experiences had a chilling influence on the ardour with which he entered on his new calling. His first voyage took him to Newfoundland; a winter before the mast off that bleak coast nearly caused him to relapse into a landsman. His second voyage, however, took him to the East Indies. This voyage, "a warm one and a long one," cured him of his last lingering desire for a life ashore.

In 1673 he engaged in the stern business of the Dutch war, serving as a seaman in *Royal Prince* under the gallant Sir Edward Spragge; and in the following year he found his way to the West Indies. Thither he went as an honest seaman in an honest trading ship. But in that quarter, in those days, from trade to piracy was a very short step. Dampier soon took it. *Facilis descensus*.

At length, in 1682, having received many hard blows and little material profit, he wearied of buccaneering adventures, and resolved to settle in Virginia. But in "the old dominion," so he darkly hints, great troubles befell him. In April 1683, therefore, he went to sea again in the *Revenge* (Captain John Cooke). The mission of the *Revenge* was trade, and her market San Domingo. Such, at least, was the tale which her captain spun in harbour. So soon as the ship was safely out of sight of land, Cooke disclosed his real intentions. The mission of the *Revenge*, he announced to a gratified crew, was piracy, and her destination the Guinea coast.

At Sierra Leone the pirates captured a larger and stouter ship. Recrossing the Atlantic, therefore, they rounded Cape Horn, and sailed northward with a view to battening on Spanish commerce in the vicinity of Valparaiso. Off Juan Fernandez their ship fell in with other vessels—among them the *Cygnet* (Captain Swan)—bound on the same lawless business, and for twelve months, as one of a fleet of ten, she cruised up and down the coasts of Chile and Peru. But the harvest reaped was meagre and hard-earned. Time, though it had not taught the Spaniards the art of seamanship, had taught them to be very wary.

In August 1685 the captain of the *Cygnet* grew tired of waiting for treasure ships that did not come. Having enlisted Dampier, therefore, as his sailing-master, he determined to part company with his fellow captains, and to visit Mexico, hoping to meet with better fortune there. Hope disappointed him. So was his pilot able to persuade him to undertake a voyage of discovery, the first attempted by an Englishman for many a long year.

The *Cygnet* left the American coast on March 31, 1686, and under the direction of Dampier sailed almost due west, 6000 miles in seven weeks, till she came to the Ladrones. She arrived at Guam with three days' provisions still in hand. This, perhaps, was well for Swan, the crew having openly avowed that, when other rations gave out, they would first break their fast by eating their "lusty and fleshy " skipper. From Guam, Dampier followed the track of the sixteenth-century navigators to the Philippines. There the company of the *Cygnet* spent half a year in idle enjoyment of Mindanaan hospitality. Then, thoroughly out of hand, they mutinied against their captain. A few remained loyal. These were left ashore with Swan. The rest, having elected as their leader one John Read, "a pretty ingenious young man, also accounted an artist," went forth, as Dampier has put it, "upon other projects," and with them they took Dampier.

For six months "the mad pickle crew of the *Cygnet*" cruised aimlessly among the "clove islands," and along the coasts of New Guinea and New Holland (Australia), meeting with astonishing adventures in lands never before visited by Europeans, but, thanks to Dampier's guiding hand, meeting with no serious mishap. At length, driven from Australia by the shortage of fresh water, they bore northward, and, on May 4, 1688, sighted the Nicobars. There Dampier, who had had enough of the escapade, took his leave of them, having only gone so far, he wrote, "knowing that the farther we went the more knowledge and experience I should get, which was the main thing I regarded."

While the company of the *Cygnet* continued their mad progress (finally running their ship on the rocks of Madagascar), Dampier made a bold voyage by canoe, with a crew of Malays, to Sumatra, and came to the English factory at Bencoolen. There he was taken into the service of the East India Company. Shortly afterward, however, "not thinking himself safe"—so he ventured to assert—"under men so brutal and barbarous" as the company's officials, he resolved to throw up his post, and, having secured a berth in a vessel bound for the Cape, quietly disappeared. Eventually, on September 16, 1691, he arrived in the Downs, and so concluded an amazing Odyssey, without a penny-piece in his pockets and with only two negotiable assets.

The first was a Melanesian islander, "Prince Jeoly," whom he tried to exhibit as an Indian potentate with a view to supplying his immediate wants.[1] The second was a long piece of bamboo. In this, with its ends carefully waxed, he carried the journal which constitutes his strongest title to fame. Little escaped Dampier's notice, and his shrewd and quaintly expressed observations, whether in the *rôle* of naturalist or navigator, show him to have been the heaven-sent explorer he was. The following description of the natives of Western Australia, "the miserablest people in the world," may be taken as a fair specimen of his style.

[1] The unfortunate 'prince' defeated this scheme by dying of smallpox at Oxford.

The Hodmadods of Monomatapa, though a nasty people, yet for wealth are as gentlemen to these; who have no houses and skin garments, sheep, poultry, and fruits of the earth, ostrich eggs, etc., as the Hodmadods have; and setting aside their human shape, they differ but little from brutes. They are tall, strait-bodied, and thin, with small, long limbs. They have great heads, round foreheads, and great brows. Their eyelids are always half-closed, to keep the flies out of their eyes. . . . They have great bottle noses, pretty full lips, and wide mouths. The two fore-teeth of the upper jaw are wanting in all of them. . . . Neither have they any beards. They are long visaged and of a very unpleasing aspect, having not one graceful feature in the faces. Their hair is black, short, and curled, like that of the negroes; and . . . the colour of their skins, both of their faces and the rest of their body, is coal black, like that of the negroes of Guinea. Their costume consists of a piece of the rind of a tree, and a handful of grass or bough. . . .

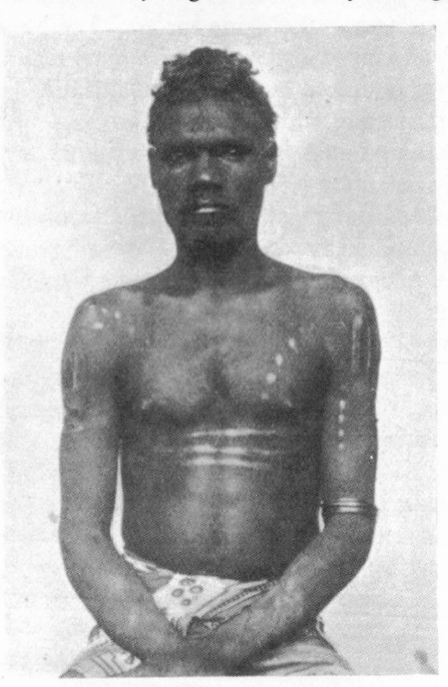

AN AUSTRALIAN ABORIGINAL
By courtesy of Dr Ramsay Smith, Adelaide

Their only food is a sort of small fish, which they get by making weirs of stone across little coves or branches of the sea; every tide bringing in the small fish, and there leaving them a prey to these people, who constantly attend there to catch them at low water. . . . When they have eaten, they lie down till the next low-water, and then all that are able march out, be it night or day, rain or sun, 'tis all one; they must attend the weirs, or else they must fast. For the earth affords them no food at all. There is neither herb, root, pulse, nor any sort of grain for them to eat that we saw; nor any sort of bird or beast that they can catch, having no instruments wherewithal to do so.

Of Dampier's doings during the six years which followed his first visit to Australia nothing is known. In the autumn of 1697, however, as a result of the publication of his *Voyage Round the World*, dedicated to Charles Montague, Earl of Halifax, President of the Royal Society, and one of the most influential politicians of the day, the pirate leapt into fame. In the following year an additional volume appeared. This brought its author the reward he desired; on Montague's recommendation he was offered the command of a sloop-of-war, the *Roebuck*, for the purpose of carrying out a further exploration of the "Terra Australis." He at once accepted the offer, and, sailing in January 1699, landed in Shark's Bay on July 26. On that same day he sighted and named the kangaroo whose tracks, "like those of a mastiff," he had observed on his former visit.

His original intention had been to make his way to Australia by the western route, round Cape Horn. Had he carried it out, he must have struck the eastern coast, and so, by anticipating the triumph of Captain Cook, would probably have antedated the opening up of Australia by half a century. But Dampier never got over that dislike of low temperatures he acquired in Newfoundland. After leaving England, therefore, he changed his plans, and, following the eastern or African route, came to the barren north-west coast. None the less, his voyage resulted in many discoveries, and, in that it also resulted in the first real mapping of the lands to the south of the East Indies, it ranks as a supremely important achievement. Incidentally, it enriched the literature of adventure with one of its strangest stories, the story told in Dampier's *Voyage to New Holland*, published in 1709.

The expedition ended in the manner of all its leader's exploits. Dampier was a great explorer, but he lacked one essential quality—the gift of command. On New Year's Day, 1701, a mutinous crew, the ravages of scurvy, and a leaking ship forced him to abandon his enterprise and hasten homeward. By using the pumps day and night, he contrived to bring the *Roebuck* to Ascension Island. Farther the old vessel would not go; her wood was rotten, her hull covered with barnacles. Next day (February 21) she sank at her anchors. Several weeks elapsed before her crew were rescued from their desolate retreat by H.M.S. *Anglesea*.

Dampier did not see the last of his troubles even then. On arrival at London, he was tried by court-martial and pronounced "not a fit person to be employed as commander of any of his Majesty's ships." The court included the two most illustrious admirals of the day, Sir George Rooke and Sir Cloudesley Shovel. But the justice of the verdict may be questioned. Censure, if it had to be passed, surely should have been passed not upon Dampier but upon those who elected to entrust an ex-pirate with the command of an expedition designed to serve scientific ends, and then sent him out in an unseaworthy ship manned by a crew of drink-sodden ruffians—murderous ruffians, too, who were "heartless enough to the voyage at best."

The temper of the men can be gauged by the fact that Dampier, not daring to sleep in his cabin, found it necessary throughout the voyage to lie on the quarter-deck with those of his officers whom he could trust, and "with small arms handy." In the circumstances it is a matter for wonder that he should so nearly have achieved the impossible; the difficulties with which he had to contend would have defeated even a Drake or a Captain James Cook. "Anyone who is sensible of those difficulties," he justly remarked, "will be much more pleased at the discoveries and observations I have been able to make than displeased that I did not make more."

Tradition says that somewhere in the sandhills of Ascension Island lies a great store of treasure which Dampier buried and never had an opportunity to recover. The tradition, were it associated with any other buccaneer, might be worth following up. The captain of the *Roebuck*, however, in all his varied career, came by very little treasure. In that respect he was the least fortunate of pirates.

Despite the findings of the court-martial which condemned him in 1702, Dampier soon received another commission. In 1703 (when the War of the Spanish Succession was at its height) he sailed as a privateer in the *St George*, in company with the *Cinque Ports* (Captain Stradling), to prey on French and Spanish ships. This, probably, is the best known of his voyages, for it resulted in the marooning at Juan Fernandez of Alexander Selkirk, sailing-master of the *Cinque Ports*, and the original of Robinson Crusoe. Viewed as a privateering expedition, however, or viewed in any light other than that of foolhardy adventure, it was, to say the least of it, a sorry failure; and the captain, on his return to England, though graciously received by Queen Anne, to whom he was permitted to recount his experiences, found himself altogether fallen from the favour of shipowners.

Unable to get another command, he made his next, and last, voyage in a subordinate capacity—as pilot of the *Duke* (Captain Woodes Rogers), a privateer, fitted out by a syndicate of Bristol merchants, which sailed in 1708 in company with the *Duchess*. This expedition turned out to be the only financial success in which he was ever concerned. During a remarkable progress round the world, the *Duke* and *Duchess* not only took and ransomed Guayaquil City, but captured no fewer than fourteen Spanish ships, including the Manila treasure galleon. Further, on February 1, 1709, they rescued Alexander Selkirk, who had been living alone on Juan Fernandez for four years and four months. Finally they returned to England, in October 1711, with £200,000 worth of spoil.

CAPTAIN WILLIAM DAMPIER
From the portrait by T. Murray in the National Portrait Gallery

Dampier, content with his share of the plunder, seems to have passed the rest of his life in retirement. History, at any rate, has nothing more to say of him. He is believed to have died in 1715 at Coleman Street, in the City of London. His wife, we are told, was "a young woman out of the family of the Duchess of Grafton."

XIX. JAMES COOK

Born 1728; *died* 1779

In 1778, while the American Colonies were in revolt against Britain, France elected to declare war on her old rival across the Channel. When doing so the French Government expressly excluded Captain Cook from hostilities, and issued an order permitting him to sail, immune from molestation, whithersoever he might list. The order proclaimed the British navigator to be the "benefactor of every nation."

This graceful tribute was richly deserved; the man who opened up to European enterprise Australia, New Zealand, and the islands of the Pacific, "the finisher"—as he has been described—"of the main tract of oceanic discovery," stands without a peer among explorers. In March 1779 Benjamin Franklin, the accredited representative of the United States in France, issued a similar mandate to American captains. Congress refused to ratify it. From Philadelphia instructions went forth that Cook was to be attacked and seized whenever the opportunity might occur. Cook, however, was already dead.

Men labouring under the handicap of humble birth and lack of education commonly amass fortunes and titles. But how often do they attain to really first-class eminence? Heaven-born geniuses are rarer than is generally supposed. To their select number Captain James Cook belongs. Though entirely self-taught, he was a mathematician who could hold his own against any, and a marine surveyor whose proficiency has never been surpassed; while, as his own accounts of his travels testify, he was gifted with a keenness and accuracy of observation, and a power of expression, which very few scientific workers have acquired. In the British Museum may be seen the time-browned pages of the journal which he kept on his last voyage. Written in a clear and running hand, with hardly an erasure, the manuscript is a model of its kind, a masterpiece of simple, graphic prose.

Success, moreover, did not turn the writer's head. Cook remained always the simple soul who knew exactly what he had to do and quietly did it. For that reason men cheerfully and trustingly followed him to the ends of the earth. For that same reason men at the ends of the earth revered him with a superstitious awe. And for that same reason he seldom had to argue points with his superiors; those set in authority over him, whether they were Baltic traders, lords of the Admiralty, or learned scholars, instinctively assumed that he was right.

The son of an illiterate peasant, James Cook was born, in the first year of the reign of George II, at Marton, in Yorkshire. His father, in due course, contrived to apprentice him in a haberdasher's shop at Staithes, near Whitby. Paternal ambition met with an ungrateful response. The boy saw beyond the bounds of a counter. About 1744 he escaped his master and ran away to sea.

For some years he toiled obscurely in the Baltic and North Sea trades. Then he volunteered as a common seaman in the Navy, and, in 1755, as chance would have it, was drafted to a survey ship bound for the coast of Labrador. For survey work he showed an immediate aptitude. His ability quickly attracted the notice of his commanding officer. So it came about that in 1759 when a skilled hand was wanted to pilot Admiral Saunders's fleet, with Wolfe and his army on board, up the St Lawrence to Quebec, Cook was recommended for the job.

The St Lawrence, between its mouth and that point on its banks—400 miles upstream—where stands Quebec, narrows from 80 miles to 1 mile. Its navigation is tricky at the best of times. In 1759 it was very tricky, for the French had removed every buoy and mark from the channel. Cook found it "not a bit worse than the Thames," and brought the fleet before Quebec without a mishap of any kind. Saunders saw to it that the pilot's achievement received recognition, and shortly afterward, to cut a long story short, the King, "reposing especial Trust and Confidence" in his loyalty, etc., entrusted the haberdasher's ex-apprentice with a commission. In those undemocratic days such promotions were rare marks of favour.

In 1762, shortly after his return to England, Cook married a certain Elizabeth Batts of Barking, and bought a home in the Mile End Road; the house, No. 88 of that road, is now a butcher's shop. His restless spirit, however, would not allow him long to remain content with a home billet. Within a year he returned to North America—this time as commanding officer of the schooner *Grenville*—to continue his surveying work. While thus employed, he wrote a remarkable description of a solar eclipse which he observed from one of the Burgeo Islands, off Cape Ray in Newfoundland. The paper was published by the Royal Society in its *Philosophical Transactions* and attracted much notice. To it the young astronomer owed his next appointment.

In 1768 the Admiralty, at the instigation of the Royal Society, fitted out a ship, the *Endeavour* (370 tons), for a voyage to the South Seas, that astronomers might observe from the island of Tahiti the transit of Venus over the disc of the sun. The *Endeavour* sailed from Plymouth on August 25, with Lieutenant Cook in command.

In the *Endeavour* also sailed Charles Green the astronomer, Sir Joseph Banks the naturalist, and other learned men. From them, no doubt, the receptive Cook acquired a liberal education. They certainly acquired a liberal education from him; and on June 3, 1769, the transit of Venus having been duly observed, he assumed command of both ship and expedition. After leaving Tahiti he cruised for five months among the islands of the Pacific. During this time he investigated that vast archipelago more thoroughly than anyone had hitherto attempted. Incidentally, by his careful study of the government, religion, habits, and morals of the natives, he gave the world a new conception of an explorer's functions.

At length, on October 7, he arrived off the north-east coast of New Zealand. Since Tasman's visit in 1642 New Zealand had been entirely neglected by Europeans. Cook circumnavigated both the main islands and, despite the ferocity of the cannibal natives, acquired a deal of very valuable information. He left New Zealand on the last day of March 1770, and sailed west till, on April 18, he sighted what proved to be the southernmost point of New Holland, or Australia, as we know it now.[1] From there he bore northward, and on May 13 effected his famous landing at Botany Bay.

On June 10, having sailed up the coast from S. lat. 38° to 10°,

[1] The name Australia was given to the country, at the suggestion of Captain Flinders, about 1800.

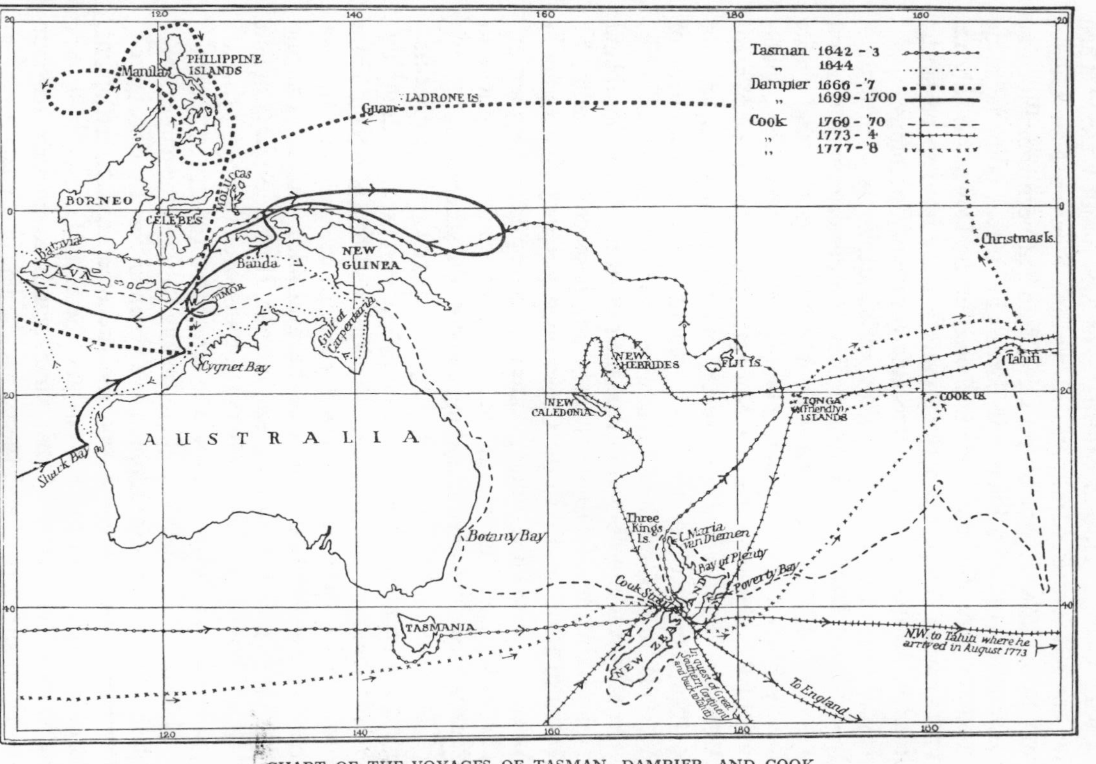

CHART OF THE VOYAGES OF TASMAN, DAMPIER, AND COOK

Cook took possession of the whole of Eastern Australia on behalf of King George III, under the name of New South Wales. Then he entered Torres Strait, and so, passing between New Guinea and New Holland (which up to this time had been thought to be one island), came to Batavia in Java. From that point he made good speed to England. He anchored in the Downs on July 12, 1771, having completed a three years' voyage fated to be hardly less fruitful than the first memorable voyage of Columbus.

With the exception of Tasman, earlier explorers—Portuguese, British, and Dutch—had visited only the desolate northern and western coasts of Australia. Cook found that rich and fertile south-eastern corner which is now the main centre of the population of the Commonwealth. Not until the close of the War of American Independence, however, did his countrymen attempt to turn the discovery to useful account. The development of Australia, in fact, resulted directly from the American War.

In 1783 it was proposed in Parliament that the Great Southland might be made to provide homes for those colonists who, by reason of their loyalty to the Crown, had forfeited their rights in America. The Government undertook to consider the question. The exiled loyalists, meanwhile, weary of waiting, migrated to Canada. So, in the end, nothing came of the scheme.

Just then another problem began to perplex the authorities. For many years the American colonies had been used as a dumping-ground for criminals, political offenders, and others who, despite a brutal legal code, had contrived to escape the gallows. In 1783 this dumping-ground ceased to be available. Again someone bethought him of Australia; and, in 1787, H.M.S. *Sirius* (Captain Arthur Phillip) was sent out with ten transports, carrying 550 male and 230 female prisoners, there to establish a convict settlement.

H.M.S. *Sirius* sailed straight to Botany Bay, and the name of this place was subsequently adopted as a synonym for 'transportation.' Yet Botany Bay never became the site of a convict settlement. Captain Phillip landed his charges there in January 1788, but he moved them later in that same month to another harbour farther to the north; and there, "at the top of a snug cove," so wrote a member of the party, "near a run of fresh water, which stole silently through a very thick wood . . . then for the first time since the Creation disturbed by the rude sound of the labourer's axe," he laid the foundations of the city of Sydney.

Save perhaps in France, the transportation system has few serious advocates to-day. We have come to share Bacon's opinion that "it is a shameful and unblessed thing to take the scum of people, and wicked, condemned men, to be the people with whom you plant." Yet there is—or was—another side to the picture. In 1787 the population of Great Britain was only slightly in excess of the present population of Greater London. Transportation, therefore, as a means of developing undeveloped lands, was infinitely preferable to its only practicable alternative, the importation of slaves. And in that it was designed to give wrongdoers the opportunity of atoning for misdeeds, and of becoming useful members of society in countries remote from old temptations and associations, it rested on a commendable theory. The theory, moreover, as a temporary expedient, was justified in practice.

In 1641 the witty Thomas Fuller observed that "it was rather bitterly than falsely spoken concerning one of our Western plantations . . . that it was very like unto England, as being spit out of the mouth of it." But can even the most fanciful hereditarian show that America has suffered in any way on account of its 'criminal taint'? As in America, so in Australia. The latter country, admittedly, was forced to receive a number of incurable ruffians who later, as bushrangers and the heroes of many a boyish romance, became intolerable pests to society. But the great majority of "indentured servants"—

> True patriots we, for be it understood,
> We left our country for our country's good—

proved themselves excellent colonists when they regained their freedom.

The transportation system led to the opening up of Australia. This, in turn, led to the discovery for which passing explorers had sought in vain—the discovery of gold. The gold finds of 1848 mark the real genesis of the Australian Commonwealth. After 1848 successive waves of free settlers, the fathers of the Australian people of to-day, quickly submerged the older convict element.

In July 1772, Cook, raised to the rank of commander, left Plymouth on his second voyage of discovery. This time he sailed with two ships, the *Resolution* (400 tons) and *Adventure* (330 tons), his object being to prove or disprove the existence of the fabled Great Southern Continent—in particular, of the so-called Cape Circumcision, which a French navigator, Benoit, claimed to have sighted, in 1709, to the south of the Cape of Good Hope, in S. lat. 54°.

The expedition crossed the Antarctic Circle in January 1773. In that same month its commander observed, for the first time, the southern counterpart of the aurora borealis. Beating east-

CAPTAIN COOK'S SHIP "RESOLUTION"
From a drawing in the possession of the Royal Geographical Society

ward, the *Resolution* and *Adventure* (Captain Tobias Furneaux) sailed 11,000 miles in 117 days, along the 60th southern parallel. But they failed to sight land. So Cook turned northward to New Zealand to rest his crews.

Later in the year he resumed his search, and sailed along lat. 45° as far as long. 140° W. Then, convinced by the great seas setting from every direction that land was not near, he went back to New Zealand. In December he set out on a final search, and, on January 27, 1774, in long. 106° 50′ W., reached his highest latitude—71° 10′ S. Turned back by ice, he proceeded to explore a vast tract of unknown sea between long. 130° and 140°. Having thus satisfied himself that the Southern Continent, if it existed, lay too near the Pole to be of practical value to man, he made for warmer climes, and on March 11, after 104 days' continuous sailing, sighted Easter Island and its strange torsos—survivals of some long-dead civilization—which a Dutch admiral, Roggewein, had discovered on Easter Day 1722. Thence he returned to New Zealand, being rewarded on the way by several finds—notably New Caledonia.

"I will not say," he afterward wrote,

> it was impossible anywhere to get farther to the south; but attempting it would have been a dangerous and rash enterprise, and which, I

THE GREAT ANTARCTIC ICE BARRIER

> believe, no man in my situation would have thought of. . . . No other reason need be assigned for my tacking and standing back to the north.

In these few words he revealed himself as the born leader he was. Though he spared neither himself nor his crews, he calculated hazards carefully and soberly. Fear of what other people might think of him never drove him to foolhardiness. Hence the implicit trust his followers placed in him; if he called on them to take risks—and he did often enough—they knew he had a more than sufficiently good reason.

After a month's stay at New Zealand the *Resolution* and *Adventure* left for America, intending to search for land to the south of Cape Horn. This venture resulted in the discovery of South

Georgia and a number of other islands. Cook then made for home; and on July 30, 1775—again after an absence of three years—he landed at Plymouth, having completed the first circumnavigation of the globe eastward. He completed it, moreover,

CAPTAIN COOK
After the painting by N. Dance

with the loss of only three men, an achievement which proved that foresight and organization could defeat the ravages of scurvy even in the eighteenth century when mariners philosophically regarded it as one of the necessary evils of the sea.

The disease had wrought havoc among the crew of the *Endeavour*. Cook insisted, therefore, that the *Resolution* and *Adventure* should be liberally supplied with provisions, such as "portable soup," lemons, conserved carrots, mustard, and "juice of wort," which were known to possess anti-scorbutic properties; and he conclusively proved the efficacy of this precaution.

On his return to England, in 1775, Cook was promoted to the rank of captain and given an appointment at Greenwich Hospital. But his restless spirit would not rest. In 1776 it drove him forth again—to solve, as he hoped, the riddle of the North-West Passage. Nearly three centuries of endeavour had failed to reveal that elusive waterway. Yet faith in its existence remained unshaken. Cook purposed to seek it from the east, following the scheme which Baffin had projected in 1621, but had not lived to attempt.

On July 12, 1776, he left Plymouth with the *Resolution*. His other ship, the *Discovery* (300 tons), under Captain Clerke, followed a month later, and the two vessels joined company at the Cape. Thence they proceeded to New Zealand, and, in February 1777, sailed north toward Bering Strait. While crossing the Pacific, Cook discovered the islands which bear his name, also the Sandwich (Hawaiian) group, which he named after the Earl of Sandwich, First Lord of the Admiralty, and, incidentally, the inventor of the sandwich. An inveterate gambler, the noble earl habitually dined off pieces of meat placed between thin slices of bread, so that meals might not interrupt his play.

The *Resolution* and *Discovery* struck the American continent at a point in California, and coasted northward till brought to anchor in Nootka Sound. There Cook compensated the Empire for "the thirteen Colonies," at that time all but lost, by annexing Vancouver Island.

Within ten years a small but prosperous settlement sprang up on the shore of Nootka Sound. In 1788 a Spanish force appeared on the scene and hauled down the Union Jack. Threatened with war, however, the Spanish Government thought better of its action and addressed a full apology to the British Crown. At the same time, it undertook to make good the English settlers' losses and to withdraw from the island. Captain Vancouver was sent out from England with two warships to supervise the departure of the Spaniards. The captain gave the island his name.

Cook left Nootka Sound on April 26, 1778, and on August 7, in lat. 66°, arrived at the most westerly point of America, the point which he named Cape Prince of Wales. Sailing west, he was off the coast of Asia ere nightfall. Then, turning north again, he passed through Bering Strait. But in lat. 71°, a solid wall of ice, stretching indefinitely from east to west, made further progress impossible. At length, therefore, in October, after a long and futile search for an opening, he retraced his course to the Sandwich Isles. There he remained more than three months, setting sail for England on February 4, 1779. But on February 12 he was back again at Hawaii. A sprung foremast compelled him thus to put about, and so to meet his tragic end.

Two days after his return, a matter of a theft involved some of his men in a scuffle with natives. An angry crowd quickly assembled at the spot. With a view to restoring peace Cook intervened. For so long as he faced the mob, not a savage dared raise a hand. Just then, however, a boat's crew, fearing for their leader's safety, opened fire from near the shore. Cook at once turned round and bade them to desist. His humanity cost him his life. While he was speaking, a savage stole up behind him, and stabbed him in the back.

This, the traditional story, can now be corrected and amplified. A chance purchaser in a London bookshop recently came upon a manuscript which proved to be the original log kept by a mate of the *Resolution*, one Henry Roberts, who was actually in charge of the boat's crew. So, after the lapse of many years, has been brought to light an eye-witness's detailed description of what happened. Roberts' entry, under the date of Sunday, February 14 (first published in the *Morning Post* of September 14, 1928), is printed below:

> The natives having stolen something from on board the *Discovery*, a canoe suspected was pursued by one of the boats, without arms in her, their crew landed and the thing stolen was brought them, afterwards our pinnace joined them, and by some means occasioned a dispute, which rose to a quarrel, when they got themselves ill-used and beat by the natives, breaking the pinnace's oars and endeavouring to stove the boat, but no other mischief. In the morning the *Discovery's* large cutter was missing from the buoy where she was moored. Boats sent from each ship in search of her, with orders to keep every canoe in the bay from paddling off till there was a likelihood of her being returned, as it was well known that the natives had taken her away.
>
> In order to make it more secure, Captain Cook went in the pinnace, manned and armed with the launch, under the command of the third Lieut., in company, to the village on the N. point of the bay, with an intention to get the Chief, Karu Oboo, on board, for which purpose

THE DEATH OF CAPTAIN COOK
From an engraving by F. Bartolozzi

> he landed with the officer of marines, the sergeant, and 8 of his people. After a little time they found the chief, and he would have willingly come off, but was hindered by his wife and those about him, who offered presents of hogs, etc., but were rejected. They afterwards were very troublesome, and began to be exceedingly insolent, and at last obliged the captain to fire on them. This occasioned a great rumour among the whole, who began to arm themselves. Shortly after the captain fired a musket, which was seconded by the marines on the boat. The captain immediately gave orders to cease fire and come in with the boat. The pinnace pulled in. The natives, on their part, had begun the attack, when the stones showered down with great violence, the whole body pressing in on our people, armed with spears, clubs, daggers, and slings, forced them into the water.
>
> The captain fell in the conflict, with four of the marines. The officer, sergeant, and others reached the boats with great difficulty, three of the number being wounded. The boats, after keeping a warm fire for a while, returned on board, not being able to get the body of our lost commander, whose death occasioned concern and sorrow in every countenance. Such an able navigator, equalled by few and excelled by none, justly styled the father of his people from his great good care and attention, honoured and beloved by those who knew or ever heard of him. The bodies of the marines, also, could not be taken, but exposed to the mercy of these savages, who were truly desperate and intrepid.

On the following day two friendly natives, "at the risk of their lives . . . brought us," wrote Roberts, "a part of the sad remains of our unfortunate captain, being a piece of his flesh from off the thigh." All other parts, it seemed, had been burnt. Subsequently, however, the bones were recovered and, on February 22, were "committed to the deep, with all the decency in our power, and the usual ceremony, fired ten minute guns."

Next morning the *Resolution* and *Discovery* weighed anchor and, with Captain Clerke in command, set sail for England. The ships arrived in the Thames in November 1780.

XX. LORD ANSON

Born 1697; *died* 1762

GEORGE ANSON (afterward first Baron of Soberton) must be accounted, next to Captain Cook, the most notable of the English navigators of the eighteenth century. A son of William Anson of Shuckborough Manor, in Staffordshire, he was born on St George's Day 1697. At the age of fifteen he entered the Navy, and in 1718, at the battle of Cape Passaro, received his baptism of fire while serving as a lieutenant in the *Montagu*, Sir George Byng's flagship.

Four years later he was given his first command, being appointed to the *Weasel*, a sloop detailed for the suppression of the smuggling trade from Holland. He showed rare judgment in the performance of this work. In 1724, therefore, he was sent out in the *Scarborough*, with the rank of captain, to protect the American colonies from the depredations of pirates and Spanish privateers.

For fourteen years he served almost continuously on the western side of the Atlantic, chiefly on the Carolina stations; the names of a county and a town in South Carolina serve to commemorate his activities. In 1739, on the outbreak of hostilities with Spain—the so-called "War of Jenkins's Ear" which in 1740 was merged into the world-wide War of the Austrian Succession—he was recalled to England and given command of eight ships, with instructions to emulate Drake's exploits in the Southern Seas. The squadron comprised:

Centurion . .	60 guns,	506 men,	Commodore G. Anson
Gloucester . .	50 ,,	374 ,,	Capt. Richard Norris
Severn . .	50 ,,	325 ,,	Capt. the Hon. E. Legge
Pearl . . .	40 ,,	250 ,,	Capt. Mitchell
Wager . .	28 ,,	160 ,,	Capt. Kidd
Tryal . .	8 ,,	81 ,,	Capt. C. Saunders

together with two 'pinks,' *Anna* and *Industry*, as victuallers.

On paper it was a formidable force. But its equipment left

much to be desired, judged even by eighteenth-century standards. The crews included some three hundred men who had been dragged out of hospital while still suffering from wounds and infirmities acquired in their country's service, and two hundred who had not had a sea-training of any sort, recruits detached from various regiments. The supply arrangements, moreover, were deplorable. The biscuit was "so worm-eaten," wrote one of the officers,

> it was scarce anything but dust, and a little blow would reduce it to that immediately; our Beef and Pork likewise were very rusty and rotten, and the surgeon endeavoured to hinder us from eating any of it, alleging it was, tho' a slow, yet a sure poison.

In the circumstances, the commodore cannot fairly be blamed for such misfortune as attended the expedition; while to him alone belongs the credit for the glorious ending to which he brought it. Indeed, as Mr John Masefield has observed, the story of Anson's circumnavigation well illustrates "the excellence of Englishmen and the stupidity of their governors."

The squadron left Spithead on September 18, 1740. Forty days afterward it reached Madeira, having been much delayed by contrary winds. Subsequently it made better speed, and on December 18 the Brazilian coast was sighted. There, at St Catherine, a long halt was called, for scurvy had already broken out among the crews, and the authorities had entirely neglected to equip the expedition with anti-scorbutics. From the flagship alone some eighty sick were put ashore. Each of the other vessels sent a proportionate number.

"As soon as we had performed this necessary duty," wrote the chaplain of the *Centurion*,

> we scraped our decks, and gave our ship a thorough cleaning; then we smoked it between decks, and after all washed every part well with vinegar. These operations were extremely necessary for correcting the noisome stench on board, and destroying the vermin; for . . . both these nuisances had increased upon us to a very loathsome degree.

The chaplain's matter-of-fact statement throws a flood of light on the conditions under which men lived in the Royal Navy in the eighteenth century.

On January 18, 1741, Anson sailed from St Catherine and

MODEL OF H.M.S. "ROYAL GEORGE"

proceeded slowly southward toward St Julian's Bay, in Patagonia, making the most careful survey of the coast that had yet been attempted. He left St Julian on February 27, and on March 7 entered the Strait of Le Maire, having narrowly escaped a meeting with an immensely superior Spanish fleet (Admiral Don Joseph Pizzaro) which had been sent to intercept him. Fortune, however, did not continue to smile on him. At the entrance to the strait his ships ran into a terrific storm, which very nearly brought the whole enterprise to naught.

"I had my topsails reefed for fifty-eight days," wrote the commodore in his official report. His men, meanwhile, were "falling down every day with scurvy." On May 8 he recorded: "I have not men able to keep the decks or sufficient to take in the topsail; and every day some six or eight men are buried." The state of affairs on board the other vessels was very much the same; and —to make matters worse—on April 24, when the storm was at its height, the fleet was scattered, with the result that the captains of the *Severn*, the *Pearl*, and the *Wager*, despairing of rounding the Horn, put about and made for England. Eventually only the *Centurion*, the *Gloucester*, the *Tryal*, and the *Anna*, pink victualler, arrived at Juan Fernandez, the appointed rendezvous, and they were in a sorry plight.

Of the *Centurion's* company no fewer than two hundred and ninety-two had died of scurvy, while the *Gloucester's* crew had been reduced from three hundred and seventy-four to eighty-two, and the *Tryal's* from eighty-one to thirty-nine. The majority of the survivors, moreover, were sick. Captain Saunders,[1] indeed, had only himself, a lieutenant, and three men to work his ship.

For a hundred and four days Anson allowed his dispirited followers to recuperate at Juan Fernandez. That island, the scene of Robinson Crusoe's adventures, seemed to them a veritable paradise. Thirty-two years had elapsed since the departure of Alexander Selkirk, *alias* Robinson Crusoe.[2] Of the latter's residence there, however, curious evidence still remained.

"He tells us," wrote Anson,

> that, as he often caught more goats than he wanted, he sometimes marked their ears, and let them go. . . . Now, it so happened that

---

[1] Afterwards Admiral Sir Charles Saunders, commander of the fleet which (piloted up the St Lawrence by James Cook) took Wolfe to Quebec.

[2] See p. 212.

the first goat that was killed by our people at their landing had his ears slit, whence we concluded that he had doubtless been formerly under the power of Selkirk. This was indeed an animal of a most venerable aspect, dignified with an exceeding majestic beard, and with many other symptoms of antiquity. During our stay on the island we met with others marked in the same manner, all the males being distinguished by an exuberance of beard and every other characteristic of extreme age.

While his crews were resting, Anson had anxiously to cogitate how best to prosecute the purpose of his voyage. Left with only three ships and scarcely men enough to navigate one, he might well have shrunk from the prospect of engaging in warlike undertakings. His bold spirit, however, to say nothing of the Drake tradition, at once ruled out counsels of caution. So on September 8, having assured his men that "nothing was to be apprehended from the naval power of Spain in this part of the world," he set sail to begin offensive operations.

The result justified his daring. The British squadron took prize after prize as it made its way up the Pacific coast of South America, the *Nuestra Señora del Carmen*, with specie on board to the value of £100,000, being among the number of its victims. In January 1742, moreover, it actually captured and burned the town of Payta, which at that time was the chief seaport of Peru. Stealing into the harbour in sundry small boats, under cover of darkness, a small company of picked volunteers completely surprised the garrison. Drake himself never planned a more daring attack.

Continuing northward, Anson cruised for two months off the coast of Mexico, in the hope of intercepting the Acapulco treasure galleon carrying the yearly hoard of the Mexican mines. But the sailing of the vessel had been postponed. So in March the British commander resolved to shape a course to China. The state of his ships forbade him to wait longer. Indeed, the *Tryal* already had become so foul that he had to abandon and scuttle her.

Before leaving England he had laboriously collected all available information regarding the navigation of the Pacific. But in those days, save to pilots engaged in the Spanish trade between Manila and Acapulco, little was known on the subject. Much of his information, therefore, proved not only false but dangerously misleading. He anticipated reaching China, with the aid of favouring trade winds, in seven weeks. Instead nearly five months passed before, with the *Centurion* alone—the *Gloucester* meanwhile having shared the fate of the *Tryal*—he at length sighted Tinian, an island in the Ladrone group. By that time water and stores alike were almost exhausted and his men again were suffering terribly from scurvy.

A month spent on the "happy isle" of Tinian effectually checked the ravages of disease. But another calamity then befell the unfortunate mariners. On September 21, while the commodore and a hundred and thirteen of his men were on shore, the *Centurion*, caught by a storm, was swept from her moorings and borne out to sea. Believing the ship to be lost, Anson at once set about to devise a plan to save himself and his companions from falling into the hands of the Spaniards at Guam. Finally he decided to have a small prize, which had weathered the storm, sawn asunder; by lengthening the barque he hoped to convert it into a vessel capable of carrying his company to China.

Fortunately, his carpenters were among the party on land, also the smith. But, though the former had their tool-chests with them, and the latter his forge, bellows had to be improvised. This proved a difficult task. Eventually a gun-barrel was made to serve as a pipe, while goats' hides were hastily tanned to provide the necessary leather. The refashioning of the barque then proceeded apace. By the middle of October the work was finished; and, having laid in a liberal supply of provisions—jerked beef, coconuts, and rice—Anson, with the aid of a pocket compass, "little better than the toys made for schoolboys," and a makeshift quadrant, undertook to pilot the vessel across the Pacific.

A happy chance spared him the necessity of making the hazardous experiment. On the very day he intended to start the *Centurion* reappeared. On October 21, therefore, he was able again to set sail in his flagship, having first destroyed the craft which he had so laboriously constructed. Three weeks later he arrived at Macao. There, despite obstacles put in his way by the local authorities, he contrived to get the *Centurion* refitted. Then, having supplemented his crew by the addition of some Dutchmen and Lascars, he retraced his course to the Philippines and, on June 20, 1743, succeeded after all in capturing the Acapulco galleon.

The Spanish ship, the *Nuestra Señora de Cabodonga*, though much larger than his own, and much more heavily armed, struck

THE BURNING OF THE TOWN OF PAYTA, 1742

after three hours' fighting, sixty-seven of her company having been killed and eighty-four wounded. The British casualties amounted to two killed and seventeen wounded. Of the latter, moreover, all recovered but one: "of so little consequence," wrote their commander, "are the most destructive arms in untutored and unpractised hands."

From the prize Anson took treasure to the value of more than £400,000. The ship itself he subsequently sold to the Portuguese

TABLE BAY AND MOUNTAIN

at Macao; and on December 15 he finally left the coast of China.

On March 11, 1744, he arrived at Table Bay, where he lay until April 3. Then, having collected forty new hands, he continued his voyage, and at length, on June 15, after an absence of three years and nine months, dropped anchor at Spithead. There he was astonished to learn that Britain was at war not only with Spain, but with France. While sailing up the Channel he had passed unobserved, under cover of fog, through the midst of a French patrolling squadron.

On the day of his return he wrote to Lord Hardwicke, the Lord Chancellor:

> Though the expedition has not had all the success the nation expected of it, which is a great misfortune to me, I am persuaded no

misconduct can justly be laid to my charge as Commander-in-Chief; and I should have great pain in returning to my country, after all the fatigue and hazard I have undergone in trying to serve it, if I thought I had forfeited either your lordship's favour and protection or the esteem of the public.

His fears proved unfounded—so far, at any rate, as the public was concerned. People at home were stirred by the story of his adventures as they had not been stirred since the days of Drake. The narrative of the voyage, *Lord Anson's Voyage Round the World*,[1] ran into edition after edition. Within a year of its publication it had been translated into seven European languages. This popularity it well deserved. As a tale of adventure, of perils bravely faced and bravely overcome, it has few rivals. Further, it is the record of a very notable naval exploit. The extent of the damage done by the British expedition to Spanish commerce and shipping may be gauged by the fact that the *Centurion* came back with treasure on board to the value of more than £1,250,000; thirty-two wagons were required to convey it from Portsmouth to London.

Shortly after his return, Anson was appointed Rear-Admiral of the Blue, and given a seat on the Board of Admiralty. In 1746 he was promoted to the rank of vice-admiral; and on May 11 of the following year, while in command of the forces detailed for the blockade of Rochefort and Brest, he overhauled, and very soundly beat, a powerful French fleet convoying transports bound for Canada and the East.

Six men-of-war, five armed merchantmen, and many privateers and other small craft fell into his hands, together with 10,000 troops, and an immense amount of specie, munitions, and stores. Among the warships taken were *L'Invincible* (74 guns), the pride of King Louis's navy, and *La Gloire*. Said the French admiral, De la Jonquière, as he handed his sword to the victor: "*Monsieur, vous avez vaincu l'Invincible, mais la Gloire vous suit.*"

The victory had far-reaching effects. It not only frustrated a French scheme for the recapture of Louisbourg (the great fortress on Cape Breton Island which had been taken by the British in 1744), but it compelled Dupleix somewhat to relax the pressure

[1] Though printed under the name of the chaplain of the *Centurion*, the book was compiled under the supervision of, and from material supplied by, Lord Anson.

he was exerting on the British in India. In recognition of a signal service thus rendered, Anson was raised to the peerage and made Vice-Admiral of England. In 1748 he became Admiral

LORD ANSON
From a mezzotint by McArdell, after Reynolds

of the Blue, and finally, in 1757, took office as First Lord of the Admiralty.

This post he held—except for a short time in 1758 when, with the *Royal George* as his flagship, he commanded at a descent on Cherbourg—during the critical period of the Seven Years' War (1756–63); and, having already shown himself a great navigator and a great fighting sailor, he proved himself perhaps the greatest of all Britain's naval administrators. While he enormously improved the conditions of service for both officers and men, he effected equally striking improvements in *matériel* and organization. Incidentally, he is to be remembered as the father of naval uniform; by 1760 officers had generally adopted the blue uniform which he first sanctioned and then ordered to be worn. Julian Corbett has written in his *Seven Years' War*:

> His reforms at the Admiralty were sweeping and active. The Articles of War which lasted in force till 1865 were started by him. The Royal Marines as they now exist owe their origin to him.
>
> Anson was the originator of the well-adapted combination of land and sea forces, and the method of employing them was the strategy which he advocated, and which Pitt approved. . . . His volunteering to leave the Admiralty at a time when the nation was dissatisfied at nothing having been done for the first two years of the war . . . show a readiness of resource and a great appreciation of the necessities of the moment. It was well planned and well executed. Under his care as First Lord, the Navy attained a pitch of power and pre-eminence to which it had never before arrived. France and Spain as sea powers were swept off the seas. The trade of England increased every year of the war, and such a scene of national prosperity while waging a long, costly, and strenuous war, a war of hard fighting, was never before shown by any people of the world.

Said William Pitt in a speech which, as Earl of Chatham, he delivered in the House of Lords in 1770: "To his wisdom, to his experience and care (and I speak it with pleasure), the nation owes the glorious successes of the last war."

The great admiral died on June 6, 1762, the last service he performed being to escort from Cuxhaven to England the Princess Charlotte of Mecklenburg-Strelitz, whom George III was about to take as his queen.

Lady Anson, a daughter of the Earl of Hardwicke, died in 1760. The highly gifted child of a highly gifted Lord Chancellor, she had been for twenty-two years her husband's guide, mentor, and friend.

XXI. WILLIAM BLIGH

Born 1754; *died* 1817

THE name of William Bligh—"Bread-fruit Bligh" as he was known in the Navy—lives in history mainly by reason of its connexion with the famous mutiny of the *Bounty*. Born at Plymouth on September 9, 1754,[1] and sprung from an old Cornish family, the owner of the name passed his early years in the mercantile marine. Subsequently he entered the Navy, and in 1772 saw service under Captain Cook.

In that year Cook set out on his second voyage, the voyage which had for its object the discovery of the fabled Great Southern Continent. Bligh went with him as sailing-master—a warrant officer—of the *Resolution*. In 1774 the *Resolution* returned to England. Shortly afterward Bligh was granted a lieutenant's commission, and in 1781 played a distinguished part in the battle fought with the Dutch off the Dogger Bank, one of the few successes which attended British arms in that year of calamitous misfortune. In the following year, at the relief of Gibraltar, he confirmed his reputation.

The daring and seamanship he displayed on that occasion brought him to the notice of Lord Howe. Thus was his future assured. In 1787 he was appointed to the command of the *Bounty*, and sent forth at the head of an expedition to the Southern Seas. Former expeditions to that quarter had aimed at the advancement of geographical and scientific knowledge. The expedition of 1787 was designed essentially as a practical undertaking; as an attempt to turn to useful account discoveries which had already been made. Bligh sailed with instructions to visit Tahiti, and thence to introduce bread-fruit into the West Indies.

This scheme, strongly urged by Anson and Cook, had been suggested by Dampier as far back as 1688. Bread-fruit formed

[1] The son of John Bligh of Tretawne, in the parish of St Kew, Cornwall. According to some authorities, he was born in 1753 at Tinten, in the parish of St Tudy, his parents being Charles and Margaret Bligh.

the staple food of the natives of Tahiti and certain other Pacific islands, and no reason could be seen why it should not grow equally well in the very similar West Indian climate. It was thought that

> The bread-tree, which, without the ploughshare, yields
> The unreap'd harvest of unfurrow'd fields,

would provide planters with a cheap and easy way of feeding their slaves.

Wrote Dampier:

> The bread-fruit . . . grows on a large tree, as big and high as our largest apple-trees; it hath a spreading head, full of branches and dark leaves. The fruit grows on the boughs like apples; it is as big as a penny-loaf, when wheat is at five shillings the bushel; it is of a round shape, and hath a thick, tough rind. . . . The natives of Guam use it for bread. They gather it, when full grown, while it is green and hard; then they bake it in an oven, which scorcheth the rind and makes it black, but they scrape off the outside black crust, and there remains a tender thin crust; and the inside is soft, tender, and white, like the crumb of a penny-loaf. . . . This fruit lasts in season eight months in the year, during which the natives eat no other sort of food of bread kind. . . . I never did hear of it anywhere else.

The *Bounty*, a vessel of two hundred and fifteen tons burden, carrying a crew numbering forty-four souls, left Spithead on December 23; and on March 10, 1788, after a swift and uneventful passage, she sighted the coast of Tierra del Fuego. Her commander had intended to put in at New Year's Harbour, Staten Island, to refresh his men. Having regard, however, to their remarkably good health, also to the lateness of the season, he changed his plans and decided to push on without delay, hoping to be able to round the American continent while conditions were favourable.

In this hope he was disappointed. Off the Horn, a headland deservedly hated by eighteenth-century navigators, the little *Bounty* encountered a terrific gale. For nine days Bligh battled with the storm. Then, finding that his ship was making no headway, he prudently determined to turn, and, by running before the wind, to cross the South Atlantic and approach Tahiti from the west.

On May 23 he arrived at the Cape. There he stayed thirty-eight days, refitting his ship and replenishing supplies. He set sail again on July 1. Seven weeks later he anchored in Adventure Bay, Van Diemen's Land, and at length, in the evening of October 25, sighted Tahiti, the *Bounty* having covered by the log

TAHITI : A TYPICAL CORAL ATOLL
Photo E. N. A.

twenty-seven thousand and eighty-six miles since her departure from England, an average of a hundred and eight miles a day.

From the Tahitians, by whom he was well remembered as one of Cook's former companions, Bligh received a cordial welcome. "There appeared among the natives in general," he observed, "great good-will towards us, and they seemed to be much rejoiced by our arrival." Poeeno, the chief of the island, went aboard to greet the visitors as soon as the *Bounty* had been secured. In the evening the ship's company was lavishly entertained on shore.

At the conclusion of the festivities, wrote Bligh,

> the ladies, for they deserve to be called such from their natural and unaffected manners and elegance of deportment, got up and, taking some of their finest cloth and a mat, clothed me in the Tahitian

fashion, and then said, ' We will go with you to your boat '; and, each taking me by the hand, led me to the waterside, and there took their leave.

This incident, trivial in itself, calls for mention, since it is largely to feminine influence that Bligh's apologists—Byron among them [1]—ascribe the untoward events which subsequently marred the success of the voyage. The sea-weary crew of the *Bounty*, we are told, left for six months to enjoy the society of the alluring daughters of a voluptuous race, were loath, when the day came, to quit the island paradise upon which they had lighted.

> Young hearts which languish'd for some sunny isle,
> Where summer years, and summer women smile;
> Men without country, who, too long estranged,
> Had found no native home, or found it changed,
> And, half uncivilized, preferr'd the cave
> Of some soft savage to the uncertain wave.

Logic may not be wholly wanting from the argument. But Bligh, it should be remembered, had no valid excuse for staying six months at Tahiti. If his followers became demoralized, he himself was largely responsible. Moreover, it would seem to have been the tyrannous methods by which he sought to restore order, rather than a rebellious refusal on their part again to submit to discipline, that led them to mutiny.

"It was Bligh's misfortune," Sir John Barrow has written, "not to have been educated in the cockpit [2] of a man-of-war among young gentlemen, which is to the Navy what a public school is to those who are to move in civil society." Though possessed of many fine qualities, and though on many occasions, when difficulties and danger had to be faced, he proved himself a consummate leader, the captain of the *Bounty* was not "to the manner born"; and a coarse, blustering nature rendered him, as it rendered many another officer of that period (when the system of selection in the service required, and was about to undergo, drastic reform), unfitted to command in the ordinary course of peace-time duty.

A long series of mutinies, culminating in the great risings of 1797 at Spithead and the Nore, forms the ugliest feature of British

[1] The relations which existed between the mutineers and the women of Tahiti form the subject of Byron's poem " The Island."

[2] The gun-room, as we should say to-day.

naval history in the second half of the eighteenth century. These incidents—the terrible mutiny of the *Hermione*, for example, or the still more terrible mutiny of the *Tremendous* at the Cape of Good Hope, and the mutiny of the *Danæ*—can be traced, with very few exceptions, to the actions of tyrannous, and therefore unqualified, officers. To the same cause must be assigned the mutiny of the *Bounty*.

Toward the end of the first week of April 1789, having at length loaded his ship with bread-fruit plants—"in seven hundred and seventy-four pots, thirty-nine tubs, and twenty-four boxes"—Bligh sailed from Tahiti. Some three weeks later, while he was bearing eastward to the north of the Friendly Islands, his men rose against him. Headed by Christian Fletcher, the master's mate, twenty-five of them took possession of the ship, and, in the early hours of the morning of April 28, turned the commander adrift in a launch, together with those who still remained loyal, eighteen all told.

The mutineers had furnished the launch with a hundred and fifty pounds of bread, thirty-two pounds of pork, some six quarts of rum, and twenty-eight gallons of water; also with a quadrant and a compass. Seized by compunction at the last moment, one of them had urged that a chart should be provided as well. The others immediately put aside the suggestion. Bligh, the compassionate one was assured, had no need of a chart. "Give him pencil and paper," said Christian Fletcher, "and he'll find his way home from anywhere."

He justified this tribute to his skill. When cut adrift, he first thought of seeking shelter at Tofoa, the nearest island of the Friendly group. But the natives for once belied their reputation for friendliness. Electing, therefore, to be drowned rather than murdered, Bligh boldly made for Timor, and thither—a distance of more than three thousand six hundred miles—he actually navigated an open boat, only twenty-three feet long and deeply laden. On the way, moreover, he discovered and carefully surveyed that part of the New Hebrides which he named the Banks Group. The story has few parallels in the annals of the sea.

The voyage lasted forty-eight days, and those who took part in it suffered terribly from hunger, thirst, and storms. During most of the time their daily ration was limited to one ounce of bread and a quarter of a pint of water a head. But not one lost his life.

THE MUTINY OF THE "BOUNTY"

Captain Bligh being cast off

From the picture by Robert Dadd

On June 14, though in the last stage of exhaustion, all landed safely at Timor.

"It is not possible," wrote Bligh,

> for me to describe the pleasure which the blessing of the sight of this land diffused among us. It appeared scarcely credible to ourselves that, in an open boat and so poorly provided, we should have been able to reach the coast of Timor in forty-one days after leaving Tofoa . . . and that, notwithstanding our extreme distress, no one should have perished in the voyage. . . . Our bodies were nothing but skin and bones, our limbs were full of sores, and we were clothed in rags; in this condition, with the tears of joy and gratitude flowing down our cheeks, the people of Timor beheld us with a mixture of horror, surprise, and pity.

The unfortunate voyagers stayed two months at Timor, recruiting their strength. Then, having procured a small schooner, they made their way to Batavia. There Bligh embarked in a Dutch packet which was about to sail for Europe, and in March 1790 he was landed on the Isle of Wight. His companions followed in various Dutch East India merchantmen.

The story of their adventures aroused immense interest at home, and not a little indignation. The Admiralty, therefore, in deference to popular feeling, decided to send out the frigate *Pandora* (Captain Edwards) to search for the mutineers and for the ship they had stolen.

The *Pandora* went straight to Tahiti, where, sure enough, the *Bounty* was found, also fourteen of the mutineers, whom Captain Edwards duly arrested. As for the others—Christian Fletcher among them—all that could be ascertained was that they had built a boat for themselves and gone forth, accompanied by Tahitian women, in quest of a safer place of refuge. On her way back to England the *Pandora* was wrecked, and four of the mutineers were drowned. The remaining ten were eventually brought to England and tried by court-martial. Three were executed.

The fate of the mutineers who had avoided arrest long remained a mystery. Not until 1808 was their retreat located. Captain Mayhew Folger, commanding an American ship, the *Topaze*, then chanced to call at Pitcairn Island, an isolated appendage of the Paumotu Archipelago—some three miles long and two miles wide —in 25° 4′ N. lat. and 130° 8′ W. There he came upon a strange community of about fifty half-castes, sprung from the *Bounty* mutineers, leading well-ordered lives under the patriarchal rule of a certain Jack Adams, the sole survivor of Fletcher's followers.

Folger's report, forwarded by the American authorities to the British Government, spoke of the Pitcairn islanders in such glowing terms that it melted even the official heart of the Crown. Adams was not only granted a free pardon for his crime, but was left to rule the island—under British protection—until his death, which occurred in 1829. The Pitcairners by that time had increased in number to eighty-seven.

"PARLIAMENT HOUSE AND CHURCH," PITCAIRN ISLAND
From a drawing made by a Pitcairn Islander
Photo E. N. A.

In 1831, owing to the scarcity of water on the island, the Colonial Office arranged for them to be shipped in a body to Tahiti. But these simple, primitive folk found the house of their maternal forbears too highly civilized for their liking; within two years they returned to their rock.

In 1853 the Colonial Office decided to transfer them to Norfolk Island. At the time, this island was still being used as a penal settlement. In preparation, however, for the coming of the Pitcairners—who, to quote from an official report,

> in the small and remote island which they occupied, had preserved an innocence of life and gentleness and benevolence of manners which had gained for them the esteem and admiration and the good-will of all by whom they had been visited

—orders were issued for it to be cleared of its convict population.

Having regard to the ignorance of the new-comers in the arts of civilization, it was proposed that one convict, a particularly clever craftsman and "an old man and a reformed man," should be left at Norfolk Island to help them. The suggestion was officially vetoed. Word went forth from Whitehall that the Pitcairners must be kept free from all danger of contamination, and the Governor of Fiji was instructed not to allow "any other class of settlers to reside or occupy land on the island."

In 1856 they moved to their new home. But they soon became as unhappy as they had been at Tahiti, and in 1859 many of them again returned to Pitcairn. They arrived at their rock just in time to prevent a French occupation. And there they—or rather their descendants—are living still. According to the latest available figures, the population of the island numbers 144 souls, living in almost complete isolation, and in blissful simplicity and innocence. They carry on a spasmodic trade in arrowroot.

In 1792, as commander of the *Providence*, Bligh revisited Tahiti. On this occasion he duly carried out the purpose of his former appointment. At the same time he did much valuable surveying work in the South Pacific, and, as a recognition of his labours, was awarded the gold medal of the Society of Arts. The results of his bread-fruit experiment, however, hardly justified the cost. West Indian settlers displayed little interest in the tree to which he introduced them; they preferred to rely on the prolific and indigenous plantain for the feeding of their slaves.

Space allows his subsequent history merely to be noted here. In 1794, on "the glorious 1st of June," he commanded the *Warrior* in the great battle won by Lord Howe off Ushant; and in 1797, as captain of the *Director* (64 guns), he contributed in no small measure to Admiral Duncan's victory at Camperdown over the Dutch. Earlier in that same year he gained for himself golden opinions by the courage and tact he showed during the critical days of the mutiny at the Nore; whilst in 1801, for the bold part he played in the destruction of the Danish fleet at Copenhagen, he earned the warm commendation of Nelson. At Copenhagen he commanded the *Glatton* (54 guns).

In 1805 he had the misfortune to be appointed Captain-General and Governor of New South Wales. For this, an administrative post, he—essentially a man of action—was wholly unsuited. In Australia, having little to do and much too much time in which to do it, he at once began to meddle in matters that lay outside his province; the colonists soon found his petty oppressions intolerable. He also offended his own immediate subordinates. So it came about that in 1808—to cut a long story short—the garrison, headed by Major George Johnstone of the 102nd Foot, arose against him. For nearly two years Johnstone held him a prisoner.

WILLIAM BLIGH
From the painting by Reynolds

The facts of the case at last became known in England. The major forthwith was recalled, tried by court-martial, and dismissed the service. Bligh, however, continued to retain the confidence of the authorities at home. In 1811 he was raised to the rank of Vice-Admiral of the Blue, and he remained on the active list down to the day of his death. He died in London on December 7, 1817, at a house in Bond Street, where his wife, a lady who aspired to a place in Society, had long been residing. He was buried in the churchyard at Lambeth.

XXII. PAUL JONES

Born 1747; *died* 1792

OF the minor characters who appear in the drama of the eighteenth century, few are more widely known than is John Paul Jones. Yet time has not been kind to his memory. In the minds of most people his name conjures up the picture of a pirate, a corsair, an unscrupulous rogue. The picture, so far from being a portrait, is a gross caricature. Paul Jones once was accounted "the ocean hero of the Old World and the New."

His mother, *née* Jean Macduff, after acting for many years as lady's-maid to the wife of Robert Craik, Member of Parliament for Kirkcudbrightshire, married her master's gardener, a certain John Paul. It will be seen presently how her son acquired the name of Jones. Despite assertions to the contrary, there is no reason to doubt that the aforesaid John Paul was his father, or that he was born on July 6, 1747, in a cottage on Craik's estate at Kirkbean.

Biographers, at a loss to explain how a yokel's son became the petted darling of the French and Russian Courts, have attempted to foist his parentage on various celebrities. Several possible fathers and several possible mothers have been named, the suggestion being that to a woman such as Mrs Paul, an ex-lady's-maid of well-proved discretion, an amorous noble dame would naturally turn when seeking a foster-mother for her unwanted son. Evidence to support the suggestion is entirely lacking.

At the age of twelve, thanks to the good offices of Mrs Craik, young John Paul was apprenticed to a local shipowner, "a merchant engaged in the American trade." Some four years later his master retired from business. The lad then obtained the appointment of third mate on the *King George*, a Whitehaven slave-ship.

For slave-trading he at once evinced a strong dislike, and in 1768, he tells us, he "became so disgusted with the business of stealing human beings" that he left his ship on its arrival at the

West Indies and took passage home in the *John*, of Kirkcudbright.

On the voyage the captain and the mate both died. The passenger, therefore, the only competent man remaining, assumed command and so, by bringing the vessel safely to port, brought himself to the notice of the owners, Currie, Beck & Co. In their service he remained till 1772. He was then made master of the *Betsy*, a London ship trading with the West Indies; a rapid rise on the part of a young man who had neither favour nor influence to aid him.

Fortune continued to smile on him. In 1773, on the death of his elder brother William, who some years before had been adopted by a wealthy planter, he found himself the heir to a considerable property in Virginia.

> Three thousand acres of prime land bordering for twelve furlongs on the right bank of Rappahannock; . . . mansion, overseer's house, negro quarters, stables, tobacco houses, threshing-floor, river wharf, one sloop of 20 tons, thirty negroes of all ages (eighteen adults), twenty horses and colts, eighty neat cattle and calves, sundry sheep and swine, and all necessary means of tilling the soil

—these were his, subject to one condition. The terms of the legacy required that he should assume the name of his brother's benefactor, the name of Jones.

Till 1775 Paul Jones—as now he styled himself—well content with his lot as a planter, enjoyed a life of "calm contemplation and poetic ease." From this he was roused by the outbreak of the War of Independence. A sincere champion of the colonists' cause, he threw himself heart and soul into the struggle, and, having offered himself for service afloat, was appointed, in December, first lieutenant of the *Alfred*, the flagship of Commodore Ezekiel Hopkins. But Virginian officers were not made welcome in the infant navy of the United States. The authorities of Virginia having taken the lead in matters military, the authorities of Massachusetts jealously guarded their supremacy in matters naval. Thus, though the most highly gifted sailor in the thirteen colonies, Jones at the outset was obstructed by a political prejudice which he was never able to surmount.

None the less, in the summer of 1776, he contrived to get a command. Thereafter for several months as captain of a sloop, the *Providence*, he gave a striking demonstration of the theory he had been preaching to deaf ears—that a small fleet, under resolute leaders, aiming directly at the destruction of commerce, could strike effectively even at the all-powerful British Navy. Long was the roll of the *Providence's* prizes. The stout little vessel, moreover, defied all efforts to capture her. Only once did a British frigate get within striking distance—the *Solebay* (28 guns), in September 1776—and she was pursued in error by Jones, who mistook her for a merchantman.

The escape of the *Providence* on that occasion ranks as a classic example of ship-handling. "The old saying," her captain wrote afterwards, "that 'discretion is the better part of valour' may in this case, I think, be changed to 'impudence is—or may be, sometimes—the better part of discretion!'"

The American colonists, in taking up arms against Britain, counted on the active support of France. This expectation did not materialize for more than two years. The French, though ready enough to engage in a war of revenge which should wipe out the stain of recent defeats, were unwilling again to challenge the British unless they could see a really good chance of success. Louis XVI decided to sit on the fence till the Americans had proved that they were able to maintain their resistance.

In October 1777, on receiving the news of General Burgoyne's surrender at Saratoga, Congress thought the French King could be given the proof he required, and decided to send it forthwith. Paul Jones was selected to act as messenger, and on November 1, in command of the *Ranger*, a new 300-ton frigate (one of the first ships, by the way, to be coppered), he left Portsmouth (New Hants) undertaking to "spread the news in France in thirty days." The crossing actually took him thirty-two days. For the delay he can hardly be blamed.

Wrote one of his officers:

> I had sailed with many captains in all kinds of voyages, but I had never seen a ship crowded as Captain Jones drove the *Ranger*. . . . As the wind hung all the time north-north-east and east-north-east, with but a few veerings outside those points, it was always forward of the beam on the true course, and often near dead ahead. Imagine, then, the situation of the *Ranger's* crew, with a top-heavy and crank ship under their feet, and a commander who day and night insisted on every rag she could stagger under without laying clear down!

As it was, she came close to beam-ends more than once, and on one occasion righted only by letting fly sheets cut with hatchets.

The *Ranger* dropped anchor in the Loire below Nantes on December 2. Some six weeks later the preliminaries of a treaty of alliance between France and the United States were duly settled. His mission thus successfully accomplished, Jones urged a scheme for showing the "stars and stripes" in British waters. Eventually, backed by influential friends whom he had made at Versailles—notably the beautiful Duchess of Chartres, whose husband, afterward Duke of Orleans, lives in history as the infamous Egalité of the Revolution—he wrung an unwilling consent from the American Commissioners in France, and sailed from Brest on April 10.

"My plan," he wrote, "was extensive. I therefore did not wish at the beginning to encumber myself with prisoners." On the 14th, however, he "took a brigantine between Scilly and Cape Clear, bound from Ostend, with a cargo of flax-seed for Ireland, sunk her, and proceeded into St George's Channel"; and on the 17th he "took the ship *Lord Chatham*, bound from London to Dublin, . . . almost within sight of her port."

On the 21st he found himself off the entrance of Belfast Lough. Learning that the *Drake*, a sloop-of-war, was lying at anchor within, he ran in under cover of dark, intending to let go his anchor on top of hers, and so to swing across her bow, and board. The plan miscarried. A strong wind was blowing at the time, and the *Ranger* did not pull up till she had passed astern of her prey. Undismayed, her captain at once cut the cable, and contrived to put out to sea without having even raised an alarm.

He decided to carry out his main project before risking a second meeting with the *Drake*. Accordingly he crossed to the English coast, and on the night of April 22–23, with two boats and thirty-one volunteers, stole into Whitehaven. There he surprised and took two forts, spiked thirty guns, and fired the shipping in the harbour. He and his followers, moreover, got away unscathed. The story of this escapade, as an instance of sheer daring, is hard to cap.

For descending on a town with which he had many associations the *Ranger's* captain had been very unreasonably censured. What he achieved at Whitehaven he could only have achieved at a place which he knew well; and war, after all, is war. The raid, again, had greater military value than the destruction of his Virginian estate by British troops in '77—a private grudge he came to avenge: at least it showed the vaunted inviolability of British coasts to be a myth, and occasioned something akin to panic from Land's End to John o' Groats. Incidentally, it had the effect of raising rates of insurance. That, its author shrewdly observed, "in the long run proved the most grievous damage of all."

From Whitehaven the *Ranger* made her way to St Mary's Island in Kirkcudbright Bay. Jones there forced an entrance to the Earl of Selkirk's house, and carried off the ancestral plate. It is not, perhaps, so easy to justify this act of 'brigandage.' Yet what were the circumstances? They cannot be better explained than in the letter—where did he learn to write such letters?—which the 'pirate' himself, a fortnight later, addressed to the countess:

MADAME, *Ranger*, Brest, May 8, 1778

It cannot be too much lamented that in the profession of arms the officer of fine feelings and real sensibility should be under the necessity of winking at any action of persons under his command which his heart cannot approve; but the reflection is doubly severe when he finds himself obliged, in appearance, to countenance such acts by his authority.

This hard case was mine when, on the 23rd of April last, I landed on St Mary's Isle. Knowing Lord Selkirk's interest with the King, and esteeming, as I do, his private character, I wished to make him the happy instrument of alleviating the horrors of hopeless captivity, when the brave are overpowered and made prisoners of war.

It was, perhaps, fortunate for you, Madame, that he was from home, for it was my intention to have taken him on board the *Ranger*, and to have detained him until, through his means, a general and fair exchange of prisoners . . . had been effected. When I was informed by some men whom I met on landing that his Lordship was absent, I walked back to my boat, determined to leave the island. By the way, however, some of my officers, who were with me, could not forbear expressing their discontent, observing that, in America, no delicacy was shown by the English, who took away all sorts of movable property. . . . I had but a moment to think how I might gratify them, and at the same time do your Ladyship the least injury. I charged the officers to permit none of the seamen to enter the house, or to hurt anything about it; to treat you, Madame, with the utmost respect; to accept of the plate which was offered, and to come away without making a search, or demanding anything else.

I am induced to believe that I was punctually obeyed, since I am informed that the plate which they brought away is far short of the inventory which accompanied it. I have gratified my men; and, when the plate is sold, I shall become the purchaser, and will gratify my own feelings by restoring it to you by such conveyance as you shall please to direct. . . .

This undertaking in due course he faithfully discharged, and Lord Selkirk wrote to him, in a letter acknowledging the return of the plate:

Some of the English newspapers at that time having put in confused accounts of your expedition to Whitehaven and Scotland, I ordered a proper one of what happened in Scotland to be put in the London newspapers, by a gentleman who was then at my house, by which the good conduct and civil behaviour of your officers and men were done justice to, and attributed to your orders and the good discipline you maintained over your people.

On April 24, the day following her departure from St Mary's Island, the *Ranger* fell in with the *Drake* off Carrickfergus, and after a short, sharp action made her a prize and took her to Brest. The British ship was under-officered and manned by a newly raised crew. Jones, none the less, could boast a very remarkable exploit. In France he found himself the hero of the hour. Only his American superiors still refused to recognize him as the great man he was. In October they gave orders for the *Ranger* to be brought back to Boston by Simpson, her first lieutenant, and left Jones without other employment than to bask in the favour of the ladies of Versailles.

At length his good friend the Duchess of Chartres again intervened on his behalf, with the result that he was given the command of an old French East India merchantman, the *Duc de Duras*, on which forty guns of various calibres, and mostly worn, had been hurriedly mounted. With this ship, which he renamed the *Bonhomme Richard* (as a compliment to Benjamin Franklin, whose *Poor Richard's Almanac* was then at the height of its popularity), manned by an ill-assorted crew of Americans, Frenchmen, and Portuguese, he left L'Orient on August 14, 1779, to make his second descent upon the coasts of Britain.

In company with the *Bonhomme Richard* sailed three other vessels—the *Alliance* (36 guns), the *Pallas* (30 guns), and the *Vengeance* (12 guns). Their equipment, however, was of an equally makeshift character; and, to render matters worse, Jones was forced, before sailing, to sign a *concordat* which, by requiring

MEDAL STRUCK IN HONOUR OF PAUL JONES

him to act on all occasions in consultation with his fellow-captains, deprived him of the advantages of superior rank. He wrote:

I am tolerably familiar with the history of naval operations from the remotest time of classical antiquity to the present day; but I have not heard or read of anything like this. I am sure that when Themistocles took command of the Græcian fleet, he was not compelled to sign such a *concordat*; nor can I find anything to exhibit that Lord Hawke in the French war, nor any English or French flag officer in this war, had been subjected to such voluntary renouncement of proper authority. These being the two extremes of ancient and modern naval history . . . I think I am entitled to consider myself the subject of a complete innovation; or, in other words, the victim of an entirely novel plan in naval operations.

THE FIGHT BETWEEN THE " BONHOMME RICHARD " AND H.M.S. " SERAPIS " OFF FLAMBOROUGH HEAD, SEPTEMBER 23, 1779

Having regard to this, one can but marvel at the power of leadership which enabled him to bring the expedition to a brilliant termination. The American squadron took prize after prize off Ireland. It then headed for Cape Wrath and, having passed through Pentland Firth, continued its triumphant progress down the east coast of Scotland. On September 14, having arrived off the Firth of Forth, Jones attempted a raid on Leith. This failed.

Failure was due, however, solely to the operation of the *concordat*, which, a few days later, also wrecked a well-laid scheme for destroying the shipping in the Tyne.

On September 23, off Flamborough Head, the *Bonhomme Richard* sighted a large fleet of merchantmen under convoy of two

SIR RICHARD PEARSON

warships, the *Serapis* (44 guns) and the *Countess of Scarborough* (20 guns). This time Jones did not wait to consult his colleagues. Signalling to them to follow, he straightway gave chase and, closely followed by the *Pallas*, came up with the convoy at 7.30 p.m. The *Pallas* at once engaged the *Countess of Scarborough*, which yielded after a very creditable resistance. Meanwhile began the memorable and long, stern duel between the *Bonhomme Richard* and the *Serapis* (Captain Pearson).

All through the night the two ships battled. At length, finding his adversary's guns too heavy for him, Jones managed to close, and, lashing the bowsprit of the *Serapis* to the *Bonhomme Richard's* mizzen-mast, used his musketry with such deadly effect that at 10 a.m. he forced Pearson to strike his colours—just in time to avoid the necessity of striking his own. The *Bonhomme Richard* could not have held out many minutes longer. Indeed, she was already sinking so fast that her crew had barely time to transfer to their prize before she finally settled down.

The *Vengeance* took no part in the fight, and the captain of the *Alliance*, who was subsequently certified insane, contented himself with firing indiscriminately on friend and foe.

On the eve of his departure from France, Jones had expressed to the Duchess of Chartres the hope that fortune might allow him some day to lay an English frigate at her feet. On his return, he craved leave to offer instead the sword of "a gallant English sailor"; the *Serapis*, he said, was too big to lay before his patron's dainty feet. The gift was graciously accepted; and thereafter, while the tongues of gossips maliciously wagged, the gardener's son, whenever he would, basked in the sunshine of the Palais Royal.

King George III was pleased to dub Pearson a knight. The captain deserved the honour; his very plucky fight had enabled a rich convoy to get safely into port. "Next time I meet him," quoth Jones, "I'll make him an earl!"

Jones, too, received his share of honours. Even Congress passed a vote of thanks to him and raised him to the rank of commodore. King Louis XVI, to commemorate his victory, gave him a gold-hilted sword, bearing the inscription, *Vindicati maris Ludovicus XVI renumerator strenuo vindici* (From Louis XVI, in recognition of the services of the brave maintainer of the privileges of the sea), and decorated him with the Order of Military Merit, "never before conferred on any one who had not actually borne arms under the commission of France."

During the closing years of the American war, the Chevalier Jones served in the French navy as a volunteer in the *Triomphant*, the flagship of the Marquis de Vaudreuil. Afterward he became an admiral in the Russian navy.

In 1785 the Czarina Catherine II, then laying plans for a war with the Turks, applied to King Louis XVI for the services of a

French admiral to reorganize and take command of her Black Sea fleet. The French Government, unwilling openly to adopt an anti-Turkish policy, suggested that the appointment should be given to Jones.

The Czarina had good reason to be grateful for the suggestion;

JOHN PAUL JONES

to the versatile Jones she largely owed the victory which her forces gained, in 1788, over the Turks at Liman. In 1790, however, the admiral resigned his commission—partly on account of ill-health, but mainly because he could not reconcile himself to Russian methods. Though it was his misfortune always to command hotch-potch, undisciplined crews, he never had a man flogged, and he refused even to carry a 'cat' in any of his ships. A more humane commander has rarely lived.

On leaving Russia, Jones lived in retirement, first in Holland and then in France, waiting for more congenial employment. In vain Catherine II urged him to return. The rank of admiral in the Swedish navy he also refused. At last, in 1792, Congress offered him a high command.

Whether he would have accepted this we cannot say, for, suddenly stricken down by illness, he died before the offer reached him. The probability is that he would have declined it. At the time of his death he was in active negotiation with the revolutionary leaders in France, and, being a man without nationality, or, as he called himself, "a citizen of the world," it can hardly be doubted that he would have looked for, and found, in the French service, the great opportunity he sought.

"How old was Paul Jones when he died?" Napoleon wearily asked Marshal Berthier, as he read the report of Nelson's victory off Cape Trafalgar.

"Forty-five," replied the chief of the staff.

"Then," said the Emperor, "he did not fulfil his destiny. Had he lived to this time, France might have had an admiral."

Napoleon remarked on another occasion :

> Our admirals are always talking about pelagic conditions and ulterior objects, as if there was any condition or any object in war except to get in contact with the enemy and destroy him. That was Paul Jones's view of the conditions and objects of naval warfare. It was also Nelson's. It is a pity that they could not have been matched somewhere with fairly equal force.

Jones's body was buried in the old St Louis Cemetery, a now abandoned burial-place for foreign Protestants, at Paris. During the revolutionary upheaval, knowledge of the site of the grave was lost. Not until 1905, after many years of fruitless endeavour, did the American Embassy at last succeed in identifying the spot. The coffin was then removed, and taken across the Atlantic under escort of an American squadron. It now lies in the Naval Academy at Annapolis.

XXIII. THOMAS COCHRANE, TENTH EARL OF DUNDONALD

Born 1775; *died* 1860

THE story of Paul Jones at once suggests that of "the great Dundonald." Contemporaries, though the one's career was ending when the other's began, these two past-masters of the navigating art had many qualities in common. Both suffered in much the same way from "the slings and arrows of outrageous fortune," and—in justice to that fickle dame—each, it must be admitted, brought her hostility upon himself.

Thomas Cochrane, 10th Earl of Dundonald, better known as Lord Cochrane, was born at Annsfield, in Lanarkshire, on December 14, 1775. His father, a highly gifted scientist, fondly thought to utilize an uncanny inventive faculty to restore the fortunes of an impoverished house, and so started on the course of reckless speculation which led him to beggary. A magician in his laboratory, the 9th Earl was a babe outside; money-lenders alone derived immediate benefit from his commercial ventures. Thus the education of this numerous offspring was left perforce to village ministers and other volunteers. Thereby hangs a tale —or, rather, a tragedy.

Thomas, the first-born, was a naval genius who, had he but acquired that something given by a public school, surely would have won for himself a high and honoured place in history. Instead—wrong-headed, saturated with half-understood doctrines of a revolutionary age—he was fated to sacrifice his talents on the altar of petty spite, and to become, like Paul Jones, "a citizen of the world," performing ill-requited service under alien flags.

While still in the nursery, he determined to be a sailor. His father, having influence at the Horse Guards, insisted on making him a soldier, and, in due course, procured him a commission in the 104th Foot. Happily, a benevolent uncle, Captain (afterward Admiral Sir Alexander) Cochrane, came to the boy's rescue.

So in 1792, despite paternal protests, the young ensign was transferred to the Navy.

After serving for six years with his uncle, mostly on the North American station, he received his lieutenant's commission, and was appointed to the *Barfleur*, the flagship of Admiral Keith, who was commanding the squadron detailed to keep bottled up at Cadiz the fleet of Spain, an ally, or helpless dupe, of revolutionary France. A rare combination of daring and prudence, which was the secret of his—as of Nelson's—greatness, quickly brought him to the notice of Keith, also to the notice of Lord St Vincent, the Commander-in-Chief of the Mediterranean station. In 1800 St Vincent gave him a command.

Cochrane made the most of the opportunity. Indeed his exploits, during the ensuing thirteen months (June 1800 to July 1801), are unparalleled in naval annals. As commander of the *Speedy*, a brig of one hundred and fifty-eight tons burden, armed with fourteen four-pounders, a species "of gun little larger than a blunderbuss," he took some fifty prizes, among them being the Spanish frigate, *El Gamo* (32 guns).

At length his little "burlesque of a man-of-war" was overhauled by three French line-of-battle ships, and, of course, she was forced to yield. But she made a very stout resistance. When, finally, her colours were lowered, the French commander declined Cochrane's proffered sword. He could not, he said, accept the sword of "an officer who had struggled for so many hours against impossibility."

Cochrane did not remain a prisoner for long. In August 1801 he had the good fortune to be exchanged, and went back to England, expecting immediate advancement to the rank of captain. None knew better than St Vincent, who was then at the Admiralty, how richly he had merited promotion. But that doughty old seaman, a stickler for tradition and discipline, was piqued by the way in which the self-assertive junior urged his claims, and made it "a point of honour" to keep him waiting. So began a quarrel which, a few years afterward, deprived Britain of the services of the most brilliant of her sailor-sons.

Wrote Admiral Collingwood, in a letter of advice to a young officer:

> You may depend on it that it is more in your power than in anyone else's to promote both your comfort and advancement. A

strict and unwearied attention to your duty, and a complaisant, respectful behaviour, not only to your superiors but to everybody, will ensure you their regard; and the reward will surely come, and I hope soon, in the way of preferment, but if it should not, I am sure you will have too much good sense to let disappointment sour you. Guard against letting discontent appear in you; it is a sorrow to your friends, a triumph to your competitors, and cannot be productive of any good. Conduct yourself so as to deserve the best that can come to you, and the consciousness of your own proper behaviour will keep you in spirits if it does not come.

EARL ST VINCENT
From a print by Barnard after a picture by Keenan

Contrast these sage words with the counsel offered by Cochrane:

If you have in the exercise of your profession acquired a right which is wrongfully withheld, demand it, stick to it with unshaken pertinacity; none but a corrupt body can possibly think the worse of you for it; even though you may be treated like myself, you are doing your country good service by exposing favouritism, which is only another term for corruption.

Cochrane punctiliously practised his own precepts. In 1801, therefore, St Vincent not merely chose to deny him promotion but, in the hope of taming him, also denied him employment. During the period of leisure forced upon him, the young firebrand divided his time between noisily airing his grievances and—more sensibly—remedying defects in his early education. With this latter object in view, he entered his name at the University of Edinburgh.

In 1803, while he was still engaged in his studies, the French war, which had been interrupted by the Peace of Amiens (1802), broke out again. Then, at last, he consented to eat humble pie; and, in the autumn of that year, he was appointed to the *Arab*, with the rank of captain, and sent to assist in the blockading of Napoleon's flotilla of invasion at Boulogne.

Cochrane was not a workman who often complained of his tools. The *Arab*, however, a collier which had been hastily converted into a warship, "sailed like a haystack"; her commander could but report that she was useless for active service. St Vincent, grimly chuckling, thereupon ordered him to convoy the Greenland whaling-fleet to the Shetlands, and afterward to protect the North Sea fisheries.

At that time the North Sea fisheries were non-existent. Yet Cochrane, "an exile in a tub at the expense of the nation," was left for a year to guard them. Lord Melville then replaced St Vincent at the Admiralty, and old animosities for a while were put aside. Early in 1805 the captain of the *Arab* was transferred to the *Pallas*, a new, fir-built frigate of thirty-two guns, and sent, with a free hand, to cruize off the Azores.

The cruise of the *Pallas* was a more splendid and more spectacular repetition of the cruise of the *Speedy*. When the frigate came back to Plymouth, with a gold candlestick five feet high (church-plate looted from a Spanish treasure ship) at each of her mast-heads, the captain found himself the hero of the hour.

Just then a general election happened to be pending, and, as ill-chance would have it, someone suggested to Cochrane that he should stand for Honiton. A sworn champion of the victims of 'naval scandals,' he jumped at the idea. The electors, however, despite his extraordinary popularity, did not return him. He refused to disgorge the necessary sums in bribes.

Said he to his protesting agent: "I, who stand as a reformer of abuses, can have nothing to do with bribes." None the less, after the poll, he gave each of his supporters ten good guineas. So it came about that in 1806, when he offered himself again as a candidate, he was returned with an overwhelming majority. On this occasion not one of his supporters received a penny. Two years later, rejected by the indignant folk of Honiton, he became one of the members for Westminster, a constituency which, in company with Sir Francis Burdett, he long continued to represent.

In action at sea he tempered his daring with cool, calculating judgment. In action in the House of Commons he was merely foolish and headstrong; and his parliamentary utterances were as verbose and ranting as his naval despatches were terse and modest. As a Member of Parliament, in fact, he proved himself an insufferable bore, who, while grievously injuring his own interests, did little to remedy the evils he denounced. For some years the business of war fortunately kept him from appearing often in his place.

Here can be noted only one of the many remarkable exploits he performed at this time. In 1809 it was suggested that the French fleet riding in Aix Roads might be destroyed by fireships, and Cochrane, notwithstanding the weight of prejudice against him, was entrusted with the task, being attached for the purpose to Admiral Gambier's blockading squadron. The sequel is writ large in history, also in the pages of Marryat's *Frank Mildmay*.[1]

The fireship idea miscarried; the vessels were badly handled, and the fuzes defective. This was a contingency which Cochrane had anticipated. Indeed, the fireships, as such, were only incidental to his plan. With them he sent into the Roads "explosion vessels" of his own ingenious designing. They duly functioned; and the French commanders, imagining that the fireships also were "explosion vessels," cut their cables in panic. The result was that thirteen French line-of-battle ships ran aground, and there, in the early hours of the morning of April 12, caught by the fall of the tide, lay defenceless on their bilges.

A few miles off was Gambier's squadron waiting, in accordance with the scheme of operations, to enter the Roads should the attack succeed. Straightway Cochrane signalled, "The enemy's fleet can be destroyed." Apart from a formal acknowledgment, the answering pennant, no reply was given. Subsequent messages—"Half the fleet can destroy the enemy," and "The frigates alone can destroy the enemy"—likewise passed unheeded. Determined to force the admiral's hand, Cochrane then signalled, "In want of assistance," and with his single frigate, sailed into the Roads. So, at last, was Gambier induced to send a few ships forward. But he very soon recalled them, and, with only five of the enemy's ships destroyed, the action was broken off.

Yet that action was a very great achievement. On his return

[1] Frederick Marryat, *alias* "Frank Mildmay," served as a lieutenant under Cochrane in 1809.

home Cochrane received an enthusiastic welcome, even in official circles. Indeed, he was rewarded with the knighthood of the Bath, a distinction rarely conferred on a man of his rank. With strange perversity he proceeded almost immediately again to wreck his prospects. Learning that the Government proposed to ask Parliament to pass a vote of thanks to Admiral Gambier, he hastened to the Admiralty and informed Lord Mulgrave, the First Lord, that he felt it to be his duty as a Member of the House of Commons to oppose the motion; Gambier, he avowed, deserved not thanks, but censure. Mulgrave strove in vain to turn him from his purpose, assuring him that his name would be included in the vote and that justice would be done to the men who had served under him. Cochrane would listen neither to reason nor remonstrance.

Anxious to save him from the consequences of his intended action, Mulgrave adopted another line of argument. "If you are on service," he said, "you cannot be in your place in Parliament. Now, my lord, I will put under your orders three frigates, with *carte blanche* to do whatever you please on the enemy's coast in the Mediterranean." Cochrane haughtily rejected the "bribe." In the circumstances, Gambier naturally demanded a court-martial; and, since the case had resolved itself into a test of strength between the captain and the Government, the verdict was a foregone conclusion. The admiral was "most honourably acquitted" on every count.

Cochrane, stigmatized as a false accuser, thus found himself debarred from all hope of immediate professional employment. So he set himself up in Parliament as a critic of naval administration, and for four years carried on a rancorous campaign which still further embittered his relations with the authorities. At length his uncle, Sir Alexander Cochrane, contrived to restore him in some measure to favour, and, in 1814, he was appointed to the command of the *Tonnant*, the flagship of the North American station. But his enemies had not done with him yet.

A few days before he was to have taken up his command he was accused of having circulated in London a lying report about the fall of Napoleon, in order, it was alleged, that he might make money on the Stock Exchange. The result of the trial—if that term can be applied to a piece of political jobbery—was that Cochrane, though manifestly innocent of the charge brought against him, was sentenced not merely to a year's imprisonment, but to stand for an hour in the pillory and to pay a fine of £1000.

The pillory was remitted. The Government feared that the carrying out of this part of the sentence would provoke a riot; indeed, so strongly ran the tide of popular sentiment that the money required to pay the fine was raised by penny subscriptions.[1] The sentence of imprisonment, however, was strictly enforced. Nor did the indignities heaped on Cochrane stop there. Struck off the Navy List, and expelled from the House of Commons, he had also to suffer the shame of having his banner as a knight of the Bath removed from Henry the Seventh's Chapel.

So it came about that the hero of Aix Roads, in righteous wrath, shook from his feet the dust of his ungrateful country. In 1818 he accepted the command of the Chilian navy.

The people of Chile and Peru, no doubt, even without his aid, would ultimately have thrown off the Spanish yoke. None the less, he was the man who gave them independence. At sea, where they were weak, he lent them strength. And who else, with the wretched fleet which he commanded, could so quickly have vanquished the vastly superior forces of Spain? For an account of what he did in Chile the reader should turn to the pages of the Hon. J. W. Fortescue's stirring biography. Even Mr Fortescue, however, cannot explain how it was done. "Raphael," he writes, "shows us his brush, Shakespeare his pen, Dundonald his sword, but we are none the wiser."

Cochrane remained in the service of Chile till 1823. Then, being hopelessly at loggerheads with the Government, he transferred his affections to Brazil. In some respects, his achievements there were even more remarkable. To him, indeed, the political severance of that country from Portugal and the establishment of the Brazilian Empire[2] were almost entirely due. But, as had happened in Chile, his relations with the authorities soon became strained to breaking-point.

Mr Fortescue has described him as "a kind of destroying angel with a limited income and a turn for politics." As such, he could not bring himself to refrain from interfering in matters which lay

[1] The note tendered in payment, bearing a defiant endorsement in Cochrane's handwriting, is still preserved in the Bank of England.

[2] Brazil became a republic in 1889 on the abdication of the Emperor Pedro IV.

outside the province of the mercenary fighting man; and his employers, while they "appreciated the destroyer, misunderstood the angel and resented the politician." In 1825, disgusted with

THOMAS COCHRANE, TENTH EARL OF DUNDONALD
From the painting by Stroehling

the treatment accorded to him, he decided to espouse the cause of the Greeks.

This, the most thankless of the tasks he undertook, was perhaps the most nobly performed by him. Though the victim of every form of corruption, intrigue, and treachery, he battled loyally for his new masters, till finally they gained their liberty. Then, in 1829, he returned to England, where justice at last was done to him. In 1830 William IV came to the throne. The sailor-king at once offered the sailor-hero redress for past wrongs.

Cochrane for some time affected to regard the granting of a 'free pardon' for an offence which he had not committed as being little short of an insult. That pardon, however, made it possible for his name to be restored to the Navy List. A few days later he was gazetted a Rear-Admiral. In due course, he was reinstated a knight of the Bath, and in 1831 he succeeded to the earldom of Dundonald. So a story, stranger than any told in fiction, ended in the manner approved by novelists. The hero lived happily ever afterward. He was spared, moreover, to achieve his highest ambition; in 1847, hoisting his flag as commander-in-chief of the North American station, he took command of a British fleet at sea.

In 1851, at the expiration of this appointment, he was in his seventy-sixth year and deemed too old for further active employment. Yet his vigour was still unimpaired. When the Crimean War broke out, he immediately offered his services, urging the Government to allow him to carry out that "secret plan" which he had submitted forty years earlier. "My dear Sir James," he wrote to Sir J. Graham, the First Lord, "were it necessary, which it is not, that I should place myself in an arm-chair on the poop, with each leg on a cushion, I would undertake to subdue every insular fortification at Cronstadt within four hours of the commencement of the attack."

In 1814 the "secret plan" had been rejected on the ground that it was "infallible, irresistible, but inhuman." In 1854 it was again considered and, after much anxious deliberation, Lord Palmerston agreed to give it a trial on a small scale at Sebastopol. Its author would not consent to this condition. The scheme, therefore, was dropped, and for a further sixty years the use of asphyxiating gas in warfare, as proposed by "the great Dundonald," remained a secret jealously guarded in Admiralty archives.

Lord Dundonald died on October 31, 1860, and was fittingly laid to rest in Westminster Abbey. The spot, in the centre of the nave, is marked by a plain white slab, bearing at its four corners the arms of Chile, Peru, Brazil, and Greece.

XXIV. SIR JOHN FRANKLIN

Born 1786; *died* 1847

SIR JOHN FRANKLIN was a Lincolnshire man, a native of Spilsby. His forbears had long been settled in those parts; they became 'franklins'—yeomen, that is to say, holding their lands direct from the king—right back in Plantagenet times. The John Franklin who was born on April 16, 1786, the last of a family of nine, was intended by his father for the Church. He held other ideas regarding his future. When quite a small boy, in his first term at Louth Grammar School, he determined to be a sailor.

In 1799, hoping to cure this perversity, his father sent him in a merchantman on a voyage to Lisbon. The remedy failed. French privateers then were active, and their activities lent to the voyage just that glamour which was needed to outbalance the discomfort. Young Franklin returned from Portugal more determined than ever to follow the profession of the sea. In the end, therefore, paternal opposition was overcome. Early in 1801 the boy found himself entered as a midshipman in H.M.S. *Polyphemus*.

A few weeks afterward, on April 2, he was given his first taste of battle. On that memorable day the *Polyphemus*, following the *Elephant*, flying the flag of Vice-Admiral Nelson, sailed into Copenhagen harbour, and there, by helping to put the Danish fleet out of action, took a hand in the frustration of one of Napoleon's little schemes. In 1805 young Franklin took part in a yet more famous fight. On October 21 of that year he acted as signal midshipman in H.M.S. *Bellerophon* off Cape Trafalgar, and was mentioned in despatches for "evincing very conspicuous zeal and activity."

In the meantime he had done a long spell of service in southern waters, having been appointed in June 1801 to a discovery ship, the *Investigator*, commanded by his cousin, Captain Matthew Flinders. Under that officer, a brilliant marine surveyor, he was employed for more than three years in exploring and mapping the coast of Australia, and he there learned lessons which subsequently stood him in good stead. The value of those lessons may be gauged by the fact that Flinders's plans still form the basis of Admiralty charts.

From 1805 to 1815 Franklin served continuously in fighting ships, and his adventures were many and varied. Space allows only one of them to be recorded here. In front of New Orleans, during the inglorious assault which brought to an end the dreary Anglo-American war 1812–14, he was wounded in a hand-to-hand fight. His gallantry and devotion to duty on that occasion received a well-earned mention in despatches.

While the French revolutionary wars were raging, the nations of Europe had little opportunity to pursue the work of discovery —of geographical conquest. The issue of the battle of Waterloo at last released pent-up enthusiasm, and from 1815 onward the nineteenth century was prolific in exploration. Napoleon's downfall, therefore, set Franklin free seriously to engage in that kind of warfare in which Flinders had taught him to exult, to fight not with men but with the forces of Nature.

In Britain, the first Age of Discovery had been inaugurated by John Cabot's quest (1497) for a northern sea-route between Europe and the East. That same quest inaugurated this new Age of Discovery. Three centuries of fruitless striving—during which no fewer than sixty-three attempts were made—had not shaken the belief of British seamen in the existence of a practicable north-west passage. Landsmen shared the conviction. In 1818 Parliament, "in the interests of commerce and science," passed an Act "for encouraging attempts to find a northern passage between the Atlantic and Pacific oceans." To him who should succeed, the Act offered a reward of £20,000.

The reward was never claimed or paid; and in 1828 the offer was withdrawn. Meanwhile, it resulted in many memorable voyages, notably those of Sir John Ross and his nephew, James Ross, and those of Parry and William Beechey. It resulted also in Franklin's expeditions of 1819–22 and 1825–27.

Franklin gained his first experience of polar work in 1818 as commander of the *Trent*, a vessel which sailed as consort to the *Dorothea* (Captain Buchan, R.N.) in an attempt to reach the North Pole. The expedition proved something of a fiasco. Franklin, however, learned many things from it. Further, it enabled him to give evidence of his peculiar fitness for command in Arctic regions—his calmness in danger, his fertility of resource, his seamanship and scientific knowledge. These qualities at once marked him out for the leadership of future ventures.

So it came about that he was put at the head of the land expedition which the Admiralty sent out in 1819 to explore the then wholly unknown central part of the northern coast of America. The other members of the expedition included Dr (afterward Sir John) Richardson, and two 'middies,' George Back and Robert Hood, each of whom subsequently became famous.

After landing in Hudson Bay, the party travelled across Rupert's Land and descended to the coast by way of the Coppermine river. In the course of a three years' journey of indescribable hardship they covered 5500 miles, passing through regions never before visited by white men, and mapped some 500 miles of coast. Their experiences may best be read in Franklin's *Narrative of a Journey to the Shores of the Polar Sea*. This book, published in 1823, is at once a classic of travel and an epic of daring and endurance.

In 1825, having been raised in the meantime to the rank of captain, Franklin—again accompanied by Richardson and Back—led a similar but more ambitious venture. This time his instructions were to descend the Mackenzie river and make a determined effort to solve the riddle of the North-West Passage in co-operation with expeditions under Beechey and Parry. Those two captains sailed in the same year, the former with the intention of fighting his way eastward from Bering Strait, and the latter with the intention of fighting his way westward from Baffin Bay.

The triple plan brought success within measurable distance. Franklin did not actually join hands either with Beechey or with Parry. Yet he very nearly joined hands with both. Furthermore, he laid down the northern coast of America through 37 degrees of longitude—from the Coppermine river as far west as the 150th meridian. In recognition of this achievement, King George IV conferred on him the honour of knighthood when, in 1828, he returned to London.

In the following year he was given the command of a warship, the *Rainbow*, and sailed for the Mediterranean. There he played a notable part in the Greek War of Independence. Subsequently, as governor of Van Diemen's Land (renamed Tasmania in 1853) he gained distinction in another *rôle*. During the seven years of his governorship, 1836 to 1843, he won for himself a place among the most illustrious of British colonial administrators. To his enterprise and far-seeing statesmanship, not only the Tasmanians, but the peoples of all the States of the Australian Commonwealth, owe a very great deal.

He returned to England in 1844. Seventeen years had elapsed since his last journey to the Arctic. But the quest for the North-

SIR JOHN FRANKLIN
From an engraving by D. J. Pound

West Passage had been steadily pursued meanwhile; and Franklin had watched its progress with eager and close attention. When, therefore, shortly after his arrival at London, he learned that the Admiralty purposed to fit out an expedition which, it was announced, would make a final attempt to find the elusive channel, he at once applied for the command.

His application was met at first with an almost cold refusal. The suggestion, he was told, that the command should be entrusted to a man sixty years of age could not be considered. "You have been misinformed, my lord," said Franklin, indignantly, "I'm only fifty-nine!" By so saying, he gained his point. On May 19, 1845, he sailed from Greenhithe with the best-equipped expedition which had ever left our shores.

His ships, the *Erebus* and *Terror*, were old friends. Commanded by Captain James Ross, they had put in at Van Diemen's Land in 1839, while on that voyage to the south which resulted, *inter alia*, in the discovery of the two volcanoes named after them. Constructed originally as bomb-ships, their timbers were enormously massive and strong. His ships' companies also were old friends, and experienced in polar work. Captain Crozier, his second in command, had been in charge of the *Terror* on Ross's Antarctic expedition. The rest were all picked volunteers from the Navy, as fine a body of men—129 all told—as ever engaged in a great adventure. The ships, moreover, were provisioned for three years, and furnished with every needful appliance which human forethought was able to suggest and science to supply —even with small auxiliary engines, driving screw propellers, and capable of developing about 20 horse-power. Success, it seemed, could hardly fail to crown Franklin's efforts.

The *Erebus* and the *Terror* passed into Lancaster Sound on July 26. In Baffin Bay, near the entrance of the sound, they were sighted that day by whalers who duly reported their movements. When, asked the London newspapers, would they be sighted in Bering Strait? The world confidently awaited the answer. A year passed. No news came. Another year passed. Still no news. But this was not to be wondered at. Silence occasioned no special alarm even at the third year's close. After this, however, as weeks grew into months, anxiety increased apace.

In June 1848 a relief ship went out. It failed to find any traces of the *Erebus* and *Terror*. Another ship was dispatched, and the Government—to stimulate private enterprise—offered a reward of £10,000 for definite tidings of Franklin and his followers, and a reward of £20,000 for their rescue. Expedition after expedition then sailed. Between 1848 and 1855 twenty or more were sent out. Lady Franklin, meanwhile, laboured unceasingly to equip auxiliary vessels on her own account.

The work of these expeditions constitutes a story of achievement unparalleled in the annals of maritime endeavour. As a result of it, the whole of the northern coast and northern archipelago of the American continent was surveyed, and scientific knowledge was enriched in a thousand ways—by Ross's charting, for example, of the exact position of the Magnetic Pole. One expedition, moreover, actually completed a north-west passage—that of Captain M'Clure who, in command of the *Investigation*, entered Bering

THE " FOX "
From a model in the Royal Naval College Museum, Greenwich
By permission of the Lords Commissioners of the Admiralty

Strait from the Pacific in 1850, and in 1854 returned to England from Davis Strait. To do this, it is true, M'Clure had to abandon his ship, and walk or sledge over hundreds of miles of ice. Still he had water under him all the way.

But, though geography and science thus gained, the fate of the missing men remained a mystery. At length, in 1855, it was decided that no useful purpose could be served by continuing the search. Lady Franklin, however, refused to give in, refused to despair; and her appeals for support met with a generous response. She had exhausted her private funds long before this. But money was sent to her by friends and sym-

M'CLINTOCK'S SEARCH-PARTY FINDING ONE OF FRANKLIN'S CAIRNS AT CAPE HERSCHEL

From *A Narrative of the Discovery of the Fate of Sir John Franklin and his Companions*

pathizers in all parts of the civilized world; the Tasmanian colonists sent £1700. So was she enabled to fit out the *Fox*, the yacht of 177 tons burden which sailed from Aberdeen in 1857.

This expedition, commanded by Captain (afterward Sir Leopold) M'Clintock, at last unravelled the story of Franklin's fate and of the gallant men who shared it. A scrap of paper—one of the printed forms supplied to the commanders of discovery ships for throwing overboard, enclosed in bottles—found in a cairn on King William's Island, provided the clue.

Written upon it was the following message, dated May 28, 1847:

> H.M. ships *Erebus* and *Terror* wintered in the ice in lat. 70° 5′ N., long. 98° 23′ W. Having wintered in 1846–47 [1] at Beechey Island, in lat. 74° 43′ 28″ N., long. 91° 39′ 15″ W., after having ascended Wellington Channel to lat. 77°, and returned by the west side of Cornwallis Island. Sir John Franklin commanding the expedition. All well. Party consisting of 2 officers and 6 men left the ships on Monday, 24th May, 1847.

Pencilled round the margin could be traced an additional report, dated April 25, 1848, and signed by Captain Crozier:

> H.M. ships *Terror* and *Erebus* were deserted April 22, 1848, 5 leagues N.N.W. of this, having been beset since September 12, 1846. The officers and crews, consisting of 105 souls, under the command of Captain F. R. M. Crozier, landed here in lat. 69° 37′ 42″ N., long. 98° 41′ W. . . . Sir John Franklin died on 11th June, 1847; and the total loss by deaths in the expedition has been to this date, 9 officers and 15 men.

Forced to desert their ships, Crozier and his men, it would seem, started for the mainland with the intention of ascending the Great Fish river to one of the Hudson Bay Company's stations. The undertaking proved too much for them. Weakened by three winters in the frozen north, and with their food supplies all but spent, they fell one by one on the way. By following in their tracks, M'Clintock was able to piece together the details of the tragic story. The corpses still lay upon the ice. These and other relics—abandoned tents, scientific instruments too heavy for dying men to carry, guns loaded to shoot game which was not there—explained all that could have been told in words.

So ended the long quest for the North-West Passage. Franklin's

[1] 1845–46 (?).

H. M. S.hips Erebus and Terror

Wintered in the Ice in

28 of May 1847 } Lat. 70°5' N Long 98°23' W

Having wintered in 1846—7 at Beechey Island in Lat 74°43'28" N Long 91°39'15" W after having ascended Wellington Channel to Lat 77° and returned by the West side of Cornwallis Island

Commander.

Sir John Franklin commanding the Expedition

All well

WHOEVER finds this paper is requested to forward it to the Secretary of the Admiralty, London, *with a note of the time and place at which it was found*: or, if more convenient, to deliver it for that purpose to the British Consul at the nearest Port.

QUINCONQUE trouvera ce papier est prié d'y marquer le tems et lieu ou il l'aura trouvé, et de le faire parvenir au plutot au Secretaire de l'Amirauté Britannique à Londres.

CUALQUIERA que hallare este Papel, se le suplica de enviarlo al Secretario del Almirantazgo, en Londrés, con una nota del tiempo y del lugar en donde se halló.

EEN ieder die dit Papier mogt vinden, wordt hiermede verzogt, om het zelve, ten spoedigste, te willen zenden aan den Heer Minister van der Marine der Nederlanden in 's Gravenhage, of wel aan den Secretaris der Britsche Admiraliteit, te London, en daar by te voegen eene Nota, inhoudende de tyd en de plaats alwaar dit Papier is gevonden geworden.

FINDEREN af dette Papiir ombedes, naar Leilighed gives, at sende samme til Admiralitets Secretairen i London, eller nærmeste Embedsmand i Danmark, Norge, eller Sverrig Tiden og Stœdit hvor dette er fundet ønskes venskabeligt paategnet.

WER diesen Zettel findet, wird hier-durch ersucht denselben an den Secretair des Admiralitets in London einzusenden, mit gefälliger angabe an welchen ort und zu welcher zeit er gefundet worden ist

Party consisting of 2 Officers and 6 Men left the Ships on Monday 24th May 1847

Gm. Gore Lieut.

Chas. F. Des Voeux mate.

25th April 1848 HM Ships Terror and Erebus were deserted on the 22nd April 5 leagues NNW of this having been beset since 12th Septr 1846. The Officers & Crews consisting of 105 souls under the command of Captain F. R. M. Crozier landed here — in Lat. 69°37'42" Long 98°41' This paper was found by Lt. Irving under the cairn supposed to have been built by Sir James Ross in 1831 — 4 miles to the Northward — where it had been deposited by the late Commander Gore in June 1847. Sir James Ross' pillar has not however been found and the paper has been transferred to this position which is that in which Sir J. Ross' pillar was erected — Sir John Franklin died on the 11th June 1847 and the total loss by deaths in the Expedition has been to this date 9 Officers & 15 Men.

James Fitzjames Captain HMS Erebus

F. R. M. Crozier Captain & Senior Offr.

and start on tomorrow 26th for Backs Fish River

REDUCED FACSIMILE OF ADMIRALTY FORM RECORDING THE DEATH OF SIR JOHN FRANKLIN glorious failure finally put to rest the old hope of a practicable northern sea-route to the Indies; and in 1906 we read in our newspapers, with hardly more than passing interest, that an intrepid Norseman, Captain Roald Amundsen, fortune's favourite, had brought a ship from Baffin Bay to Bering Strait along the very route which Franklin had meant to follow. But that is another story. . . .

Franklin married twice. In 1823 he wedded Miss Eleanor Porden, an architect's daughter, and in 1828, just before he received his knighthood, a Miss Jane Griffin. Lady Franklin survived him many years. She died in 1875, aged eighty-three. Shortly afterward, in Westminster Abbey, was unveiled that memorial which has enshrined Sir John among the heroes of our race. A master navigator, an indomitable fighter, scholar and scientist, statesman and courtier, he was a worthy successor of the great Elizabethans, the true heir of Sir Humphrey Gilbert, Sir Richard Grenville, and Sir Walter Ralegh.

The relics brought back by M'Clintock were presented by Lady Franklin to the United Services Museum. Other relics may be seen at Greenwich Hospital.

INDEX